37INK

SIMON & SCHUSTER

ALSO BY SCOTT S. GREENBERGER

The Unexpected President:
The Life and Times of Chester A. Arthur

THE FORSAKEN FOUNDER

GOUVERNEUR MORRIS,

the Unsung Patriot Who Wrote the Constitution, Stood Up to Slavery, and Survived the Reign of Terror

SCOTT S. GREENBERGER

37INK

SIMON & SCHUSTER

NEW YORK AMSTERDAM/ANTWERP LONDON
TORONTO SYDNEY/MELBOURNE NEW DELHI

37INK
SIMON & SCHUSTER

An Imprint of Simon & Schuster, LLC
1230 Avenue of the Americas
New York, NY 10020

The authorized representative in the EEA is Simon & Schuster Netherlands BV, Herculesplein 96 3584 AA Utrecht, Netherlands. info@simonandschuster.nl

First 37 INK/Simon & Schuster hardcover edition September 2026

37 INK/SIMON & SCHUSTER and colophon are registered trademarks of Simon & Schuster, LLC

Interior design by Ruth Lee-Mui

Manufactured in the United States of America

1 3 5 7 9 10 8 6 4 2

Library of Congress Cataloging-in-Publication Data is available.

ISBN 978-1-6680-9494-5
ISBN 978-1-6680-9496-9 (ebook)

For my children, Sydney and Eli

In memory of my father, Robert S. Greenberger

Why are we here? We are here to save the people from their most dangerous enemy—to save them from themselves.

Gouverneur Morris, 1802

CONTENTS

AUTHOR'S NOTE

Gouverneur Morris and his contemporaries wrote and spoke English differently than we do today. In quoting from letters, diaries, and other documents, I have faithfully reproduced the exact wording in the original source. However, in some cases I have modernized the spelling, punctuation, and capitalization to make the language more accessible to a twenty-first-century reader.

PROLOGUE

On July 6, 1816, a sixty-four-year-old man with a wooden leg and a shriveled arm sat down to write a letter to an old friend. Nearly seventeen years had passed since their parting at the edge of the Elbe River, in Hamburg. European adventures were beyond the writer now, as flare-ups of gout kept him close to home. But his elegant manor house, filled with French finery and fringed by flatlands and marshes, was a pleasant hermitage. Death was drawing near, but it was not in his nature to be morose. Marriage and fatherhood had finally arrived, and both had enriched him in ways he scarcely could have imagined during his long and libidinous bachelorhood. He loved his wife, a woman with much genius and an affectionate temper unscarred by the scandal that had nearly ruined her. As for his charming three-year-old son—well, the sentiments of a father regarding his only child are hardly objective, but even those who wished the boy had never been born acknowledged his beauty and promise. The playboy who had notched conquests in carriages and convents was now a contented family man.

He gazed out the window, and the cool breeze blowing off Long Island Sound carried memories of his consequential life: huddling with George Washington at frozen Valley Forge, strolling with Thomas Jefferson in muddy Paris, comforting Alexander Hamilton as he agonized on his deathbed. As America's ambassador to France, he had plotted with King Louis XVI and Marie Antoinette to save them from the guillotine. When the Marquis de Lafayette's folly landed him in an Austrian prison, he loaned him money and lobbied for his release. He had designed Manhattan's street grid and even now, at his advanced age, he was fighting for his vision of a great canal connecting the port of New York to the interior of the continent.

For all that, he was most proud of this fact: The hand moving across this very page had written the words that were the bedrock of the nation. James Madison? The president was often drunk on wine or high on opium and so withered that his wife had signaled her openness to an affair. *He* was the penman of the Constitution, and the sole author of its eloquent Preamble. And while he had failed to excise slavery from the document, he had surreptitiously shaped the final draft in ways that would embolden abolitionists in decades to come.

His antislavery views offended many of his contemporaries—especially the slave-owning Virginians who had a stranglehold on the presidency. His amorous adventures and high living, his effortless wit and good looks also aroused resentment, as did his firm belief that it was a divine imperative to enjoy superb meals and bawdy jokes. If all of that denied him a place in the nation's pantheon of founders, so be it.

In revolutionary Paris, he had seen people brandishing bloody heads on pikes; he knew what human beings were capable of. Unlike Jefferson, who elevated mankind but assigned too many individual men to the humble rank of fools, he understood that each one of us has strengths and weaknesses. He also believed, despite two crippling injuries, that incidents of pleasure and pain were scattered among human beings more equally than most people imagined. The cards were dealt with fairness; the only thing to do was play the game.

Gouverneur Morris picked up his pen. "Looking back, I can with some little self-complacency reflect that I have not lived in vain; and at the same time look forward with composure at the probable course of future events," he wrote. "At sixty-four, there is little to desire and less to apprehend. Let me add that, however grave the form and substance of this letter, the lapse of so many years has not impaired the gaiety of your friend."

★

Gouverneur Morris is our forsaken Founding Father. Morris reorganized the ragtag Continental Army into a force that vanquished the preeminent military power of the age. He played a pivotal role in putting the new nation on solid financial footing and conceived the country's first bank. At the Constitutional Convention, he was the delegate who fought hardest to abolish slavery, even as Benjamin Franklin, Alexander Hamilton, and other opponents of slavery sat silently. Abraham Lincoln, in his famous 1860 speech at the Cooper Institute in New York City, hailed Morris as one of the "most noted antislavery men of those times." It was Morris, not James Madison, who composed the soaring Preamble to the Constitution and rewrote the final draft so that it did not endorse slavery—either explicitly or implicitly. His changes transformed the Constitution into a blueprint for a better America, one wielded by Frederick Douglass, Susan B. Anthony, Martin Luther King Jr., and many others. Morris succeeded Thomas Jefferson as minister to France and perceived—as his predecessor did not—that that country's bid to emulate America's revolution would be drowned in blood.

"There has never been an American statesman of keener intellect or more brilliant genius," Theodore Roosevelt wrote in his 1888 biography of Morris, describing his fellow New Yorker as "gallant and fearless" and "absolutely upright and truthful." Roosevelt ended his book with this definitive declaration: "With all his faults, there are few men of his generation to whom the country owes more than to Gouverneur Morris."

So why have we forgotten him? Many of Morris's contemporaries resented his brilliance, his larger-than-life personality, and what Roosevelt called his "extreme, aggressive frankness," especially in opposing slavery. He was an unabashed ladies' man, and his romantic adventures scandalized some of his peers and ignited jealousy in others. The rancor these men expressed in their letters and memoirs seeped into the earliest histories of the period, poisoning the perceptions of later generations. Some critics have tarred him—erroneously—as a monarchist. Morris's activities during the War of 1812 also tarnished his legacy. He perceived the war as a wicked plot by slave-owning Southerners to impoverish the Northeast—and maybe even ally America with Napoleon. That led him to consider (briefly) whether New York and New England should secede from the Union—a stance that did not age well, even though it preceded by nearly fifty years Lincoln's own observation that the country could not endure half-slave and half-free. For these reasons and others, our most colorful Founding Father has been denied his rightful place in American history. It's time to set the record straight.

ONE
CHOOSING SIDES

At ten o'clock on the night of April 18, 1775, rebel spies watched eight hundred British soldiers assemble on a moonlit beach below Boston Common. Twenty longboats bobbed in the surf, oarsmen at the ready. Silently, the red-coated troops boarded the boats, sitting face-to-face in two rows with their muskets propped between their knees. The boats ferried the men a mile across Back Bay to Lechmere Point in Cambridge, where they sloshed through marshland to reach a dirt road. From there, the British marched toward Concord—flowing past apple and plum orchards, cider mills and smokehouses, like blood coursing through the countryside.

King George III and the British Parliament had decided it was high time to arrest and imprison the leaders of the rebellion roiling Massachusetts. The British knew local militiamen had been training, and that units of roughly seventy-five hundred so-called minutemen were ready to mobilize quickly. But Lord Dartmouth, the colonial secretary, believed that "with proper preparation and secrecy," British forces might be able to seize the rebel leaders—Samuel Adams, John Hancock, and Dr. Joseph Warren—and crush the uprising without shedding much blood.

British Lieutenant General Thomas Gage, who had taken the reins as royal governor of Massachusetts in the spring of 1774, agreed that force would be required, but he wanted to focus on the patriots' arms and ammunition, which his spies told him had been hidden in towns west of Boston. An especially large cache was stashed in the town of Concord, eighteen miles northwest of the city. Gage even had a hand-drawn map showing exactly where the supplies could be found. On the night of April 18, 1775, he dispatched a force to destroy the military stores concealed there.

Through their own informants in London, the Americans knew British troops were preparing to deploy, and that Gage had received orders to stamp out the rebellion. Warren remained in Boston, but Adams and Hancock decamped for Lexington, about seven miles east of Concord. In mid-April, several dozen patriots who met regularly at Boston's Green Dragon Tavern to organize surveillance of British troop movements realized that something was afoot: British longboats, grenadiers, and infantry companies were getting ready for action.

Bostonians were watching the British troops—most colonists called them "redcoats" or "lobsterbacks," because of their bright red uniforms—as they boarded their boats. Even before they pushed off, Warren summoned two riders to alert Adams and Hancock, and the countryside, that the British were coming. The first messenger was William Dawes Jr., a thirty-year-old smuggler and spy who eavesdropped on British officers by pretending to be a vegetable peddler, a miller, or a drunk. The second was Paul Revere, a forty-year-old metalworker who had already made nearly a dozen rides to Philadelphia, New York, and New Hampshire in service of the rebellion, delivering news of the dramatic doings in Massachusetts to other colonies. After receiving his instructions from Warren, Revere rushed home to grab his riding boots and overcoat, then scurried through the North End to the waterfront, where two patriots were waiting for him with a dinghy that would take him across the Charles River to Charlestown. The British sailors on the *Somerset*, a seventy-gun warship that was supposed to be guarding the route, somehow failed to notice the tiny vessel skittering past the stern. Revere stepped onshore and rendezvoused with patriots in town who gave him a brown mare—"a very good horse" that he proceeded to ride into history.

Elsewhere in the North End, another patriot carrying two tinplate lanterns climbed a set of stairs and a shaky ladder in the steeple of the Old North Church on Salem Street. Navigators entering Boston Harbor had long used the steeple as a reference point; now it would serve a different purpose. Revere had instructed a confederate to set a single lantern in the north-facing window if the British were coming by land, two if by sea. The man placed both lanterns in the window, signaling to rebel leaders that the British had crossed Back Bay.

As it turned out, the signal from the steeple wasn't necessary: Dawes and Revere roused patriots in every town and village on the way to Concord. It took Revere about two hours to reach Lexington, where he warned Adams and Hancock to flee. Half an hour later, Dawes arrived with the same message. Adams was already packing his things, but Hancock growled that he would stay and fight before he finally agreed to escape in his elegant carriage. As Revere and Dawes galloped toward Concord, other patriots swung into their saddles to spread the word.

At dawn on April 19, the redcoats marched into Lexington, where about seventy patriot militiamen were assembled on the town common. The British commander ordered his troops to surround the rebels, but not to fire. "Keep your ranks," Major John Pitcairn instructed. "Form and surround them." When the redcoats were about fifty yards away, the American commander, Captain John Parker, ordered his men to scatter. Then a shot rang out—nobody knows who fired it—and the British muskets exploded. Pitcairn swung his sword above his head in a vain attempt to get his troops to stop shooting. When the smoke cleared, eight Americans were dead—several had been shot in the back—and nine were wounded. On the British side, only two men were slightly wounded. The redcoats fired a volley and shouted three "huzzahs" before continuing west.

As the first British troops approached Concord shortly after eight in the morning, the rebels withdrew to a hill near the North Bridge, which spanned the Concord River just north of the village. The British searched Concord for arms and ammunition but didn't find much—the patriots had already removed most of it. After making a bonfire of what they had seized, they decided to cross the river to search the farms on the other side. At around nine, they crossed the North Bridge. The patriots, seeing the smoke billowing from Concord, thought the British had torched the town; enraged, they began to advance. A British soldier fired into the river, igniting a flurry of shots from both sides. In the next three minutes, two Americans were killed and three wounded; on the British side, there were two men killed and eight wounded. As one battered and bloody British soldier struggled to stand up, a minuteman crushed his skull with a hatchet. The redcoats fell back toward Concord. "Now the war has begun, and no one knows when it will end," one patriot remarked.

As the British retreated, the rebels shot at them from behind stone walls, homes, and hedges. "I had my hat shot off my head three times," a British soldier later reported. "Two balls went through my coat and carried away my bayonet from my side." The day's final toll revealed the absurdity of the idea that the rebels would be easily subdued: Seventy-three redcoats were dead or would die from their wounds and another two hundred were wounded. Forty-nine Americans had been killed, another forty-six wounded. "Whoever looks upon them as an irregular mob will find themselves much mistaken," British Brigadier Hugh Earl Percy wrote of the Americans. "You may depend upon it that, as the rebels have now had time to prepare, they are determined to go through with it."

★

The dramatic events at Lexington and Concord forced the many Americans who were undecided about seeking independence from Britain to make a choice. Gouverneur Morris, a twenty-three-year-old New Yorker, was one of them.

Morris's own family was split: His half brother Lewis supported the patriots (a member of the Continental Congress, he would sign the Declaration of Independence), and his half brother Richard resigned his judgeship because he didn't want to serve under the British; after some hesitation, he joined the revolution. Morris's maternal uncles, both West Indies merchants, would send cannons to the patriots.

But Morris's third half brother, Staats Long, lived in England, was married to a duchess, and was an officer in the British army. Morris's mother remained loyal to the Crown, and two of his married sisters—Sarah and Isabella—had Loyalist husbands.

Gouverneur had long claimed to be uninterested in politics, expressing hope that America and its mother country could mend their widening rift. After Lexington and Concord, it was evident that wouldn't happen. He had to choose a side, and the decision he made would determine the course of his life—and the fate of a new nation.

TWO

A SLOOP IN THE FOREST

The bewigged men wore waistcoats, cravats, breeches, and stockings, accented with pocket watches and sometimes swords. The ladies, perched properly on the silk-bottomed chairs, styled their hair into towers, and their cloaks and hooped petticoats were made of Venetian poplin, German serge, or Genoa velvet. Having returned from his rambles through the woodlands and meadows of the estate, young Gouverneur watched them from the shadows of his parents' Wilton-carpeted, black-walnut parlor. They conversed confidently on a range of subjects—the ongoing French and Indian War, history and literature, music and science. Most read some Greek and Latin, and spoke at least one language other than English, preferably French. All the men could ride and hunt, the women were skilled at needlework, and both sexes could dance and play cards competently. Anyone naturally deficient in any of these had paid elocutionists, music teachers, and dancing instructors to help them polish their skills.

Twenty-three years before the gunshots in Lexington and Concord echoed around the globe, Gouverneur Morris was born into one of the elite families of colonial New York. The Morrises resided in a social stratum that included just a handful of other clans, among them the De Lanceys, the Schuylers (later to claim Alexander Hamilton as a son-in-law), the Van Rensselaers, the Van Cortlandts, and the Livingstons (whose family tree would sprout branches of Roosevelts and Bushes). By the middle of the eighteenth century, these wealthy landowning families had dominated the social and political life of colonial New York for generations. They lived in elegant manor houses on sprawling estates and were often tied by blood or marriage to English aristocrats.

The first Morrises to gain a foothold in America were two Welsh brothers, Richard and Lewis, who emigrated to Barbados in the 1640s after serving in Oliver Cromwell's army. In the late 1660s, several years after the English seized New Amsterdam and renamed it New York, Richard, now married and prospering as a merchant, moved there. Soon after arriving, he purchased jointly for Lewis and himself a five-hundred-acre tract from a Swedish farmer named Jonas Bronck about ten miles north of Manhattan, stretching east from the Harlem River to Long Island Sound. (Centuries later, the land would be included in the New York City borough named after Bronck: the Bronx.)

Richard and his wife both died in 1672, leaving a son who was only six months old—Gouverneur's grandfather, also named Lewis. The orphan was placed in the care of his uncle and namesake, who came from Barbados to take charge of him. Uncle Lewis expanded the family's holdings by buying additional land in New Jersey. When he died in 1691, his twenty-year-old nephew inherited all of it. That same year, the young heir married Isabella Graham, the daughter of the New York attorney general. Isabella's connections helped Lewis secure an appointment to the governor's council of New York, and he went on to become chief justice of the colony's highest court. He never had any formal education, but he was a voracious reader and assembled one of the largest private libraries in America.

Lewis was an odd man. Once, he constructed a sloop in the middle of a New Jersey forest and proudly led a group of men into the woods to show them his handiwork. He was taken aback when one of them asked how he planned to transport the ship to the water, roughly ten miles away. "My God," Morris responded, "I never thought of that." The sloop ended up rotting under the trees. Another oft-told tale about Lewis also involved water. One day the panicked miller of his estate, Morrisania, alerted him that a torrential rainstorm was coming, so he'd better open the floodgates of the dam to prevent its destruction. Instead of taking quick action, Morris calmly sat down to calculate how many cubic inches of water the dam could hold; he was still scribbling figures when it burst. Lewis and his offspring were so fond of telling tall tales that throughout Westchester, New York City, and Long Island, people referred to suspect stories as "Morrisanias."

Judge Morris relished political combat. In 1733, he became embroiled in the fight of his life when he crossed the royal governor of New York, William Cosby, in a case involving Cosby's attempt to claim his salary for the thirteen months that elapsed between his appointment by King George II and his arrival in New York. After Morris wrote an opinion denying Cosby's suit, Cosby fired him. When Morris enlisted a poor German printer named John Peter Zenger to publish newspaper articles attacking Cosby and his administration, Cosby had Zenger arrested for seditious libel. But Zenger was acquitted, in a decision many hailed as a victory for freedom of the press. The rebellious judge landed on his feet, winning an appointment as governor of New Jersey.

When Judge Morris died in 1746, he left Morrisania to his eldest son, Lewis Jr., who had already inherited his eccentricity: Instead of a hat, Lewis Jr. wore a cap made from the skin and feathers of a loon, the waterfowl known for its tremolo call that sounds like a maniacal laugh. A judge like his father, he wore it both in social settings and in the courtroom over which he presided.

Unlike the slave-owning planters who dominated society in the South, the Morrises and other New York landowners were less interested in agriculture than they were in trade and the law. But they did enslave Black people. A tally of Lewis Jr.'s property in 1762 listed seventy-nine cattle, sixteen horses, one hundred and nineteen sheep, eighty-four hogs, and forty-six enslaved people whom Lewis Jr. likely depended on to run his household, maintain his estate, raise livestock, and grow fruits and vegetables.

When Lewis Jr. became lord of Morrisania, about a fifth of New Yorkers were Black—the largest percentage in any colony north of Virginia—and enslaved people were present in at least half the city's households. In wealthy homes they were domestic servants, but they also built ships, manned crews, owned food carts, toiled on the docks, and worked as coopers, butchers, fishermen, carpenters, barbers, and blacksmiths. Their lives might have been less severe than what the enslaved experienced in the tobacco and rice fields of Virginia and the Carolinas, but they, too, hungered for freedom. In 1712 and 1741, they rebelled. The second revolt, known as "the Great Negro Plot," was sparked by a series of thirteen suspicious fires that might have been the prelude to an insurrection. White New Yorkers were terrified, and after an investigation the colonial authorities executed thirty slaves—burning thirteen of them at the stake, an extraordinary punishment for the time—and hanging seventeen along with four white people alleged to be ringleaders. Fifty enslaved people were publicly flogged, and seventy more were carted off to Caribbean slave markets. As a member of the colony's ruling class and a slave owner himself, these uprisings likely terrified Lewis Jr. At the same time, he must have been aware that many in the English-speaking world were beginning to question the morality of slavery. A growing number of books, pamphlets, and newspapers were making the case for abolition.

When Lewis Jr. inherited Morrisania, he was a forty-seven-year-old widower with four children. His first wife, Katryntje Staats, had died fifteen years earlier, after giving him a daughter and three sons. The same year his father died, Lewis Jr. finally remarried. His second wife was thirty-one-year-old Sarah Gouverneur. Sarah gave birth to two daughters, one in 1748 and one in 1749. At one thirty in the morning on January 30, 1752, the couple welcomed their first and only son. They named him Gouverneur, in honor of his mother's family.

Gouverneur's half brothers were relatively successful men—the eldest was a landowner and developer, the second a British army officer, and the third a rising lawyer—but Lewis Jr. was disappointed with the education they had received at Yale College. He held an unspecified grudge against the Congregationalists who had founded Connecticut and Yale and didn't want Gouverneur to absorb their "low craft and cunning." But he detected greatness in Gouverneur. Thomas Jones, a Tory judge who wrote an account of his experiences in revolutionary New York, agreed that Gouverneur was the best of the brood, describing him as having "more knowledge (though still a youth) than all his three brothers put together."

To begin Gouverneur's formal education, Lewis Jr. sent him to New Rochelle to live and study with a Swiss Huguenot minister who taught him French and the basics of mathematics, botany, geography, navigation, and surveying. Then, when Gouverneur was only nine, Lewis Jr. sent him to the Academy of Philadelphia. Founded by Benjamin Franklin, the academy was the foremost college preparatory school in the colonies. The trustees of the school wanted students to have the classical education they had received—that meant Latin and Greek grammar and poetry, history, logic, rhetoric, geometry, astronomy, and music. At Franklin's insistence, the school also gave its students more modern, practical skills that would prepare them for useful careers. All classes were taught in English, and the students learned how to write, survey, navigate, draw in perspective, and keep merchants' accounts.

In 1762, when Gouverneur was ten, his father died. Lewis Jr. had been troubled that the children from his first marriage resented his new wife and their half siblings, largely because their father's second family meant smaller inheritances for them. Anticipating strife, Lewis Jr. made a plea in his will for family harmony, urging his children to "use their best endeavors to cultivate a good understanding with each other," while displaying the quirkiness for which he was well known. "My desire is that nothing be mentioned about me," he wrote, "not so much as a line in the newspaper to tell the world I am dead."

His will divided Morrisania into two estates. His eldest son from his first marriage (yet another Lewis) got the western part. His widow Sarah got the eastern portion, which was to be passed to Staats Long, the second oldest son, when she died. Though Gouverneur didn't inherit any land, Staats Long was to pay him two thousand pounds (about a half a million dollars today) after he took possession of Morrisania. Lewis Jr. also left a number of enslaved people to his children and relatives. The will stipulated that Gouverneur was entitled to take possession of "a Negro boy called George" upon his mother's death, but there is no evidence that he ever did so.

Lewis Jr. also included specific instructions regarding Gouverneur's education. "It is my desire that my son Gouverneur Morris have the best education that is to be had in Europe or America," he wrote. Gouverneur was *not*, he emphasized, to be sent to Yale.

The instructors at the Academy of Philadelphia recognized Gouverneur's brilliance almost immediately. When he was only twelve—three years younger than the typical first-year college student—they determined he was ready to attend King's College, later renamed Columbia University. King's College prided itself on teaching "the arts of reasoning exactly, of writing correctly, and speaking eloquently," according to a newspaper advertisement published in 1754, the year it was founded. The school also promised to teach students the basics of surveying, navigation, geography, history, husbandry, commerce, and government, and to impart "knowledge of all nature in the heavens above us, and in the air, water and earth around us." King's College was committed to equipping its graduates with "everything useful for the comfort, the convenience and elegance of life."

There were nine students in Gouverneur's class, but only seven would make it to graduation. They all came from upper-class families, and they became a tight-knit group. Gouverneur was particularly skilled at math and amused himself and his classmates by completing complex calculations in his head. He enjoyed solving problems related to the speed and power of running water, and the motion of machinery. The prodigy was so sharp he didn't have to work very hard to complete his assignments, so he didn't.

Located on the wooded northern edge of New York City, King's College impressed one Scottish traveler as one of the most beautiful schools in the world—with a single caveat. "One circumstance I think is a little unlucky," he observed. "The entrance to this college is through one of the streets where the most noted prostitutes live. This is certainly a temptation to the youth that have occasion to pass so often that way." King's College students also didn't have to go far to get a drink, and the pampered Morris probably got his first taste of New York's boisterous tavern life at one of the many drinking establishments surrounding the school. It was the beginning of a lifelong affinity for wine, women, and boozy late-night socializing.

★

Distracted by the delights of college life, Gouverneur was largely oblivious to the increasingly strained relationship between Britain and her American colonies.

In April 1764, Britain's Parliament approved a broad revenue-raising measure, popularly known as the Sugar Act. The law increased the duties colonists had to pay on imports such as wine, coffee, and textiles and ratcheted up enforcement of the collection of duties on sugar and molasses imported from the West Indies. New York's merchants drew up petitions opposing the Sugar Act, but the British ignored their appeals and went even further. In March 1765, Parliament approved the Stamp Act, levying new taxes on a wide array of paper and paper products, including newspapers, pamphlets, legal documents, and playing cards. The Americans are "children planted by our care, nourished up by our indulgence . . . and protected by our arms," scoffed Charles Townshend, a member of Parliament who would soon become chancellor of the exchequer. Why shouldn't they help the mother country pay its debts from the French and Indian War?

Just two days after approving the Stamp Act, Parliament passed the Quartering Act, which required colonial governments to house and supply British troops stationed in America. Having to fork over more money for essentials like sugar and paper was bad enough; having to provide room and board to the redcoats enforcing the rules was infuriating. In October, most of the colonies sent representatives to New York to formulate a unified response. They issued a declaration laying out the basic principle underlying their opposition to the new taxes: They did not have a voice in Parliament, and therefore it was unjust for Parliament to tax them. Their pronouncement, issued on October 19, 1765, began with a profession of loyalty to the king and his government. As loyal Englishmen, they argued, "no taxes should be imposed on them, but with their own consent, given personally, or by their representatives."

Three days later, frigates in New York Harbor fired their cannons to herald the arrival of the *Edward*, which carried two tons of stamped paper, parchment, and vellum in its hold and was about to test New Yorkers' willingness to abide by the Stamp Act. Escorted by two British warships, the *Edward* dropped anchor off the Battery, on the southern tip of Manhattan, near Fort George, as two thousand protesters seethed on the shore. Other ships in the harbor flew their colors at half-mast, to signify "mourning, lamentation and woe." Under cover of darkness on the twenty-fourth, the crew of the *Edward* deposited the stamped paper in the fort, but handbills posted on doors, shops, and street corners threatened dire consequences for anyone who deigned to use it.

The Stamp Act went into effect on November 1. At dusk, a stream of sailors, artisans, and laborers flowed toward the city Common, in what is now City Hall Park in Lower Manhattan, collecting candles and torches from homes on their way. By seven that evening, there were two thousand people gathered in the field, their faces half-shadowed by the wavering light. They quickly erected a scaffold and hung an effigy of the royal governor holding stamped paper in his hand; next to it, they strung up an effigy of the devil. At the same time, a second group of marchers snaked through the lanes and alleys of Manhattan, heading for Fort George. When they reached the fort, they hurled insults at the soldiers, daring them to open fire. Emboldened by the guards' inaction, some demonstrators broke into the governor's coach house and seized one of his carriages. Later, the two groups merged at Bowling Green, where they ignited a huge bonfire and burned the gallows, the effigies, and the coach. After all were reduced to ashes, some members of the mob reassembled at the home of Major Thomas James, the commander of the fort, who had vowed to the colonists that he would "cram the stamps down their throats with the end of [his] sword." They broke into the major's house, snatched mirrors, doors, furniture, curtains, and books, and smashed them in the street. They drank James's wine, "destroyed the beef, threw the butter about," and stole the royal colors, which they paraded through the streets until four in the morning.

New Yorkers had made it clear they did not like being taxed without their consent.

THREE

WIT AND BEAUTY

Less than a year later, in August 1766, Gouverneur was back at Morrisania on a break from school when disaster struck.

Surely, he had been warned to stay out of the kitchen. It was a place of hazards—sharp knives, swinging pots, open flames—but such cautions carried less force for a confident young collegian than for a child. Now a sophisticated college student, Gouverneur was old enough to know better yet young enough to ignore the risk. He and his friend Morgan Lewis were wrestling or chasing each other through the Morris household when one of them toppled a kettle of boiling water. It pitched forward, spilling scalding liquid across Gouverneur's right side.

The results were catastrophic. The boiling water stripped away much of the flesh on his arm and ravaged the nerves beneath. Caregivers likely turned to the few remedies available: vinegar, or soap made from limewater and oil, to fend off inflammation, then exposure to open air to harden a protective scab and coax new tissue beneath it. Morgan Lewis would later recall that Gouverneur bore the agony with "a fortitude that would have done honor to an Indian brave," but the ordeal lasted months. He withdrew from King's College for a full year to convalesce at home, and though he healed, the arm never wholly recovered. The scars would remain visible all his life—a physical reminder of mischief, pain, and resilience.

The injury was slow to heal, but his mind stayed quick. Though one of the youngest of his cohort, Gouverneur made up a year's lost work and graduated with his peers. On May 17, 1768, in the still-new St. Paul's Chapel, Gouverneur and five classmates received bachelor of arts degrees. In Gouverneur's commencement speech—"Wit and Beauty"—he took up a theme that would anchor his future politics: Human beings, he said, were ruled by "the passions of barbarians," but wit and beauty could elevate them toward civilization. The question implicit in his speech—what form of government could restrain those passions while honoring "the love of liberty so natural to all"?—was one he would spend the rest of his life trying to answer.

Like his father and grandfather, and many of New York's leading men, Morris chose to pursue a career in the law. He clerked in the office of an old family friend, William Smith Jr. Under the rules of the time, Morris would be eligible for admission to the bar after serving a three-year apprenticeship in Smith's office. During this period, Gouverneur likely lived in Smith's house, at No. 5 Broadway.

Smith offered a formidable education by example, if not by formal instruction. Scholar, historian, lawyer, councilman—he read Greek philosophy, Hebrew commentary, medical treatises, mathematics. He believed Parliament had overstepped with the Stamp Act, yet he remained wary of the masses, preferring limits on public influence. His clerks, meanwhile, were consigned to copying legal documents with scant explanation. Peter Van Schaack, a fellow King's College graduate who was completing his apprenticeship when Morris started his, befriended the new arrival. Later, Van Schaack described the drudgery of the job. "How many hours have I hunted, how many books turned up for what three minutes of explanation from any tolerable lawyer would have made evident to me!" Gouverneur persevered and even flourished.

He bonded with Smith, devoured law, and used his keen mathematical mind to master public credit and currency—expertise the young republic would one day desperately need. In 1769, he published an anonymous article asserting that a bill before the New York colonial assembly would trigger inflation. When his authorship was revealed, the teenager was hailed as a fiscal prodigy.

In October 1771, not yet twenty, Morris received his law license and took the attorney's oath. Restless, ambitious, still boyish, he longed to see England before settling into his profession. In February 1772, he wrote to Smith for advice. The journey, he said, would help him "rub off in the gay circle a few of those many barbarisms which characterize a provincial education." He admitted, wryly, "a taste for pleasure" (a taste that would only deepen as he moved through the salons and drawing rooms of the Atlantic world), and worried that London might overwhelm his self-discipline. Yet it was, he said, his last chance to "pause before I tread the great stage of life."

Smith urged caution. Build your career first and stabilize your finances, he counseled. Knowing the young man's temperament, Smith warned that London's charms could swallow him whole. "If you mean to adorn your character, I say, go," he wrote. "But considering your time of life, and the country you go to, I tremble at every step you are to take."

In the end, Morris stayed in a city that was also on the rise: New York was energetic, cosmopolitan, and already the second-largest city in British America, with nearly twenty-five thousand residents. (Only Philadelphia, with forty thousand people, was larger.) Geographically, it hugged the southern tip of Manhattan from Bowling Green to Catherine Street, just over a mile away. Broadway was paved and lined with poplars and elms, but most side streets were narrow and ill-kept. Three-story brick houses jostled against workshops, stores, and lawyers' offices. Public water came from carts, as wells were often fouled. Light came from oil lamps along the major streets.

The city's diversity set it apart from Philadelphia and Boston. Less bound to religion, more devoted to commerce, New York welcomed people of a range of faiths—Catholics and Jews among them—and immigrants of all origins. This openness would shape its character and fuel its dynamism for centuries to come. The city's hard-charging personality bred its own roughness. John Adams of Massachusetts noticed it when he visited during Morris's early years at the bar. "With all the opulence and splendor of this city, there is very little good breeding to be found . . . I have not seen one real gentleman, one well-bred man since I came to town," Adams recorded in his diary. "There is no modesty—no attention to one another. They talk very loud, very fast, and altogether."

Still, Morris fit the place. Tall—about six foot four—broad-shouldered, with light-brown hair, blue eyes fringed with long lashes, and an aquiline nose, he had the looks of an aristocrat and the wit of a charmer. His legal reputation grew steadily, helped by his membership in the Moot, a lawyers' club that met at the King's Arms Tavern, on what is now Whitehall Street. There he joined Smith, Robert R. Livingston, John Jay, Van Schaack, and other rising attorneys in spirited Friday night debates over law, politics, and philosophy.

Soon after joining the Moot, Gouverneur fell in love.

The Livingston family—wealthy, influential, and prodigiously large—opened their doors to New York's brightest young men. Morris's friend John Jay soon courted Sarah Livingston. Morris became captivated by her sister Catherine ("Kitty"), a year older than him. He sent her poems declaring his "hopeless passion." He asked, in a letter, for a lock of her hair "to wear devoutly as a sacred relic." But his ardor outpaced his prospects. Financially unsteady, professionally just beginning, he could not offer what Kitty required. By late summer 1772, their romance had dissolved. Morris consoled Kitty—and himself—with characteristic cheer. "I am (as you know) constitutionally one of the happiest of men," he wrote. "A heart like yours deserves to be happy, and depend upon it, it will be so."

★

Less than a year after Gouverneur abandoned his pursuit of Kitty Livingston, the passions of the colonists were aroused by an especially odious new tax.

In May 1773, Parliament approved the Tea Act. The law granted the British East India Company the right to ship its tea directly to North America, without paying export duties. Its main goal was to help the floundering company, which had seventeen million pounds of surplus tea in its warehouses. The colonists mostly drank Dutch tea, which was cheaper. Now the British tea would be less expensive than the Dutch, but to purchase it the colonists would have to pay a tax. Britain's goal, many colonists believed, was to force them to recognize the legitimacy of taxation without representation.

On December 16, 1773, more than five thousand people jammed into Boston's Old South Meeting House. Many were Bostonians, but some had come from the surrounding towns, traveling in carriages, on horseback, and on foot to attend one of the largest political gatherings in the history of the colony. Months of rising tension over the Tea Act had pushed the city to the edge. Three tea-laden ships had arrived in Boston Harbor—the *Dartmouth*, the *Eleanor*, and the *Beaver*—each carrying East India Company tea that Parliament insisted must be taxed upon landing. Midnight was the deadline for the *Dartmouth*, the earliest arrival, to unload its cargo and pay the required duties.

All day, the men at the Old South Meeting House debated what to do. It was nearly sundown when Francis Rotch, the Quaker who owned the *Dartmouth*, walked through the doors. The candles flickering inside the Old South Meeting House couldn't chase the gloom that crept over the pews as another rainy, raw New England day receded through the arched windows. Rotch had left the meetinghouse several hours earlier to make a personal plea to Thomas Hutchinson, the royal governor, but Hutchinson had not budged: He wanted the tea unloaded and the tax paid. A murmur passed through the crowd. Then John Rowe—merchant, smuggler, and owner of the *Eleanor*—spoke up: "Who knows . . . how tea will mingle with salt water?"

The room erupted: "A mob! A mob!" John Hancock, who was presiding from the pulpit, struck his gavel to restore order, counseling calm. Now the firebrand Samuel Adams rose, his head and hands trembling. The fifty-one-year-old had frittered away a fortune by running his family's malthouse into the ground, but had reinvented himself as a political organizer. "This meeting can do nothing more to save the country," he declared.

That was the signal. Men disguised as Mohawk warriors appeared, wrapped in blankets, painted in lampblack. From the meetinghouse, the band made its way down Milk Street, toward the wharves. There they divided into three groups, one for each of the tea-laden ships. On each ship, some men descended into the hold to attach pulleys to the heavy tea chests. A second group hoisted the chests onto the deck. Then a third group used their hatchets to break open the chests so they could shovel and pour the tea over the side, tossing the demolished chests after it. The men worked silently in the moonlight; the only sound was the thwack of their blades splitting the wood. The work was done in less than three hours, and it was done thoroughly: When the tide receded the next morning, long windrows of drenched tea leaves reached far out into the harbor.

The next day John Adams, who was Samuel's second cousin, wrote in his diary: "This destruction of the tea is so bold, so daring . . . that I can't but consider it as an epoch in history." News of the Boston Tea Party quickly spread to New York and Philadelphia, which would have to decide what to do when tea-laden ships arrived in their ports. In New York, crowds pledged to follow the Bostonians' lead. "They highly extolled the Bostonians," one messenger reported on January 3, 1774. Philadelphia received the news soon after.

Gouverneur Morris, still at the beginning of his career as a young lawyer, felt the world shifting beneath his feet. New York was in an uproar, and yet he still professed indifference. "Politics I dislike," he wrote in January 1774, "and only look on with pity, while the madness of so many is made the gain of so few." But events would not let him stay on the sidelines.

★

Back in London, King George III sniffed that he was "much hurt" by the Boston Tea Party, but that hurt quickly hardened into fury. His subjects were similarly enraged; Benjamin Franklin, who had been a colonial agent in London for nearly two decades, described "a great wrath" sweeping the country. The colonists' defiance threatened the very underpinnings of the British Empire. Retreat from America might inspire similar rebellions in Ireland, the Caribbean, and India. And if Britain lost its empire, as one member of the House of Commons warned, it would "revert to her primitive insignificancy in the map of the world." It was time for harsher measures.

In the spring of 1774, Parliament approved the Coercive Acts—immediately christened by Americans as the Intolerable Acts. "The die is now cast," the king wrote. "The colonies must either submit or triumph. We must not retreat."

Under the first law, which took effect on June 1, 1774, British warships blockaded Boston Harbor, strangling the city's commerce. The port would remain closed, the British vowed, until the colonists reimbursed the East India Company for the tea they had destroyed. Under the second law, the British replaced elected officials in Massachusetts with appointed ones and restricted town meetings and jury selection. The third law gave the royal governor the power to move a trial to another colony—or even to Britain—if he determined that an impartial proceeding could not be held in Massachusetts. After the 1770 Boston Massacre, British troops had withdrawn from the city. But under the fourth Coercive Act (which applied to all the colonies), the redcoats returned, and British officers were empowered to seize unoccupied buildings to house their men.

New York was convulsed by the news. In mid-May, New Yorkers

convened a series of public meetings to discuss what to do next. Despite his avowed lack of interest in politics, Morris attended one of the gatherings in Fraunces Tavern, but he remained deeply skeptical of a revolutionary course. "Yesterday I was present at a grand division of the city, and there I beheld my fellow citizens very accurately counting all their chickens, not only before any of them were hatched, but before above one half of the eggs were laid," he wrote to a friend on May 20, 1774. Morris maintained hope that the colonists could repair their rupture with the mother country. Standing in the balcony at Fraunces Tavern, he couldn't help noticing that property owners were arrayed on one side of the room, tradesmen on the other. Morris feared the gentry would lead the masses into open revolt. Concerned about the volatility of the public, he feared chaos more than oppression. "I see it, and I see it with fear and trembling, that if the disputes with Great Britain continue, we shall be under the worst of all possible dominions. We shall be under the domination of a riotous mob," he wrote.

Massachusetts argued that the colonies might sway Britain if they acted together. Its leaders called for a colonial convention, to be held in Philadelphia in September, to coordinate a collective response, present a united set of grievances, and explore common measures short of outright independence. Twelve of the thirteen colonies—all except Georgia—sent a total of fifty-six delegates to the First Continental Congress. They included John and Samuel Adams, George Washington, Patrick Henry, and John Jay. Two prominent patriots, Benjamin Franklin (who was still in England) and Thomas Jefferson, did not attend.

The delegates convened in solidarity and hope. They laid out their objections to the new laws and reiterated their opposition to taxation without representation. After seven weeks of debate, they approved a boycott of British goods and pledged to halt exports to Britain until the Intolerable Acts were repealed.

This demonstration of unity only stiffened British resolve. In

November 1774, King George III told Parliament that the colonists were exhibiting "a most daring spirit of resistance and disobedience," with "fresh violences of a very criminal nature." In February 1775, Parliament presented a petition to the king declaring that "a rebellion at this time actually exists" in Massachusetts. The lawmakers asked the king to bring the colonists to heel. "You may depend on my taking the most speedy and effectual measures for enforcing due obedience to the laws," he told them. Soon after, an American artist visiting London watched as the British loaded tents, wagons, cartridge boxes, and kegs of flint marked "Boston" onto warships bound for America. One of the redcoat regiments tramping toward Tower Wharf wore caps decorated with an embroidered skull and an inscription: "Death or Glory."

The rebels in Boston, where dedication to the patriot cause was nearly universal, were girding for a fight. New York remained divided—more Loyalist, more mercantile, more conflicted than Boston. Tory placards, handbills, and broadsides sprouted in the streets of the city in the spring of 1775, many of them churned out by James Rivington, publisher of the *New-York Gazetteer*, the most influential Loyalist newspaper in the colonies. "The people here are very much divided, and party spirit is very high," a Scots visitor noted in March 1775.

Gouverneur still might have been undecided when the Scotsman wrote those words. A month later, after the April clashes at Lexington and Concord, he no longer was: He cast his lot with the patriots. It was a choice prefigured by the speech he gave when he graduated from King's College, when he included himself among those "who can boast the glorious title of free-born Americans." And it was a choice made in the spirit of his eccentric grandfather, who had stood up for the freedom of the press in the trial of the printer John Peter Zenger, way back in 1735. That trial, Morris later said, "was the germ of American freedom—the morning star of that liberty which subsequently revolutionized America." Much later, he explained why he concluded that violent revolution was America's only recourse. "Could the American contest have been decided without blood, I should have been happy," he wrote. "While the appeal lay to reason, I reasoned; when it was made to the sword, I thought it my duty to join in the great issue."

In May 1775, prominent Westchester County patriots convened in White Plains to choose representatives to the new Provincial Congress—the provisional government New York revolutionaries formed to replace the colony's royalist General Assembly. At this time, Westchester included Morrisania, and Gouverneur Morris, still only twenty-three years old, was one of the men they chose.

FOUR

THE COMMANDER IN CHIEF

In June 1775, with British and American forces staring each other down around Boston, the Second Continental Congress did something unprecedented. It took the unruly New England militias besieging British General Thomas Gage and consolidated them into a single Continental Army, a force that would fight not just for Massachusetts but for all thirteen colonies.

Congress then did something even bolder: it placed that army in the hands of a tall, reserved Virginian in a blue and buff uniform—George Washington.

A few New England delegates thought one of their own should command the troops outside Boston, and some patriots grumbled that a man who enslaved people should not lead a fight for freedom. But the appointment of the forty-three-year-old Virginian signaled that this would be an army of all the colonies, and that the wealthiest and most populous colony, Virginia, was fully in the fight. Washington had genuine military experience, having risen to lieutenant colonel in the Virginia militia during the French and Indian War. In that conflict he had shown both leadership and nerve under fire. "I heard the bullets whistle; and believe me there is something charming in the sound," he wrote in a 1754 letter later printed in *The London Magazine*.

Washington had never commanded more than a regiment and had known disasters as well as successes. He possessed, nonetheless, a quality many other veterans of that war did not: a stately, almost majestic presence. He looked and acted like the commander of an army, with "so much martial dignity in his deportment that you distinguish him to be a general and a soldier from among ten thousand people," the Pennsylvania delegate Dr. Benjamin Rush remarked.

For all his outward confidence, Washington was uneasy about the task Congress laid on his shoulders. "Though I am truly sensible of the high honor done me in this appointment," he told the delegates, "yet I feel great distress, from a consciousness that my abilities and military experience may not be equal to the extensive and important trust." He insisted he would take no salary—only reimbursement of expenses—and then, aware that defeat was entirely possible, tried to inoculate himself against future blame. "Lest some unlucky event should happen, unfavorable to my reputation," he said, "I beg it may be remembered . . . that I, this day, declare with the utmost sincerity, I do not think myself equal to the command I am honored with."

On June 23, 1775, the reluctant general left Philadelphia to take command of the troops around Boston. Two days later, on Sunday the twenty-fifth, Gouverneur Morris and other delegates from the New York Provincial Congress met Washington in Newark, New Jersey. From there they traveled to Hoboken and boarded a ferry across the Hudson. At about four o'clock they disembarked at the country estate of Colonel Leonard Lispenard, two miles north of the city. Local patriot leaders and nine companies of uniformed New York militiamen greeted Washington as he strode onto the beach. With "shouts and huzzas," they guided him to Lispenard's house for a meal and then escorted him into town. Church bells rang and citizens shouted themselves hoarse as the procession made its way down Broadway to Hull's Tavern, where Washington would spend the night. Ministers threw up their hands as parishioners bolted from the pews to see the spectacle.

The fanfare suggested a unity that did not exist in the army that Congress had cobbled together.

From the beginning, Washington's Continental Army—patched together from local militias with provincial habits—was riven by regional rivalries. One wintry day, the general had to gallop into Harvard Yard to break up a snowball fight that had devolved into a biting, gouging brawl between backwoods Virginia riflemen, newly arrived to join the army, and a Marblehead, Massachusetts, regiment. The conflict began after the Marblehead men mocked the rustic clothing of the Virginians, who wore ruffled and fringed white linen frocks. "With the spring of a deer, [Washington] leaped from his saddle, threw the reins of his bridle into the hands of his servant, and rushed into the thickest of the melee, with an iron grip seized two tall, brawny athletic, savage-looking riflemen by the throat, keeping them at arm's length, alternating shaking and talking to them," one witness recalled. "Seeing this, the others took flight at the top of their speed in all directions from the scene of the conflict."

There was no mistaking why it worked. Washington stood six foot three and weighed close to two hundred pounds. A superior horseman—Jefferson called him "the best horseman of his age"—he loved foxhunting so much he sometimes rode for seven hours straight. Tales circulated of his prodigious strength: He was said to have hurled a stone more than two hundred feet from the bed of a stream to the top of Virginia's Natural Bridge, and to have easily bested a circle of young men on the Mount Vernon lawn who were competing to see who could throw an iron bar the farthest. Washington ambled up, the portraitist Charles Willson Peale remembered, and without even removing his coat, threw the bar "far, very far beyond our utmost limit."

He was rich—largely because he had married the attractive and wealthy widow Martha Dandridge Custis in 1759—and had the tastes of an English gentleman. He rode in an elegant green coach with leather lining and brass bolts and brackets, manufactured in the mother country to his exact specifications. He dressed impeccably in the finest English wools and linens and wore custom-made shoes and boots imported from London.

Yet beneath the power and polish, Washington shared some of the very prejudices he was forced to manage. A month after assuming command, he complained to fellow Virginian Richard Henry Lee about an "unaccountable kind of stupidity" in the common Massachusetts soldier. "It is among the most difficult tasks I ever undertook in my life to induce these people to believe that there is, or can be, danger till the bayonet is pushed at their breasts," he wrote.

To the New Englander John Adams, the root of the discord lay in slavery and social hierarchy. "Gentlemen in the other colonies have large plantations of slaves, and the common people among them are very ignorant and very poor," Adams observed. No wonder Southern colonists were "habituated to higher notions of themselves and the distinction between them and the common people than we are."

Military necessity—or an instinct for survival—forced Washington to set aside at least one of his prejudices. Black soldiers had already served in the Massachusetts militia and fought at Lexington and Concord. At first, Washington resisted the idea of including them in the Continental Army, grouping them with children and old men as unfit for service. But as desertions mounted and enlistments lagged, he listened to Northern generals who attested that Black soldiers had fought bravely in early battles—and warned that if the colonists refused them, they might join the British instead.

★

Despite his youth, Morris quickly emerged as a leader of the New York Provincial Congress. Now that war had come, raising money to build and sustain a capable military was the top priority. Morris took the lead in drafting a plan under which the Continental Congress would issue a common currency and distribute it among the colonies. At his suggestion, the Provincial Congress opened its doors to merchants and other interested citizens so they could hear the delegates debate the idea, and many walked away dazzled by the young man's eloquence and mastery of the subject. Morris "appeared to have comprehended it throughout, and as it were by intuition," a friend remarked. "He advanced and maintained opinions new to all. There was none who did not ultimately perceive and acknowledge them to be just."

Even as New Yorkers braced for more bloodshed, they made a final attempt to persuade the mother country to relent. Morris helped draft a plan of reconciliation to be submitted to the Continental Congress. It proposed that the colonies be permitted to tax themselves, with all revenues funneled into American coffers.

The inclusion of an anti-Catholic provision condemning the "indulgence and establishment of popery all along the interior confines of the old Protestant colonies" gave Morris an opportunity to stand up for religious freedom. The delegates had added the language to protest the Quebec Act of 1774, which extended the province of Quebec to the Ohio River, but Morris called it the "most arrant nonsense." In a letter to John Jay, he wrote that "the foolish religious business I opposed until I was weary; it was carried by a very small majority, and my dissent entered."

The plan of reconciliation went nowhere—events had already moved far beyond such a solution.

★

In October 1775, King George III replaced the luckless General Gage with General William Howe. Two weeks later, the monarch told Parliament that the rebellion in America had spread beyond Massachusetts and that its goal, incredibly, was independence. The colonists had raised an army, were trying to form a navy, and had illegitimately seized legislative, executive, and judicial powers, he said. Many colonists remained loyal, he added hopefully, but "the torrent of violence has been strong enough to compel their acquiescence till a sufficient force shall appear to support them."

New Yorkers expected that force to be deployed against them, because Boston had become untenable for the British. Crammed into overcrowded camps, the redcoats were running short of food, fuel, and tents; smallpox and dysentery were rampant. "The cold is so intense that the ink freezes in the pen whilst I write by the fireside," a British officer in Boston wrote on the last day of 1775. "Our little army has suffered severely from the dampness of the season, and from living totally on salt provisions."

After the disasters at Lexington and Concord, the British had little appetite for marching deep into a hostile Massachusetts countryside. New York offered a more promising prize. Near the center of the Eastern Seaboard, with a wide harbor and superior port facilities, it could not be effectively defended by the rebels' fledgling navy. If the British could seize the city, they might command the Hudson River all the way to Lake Champlain—a major coup that would let them cleave fractious New England from the other colonies. And though many Tories had fled, enough remained in the city and its hinterlands to aid a British force.

The conquest of New York seemed not just likely, but inevitable.

FIVE

WAR COMES TO NEW YORK

By the winter of 1775–76, the American rebellion had ceased to be a skirmish and become a war: a new Continental Army under George Washington ringed Boston; provincial congresses had replaced royal governments; and both sides braced for the next blow. Everyone knew that New York—wealthy, strategic, and dangerously divided—would be the British Empire's next target.

The man sent to defend the city arrived in characteristic fashion.

Moody, coarse, and unkempt, General Charles Lee was rarely seen without his beloved dogs—especially Spada, his Pomeranian, with whom he communicated in what he called "the language of doggism" as they dined together. The forty-four-year-old patriot commander, a veteran of the French and Indian War with a military record that nobody else on the American side could match, had helped Washington besiege Boston in the summer and fall of 1775. Now Lee had been tasked with preventing New York from falling into British hands. Logistically, it was nearly an impossible mission, but he was determined to make the enemy pay dearly for its trophy.

Lee's arrival on February 4, 1776, was a harbinger of the violence to come, and it prompted New Yorkers to flee the city in droves. On the Sunday after he appeared, people flooded into the streets to load carts with their belongings, creating so much commotion that the few who ventured to church that day had a hard time hearing clergymen over the din. "To see the vast number of houses shut up, one would think the city almost evacuated," one resident observed. "Women and children are scarcely to be seen in the streets. Troops are daily coming in; they break open and quarter themselves in the houses they find shut up. Necessity knows no law."

Lee immediately got to work. He ordered the construction of thirteen forts and batteries on Manhattan and Long Island, to defend against British warships sailing up the East River. He erected barricades to block major streets, and six more forts and gun batteries between the city and King's Bridge at the northern end of Manhattan. Laborers, most of them enslaved, constructed another string of forts on Brooklyn Heights—a strategically vital high ground—linked by trenches and breastworks.

Only twenty-four, Morris was prime military age, and he wanted to help defend New York—but on his terms. At the time, it was not uncommon for men of wealth and influence to raise their own battalions. In a plan they presented to the Provincial Congress, Morris and other members of the New York gentry said they would raise a battalion of fifteen hundred men, on the condition that they be allowed to appoint their own officers. The Provincial Congress agreed to name Morris—who was slated to be a lieutenant colonel—and shoemaker John Lasher, who was already a colonel in the New York militia, as the commanding officers of the force, but it refused to accept the other would-be officers. Morris thought it was wrong for him to accept his commission if the other men didn't get theirs, so when the Provincial Congress forwarded the plan to the Continental Congress for its final approval, he persuaded his brother Lewis, who was serving as a delegate in Philadelphia, to scotch it. Morris never served as a soldier, but his contributions to the Continental Army would far outweigh anything he might have done in a uniform.

On March 17, 1776, Howe and his troops finally evacuated Boston under pressure from American artillery. The British retreated to Halifax, Nova Scotia, to regroup and prepare for their inevitable attack on New York. In response, Washington immediately moved eight thousand troops south to defend the city, and on April 13, he joined them. The commander in chief set up his headquarters at No. 1 Broadway, a town house at the southern tip of Manhattan, and contemplated his grim predicament. New York's spacious harbor could accommodate a huge invasion fleet, and Washington expected British warships to sail up the two rivers that bounded the city to pummel it. He added more gun batteries to the ones Lee had deployed and ordered the construction of two forts on either side of the Hudson River—Fort Washington in New York, and Fort Lee in New Jersey. The work occupied nearly every able-bodied man in the city, free and enslaved.

Despite chasing the British from Boston, the Americans hardly seemed ready to take on an empire. The farmers and artisans who made up the bulk of the Continental Army were hardy, resourceful, and handy with tools, but they were poorly trained and undisciplined. Unwashed and unshaven, clad in mismatched shirts, coats, breeches, and hats, the rebels carried a wide variety of muskets, rifles, and fowling pieces (light shotguns for shooting birds)—to say nothing of the aforementioned prejudices, with soldiers of one colony looking askance at soldiers of another. Officers wore different colored cockades on their hats, but otherwise they were indistinguishable from their men. To make matters worse, some soldiers were less motivated by patriotism than the prospect of a paycheck.

★

On May 15, 1776, the Continental Congress directed the colonies to make a clean break from Britain by forming new state governments. Nine days later, Morris urged the New York Provincial Congress to follow the order, arguing that the colonies had traveled too far down the road of independence to turn back. Believing otherwise, he said, reminded him of "a common story of a certain juggler who would undertake to cut off a man's head and clap it on again so neatly as to cure him without a scar." Morris acknowledged that the patriots were embarking on a risky course, but "as a connection with Great Britain cannot again exist without enslaving America, an independence is absolutely necessary. I cannot balance between the two. We run a hazard in one path, I confess, but then are infallibly ruined if we pursue the other." He predicted that Britain's attempt to subdue America would fail. Then he painted a portrait of a glorious future: A united and economically thriving republic, enlarged by western settlements and blessed with a growing and educated population. He and other members of the upper classes would relinquish some of their privileges for the new nation, and America would emerge as "an asylum from oppression" for people around the globe.

Even at this late date, however, many people in New York City and the surrounding region rejected Morris's vision of an independent America. Loyalist sentiment was especially prevalent on Long Island, in Queens County, and on Staten Island—and it grew bolder as Howe's expected invasion loomed closer. The Provincial Congress formed a committee to investigate suspected Loyalists and appointed Morris to serve on it. His commitment to the cause was tested when he had to sit in judgment of a familiar Tory: his mentor William Smith.

Responding to a summons to appear before the committee, Smith wrote to Morris that he still believed that an "unnatural and destructive war" between Britain and America could be avoided, and that he had "always considered the two countries as under a great covenant." But Morris warned Smith that he was taking a huge risk by swimming against the tide of rebellion. "The future consequence of every gentleman in the country depends upon the decision of his present conduct," he wrote. Morris urged Smith to reconsider, to "cross over into the road whither you are beckoned by your countrymen."

Despite Smith's recalcitrance, Morris's committee declined to punish him. A plot targeting the most important man in the colonies—George Washington—was a more serious matter. The ringleaders were royal officials: William Tryon, the royal governor of New York, who was cloistered aboard the *Duchess of Gordon* in New York Harbor, and David Mathews, New York City's Tory mayor. Tryon and Mathews recruited and paid men to organize an underground force that would aid the British when they invaded New York. Witnesses later testified that each man who joined the plot got five guineas, plus a promise of two hundred acres of land for himself, a hundred acres for his wife, and fifty for each of his children.

Tryon and Mathews also hoped to kill or capture Washington. That goal appeared within reach when they recruited one of Washington's bodyguards, an Irish native named Thomas Hickey. Five foot, six inches tall, with a dark complexion, Hickey was a former British soldier who had deserted. Now, considering a British victory to be inevitable, he had returned to the king's service. As a member of Washington's protective force, known as the Life Guards, Hickey was an especially valuable recruit, and he corrupted several of his comrades.

The plot came to light when Hickey and another Life Guard, Michael Lynch, were arrested and imprisoned for passing counterfeit money. Counterfeit bills were circulating widely, and the soldiers would have been returned to their unit for military discipline if they had kept their mouths shut. But Isaac Ketcham, a counterfeiter himself who was sharing a cell beneath city hall with Hickey and Lynch, heard them discussing the plot. Ketcham was able to pull key details out of them by presenting himself as a fellow Loyalist. Eager to return to his children, who were on their own on Long Island after the death of their mother, Ketcham wrote a letter to the Provincial Congress asking for leniency and indicating he had important information he'd like to share with them. Morris and his colleagues on the committee, John Jay and Philip Livingston, summoned Ketcham to testify and were horrified by the tale he told. At one in the morning on June 22, they sent troops to arrest Mathews at his home in Flatbush and that night, they arrested gunsmith Gilbert Forbes, another alleged conspirator. But the committee had the strongest evidence against Hickey, and he was the one they marked for the harshest punishment. A court-martial was convened, and it found Hickey guilty of mutiny and sedition and sentenced him to be hanged. Washington signed the death warrant. At ten in the morning on June 28, twenty thousand witnesses watched Hickey pay for his treachery.

At about nine the next morning, a humid and overcast Saturday, officers clambered onto the roof of Washington's headquarters to get an unobstructed view of the harbor. Turning their telescopes toward Staten Island, they spied three red-and-white-striped flags flying from a hilltop and quickly sent word to their commander in chief. Daniel McCurtin, a soldier from Maryland, learned the news while relieving himself in a second-floor outhouse. Gazing through the window, McCurtin saw "something resembling a wood of pine trees trimmed." He could not believe his eyes. Within ten minutes, "the whole bay was as full of shipping as ever it could be," he recorded in his diary. "I do declare that I thought all London was afloat."

The full might of the British Empire had arrived in New York.

SIX

A NARROW ESCAPE

By midsummer 1776, Washington expected the British to attack at any moment. Instead, the armada lingered off Staten Island, swelling almost daily with more ships. Swarms of redcoats disembarked on the island and set up encampments.

On July 9, Washington ordered his anxious men to assemble at six in the evening at parade grounds around the city, from Governors Island to King's Bridge. At the appointed time, he rode into the city Common, where troops from New York and Connecticut had convened. Without dismounting, he unfolded a broadside he had received from Philadelphia. "In Congress, July 4, 1776," he read aloud. "When in the course of human events, it becomes necessary for one people to dissolve the political bands which have connected them with another . . . a decent respect to the opinions of mankind requires that they should declare the causes which impel them to the separation."

"We hold these truths to be self-evident," Washington continued, "that all men are created equal, that they are endowed by their Creator with certain unalienable rights, that among these are life, liberty, and the pursuit of happiness." Washington's troops were no longer simply rebelling against British authority—they were now soldiers of an independent nation.

Washington duly recited the twenty-seven separate grievances Congress had enumerated in the Declaration of Independence before concluding with words that must have sounded ominous to men awaiting an invasion by the most fearsome expeditionary force Britain had ever assembled. "With a firm reliance on the protection of divine Providence, we mutually pledge to each other our lives, our fortunes and our sacred honor."

The oration was met first by silence, then by a rising murmur that swelled into cheers. Hats flew into the air and muskets barked in salute. Some soldiers, energized by the declaration, drifted to Bowling Green and toppled the mounted statue of King George III. They decapitated the king, knocked off his nose, and riddled his torso with musket balls. Then, as fife and drums played "The Rogue's March," they used a wheelbarrow to transport the severed head to Washington's residence, before taking it to the Blue Bell Tavern, where they mounted it on a spike.

But their elation was short-lived. Three days later, five British warships fired a barrage at the southern tip of Manhattan, blasting holes in houses and forcing terrified New Yorkers to scamper into their cellars or dash uptown. Then the ships glided up the Hudson River, sailing with impunity past eleven rebel gun batteries. About half the would-be defenders were in bars or brothels when the attack began and never showed up for duty. One battery, six rebel gunners who were probably drunk, blew themselves to bits when they rammed a new cartridge down the smoking barrel of their cannon without properly sponging it, prematurely igniting the powder. A mere five warships had wreaked havoc; New Yorkers shuddered to think what might be in store for them once the British fully flexed their muscles.

More British ships arrived throughout July and August. Now there were about four hundred vessels anchored off Staten Island, and thirty-two thousand troops encamped there. On August 22, the British finally made their move, sending fifteen thousand British and Hessian soldiers ashore at Gravesend Bay on Long Island. There was no rebel resistance, and local Loyalists gave them a hearty welcome. Four days later, the invaders split their force into three columns and attacked. Two columns made a frontal assault on the Americans entrenched on the Heights of Guan, a line of wooded hills extending across modern-day Brooklyn and Queens. The third and largest column advanced through an unguarded pass to the left of the rebel line, outflanking the Americans. It was a perfectly executed plan: In the largest battle of the war to date, the redcoats and their Hessian allies routed the unsuspecting patriots, sending Washington's inexperienced troops fleeing for their lives. The rebels awoke the next morning to a depressing reality: They were trapped in Brooklyn, with their backs to the East River. That afternoon, the skies opened and the defeated Americans were drenched by a violent downpour. As the storm raged the next day, it created more misery—but also an opportunity: While it continued, British warships could not sail up the East River to finish off the patriots. Washington decided to cut his losses and retreat. That night, aided by fog and a favorable wind, nine thousand American troops escaped across the river to Manhattan.

Washington's army had survived, but it was in a desperate state, its confidence shattered. "The merry tones on drums and fifes had ceased," Pastor Ewald Shewkirk recorded in his diary. "Many looked sickly, emaciated, cast down . . . the wet clothes, tents—as many as they had brought away—and other things were lying about before the houses and in the streets." Two weeks later, Washington met with his war council and made the painful decision to withdraw from the city. He ordered the main part of his army to retreat to the north as quickly as possible, while leaving a smaller force to hold off a British attack from the rear. By the end of October, the British had effectively expelled the Continental Army from New York.

★

The British victories in the summer and fall of 1776 forced the New York Provincial Congress to flee Manhattan, first for White Plains and then to the Dutch Reformed Church in the town of Fishkill, in the Hudson Valley about sixty-five miles north of Manhattan. But as events in the city reached a crescendo, Gouverneur Morris had gone missing.

Early in September, Morris told his fellow delegates he had to leave to attend to some personal business and would be back shortly; a month later, he was still absent. "Gouverneur, through what cause God alone knows, has deserted in this hour of danger, retired to some obscure corner of the Jerseys where he enjoys his jest and his ease while his friends are struggling with every difficulty and danger & blushing while they make apologies for him which they do not themselves believe," Robert R. Livingston wrote to Edward Rutledge, a South Carolina delegate to the Continental Congress, on October 10. Rutledge shared Livingston's annoyance. "I am amazed at Gouverneur! Good God what will mankind come to!" he responded. "Is it not possible to awaken him to a sense of his duty? Has he no one virtue left that can plead in favor of an oppressed & bleeding country?" Shocked, Rutledge said that Morris had abandoned his friends Livingston and Jay to face "the attacks of open and secret enemies" alone. "One would think he would find solid satisfaction in acting and even suffering with such men in such a cause—does he desire to live forever in obscurity, or would he prefer being 'damned to everlasting fame' to a life devoted to his country?"

Gouverneur spent at least some of his time away visiting his sister Euphemia and her husband in Boonton, New Jersey. In a letter dated October 13, he breezily and perhaps spuriously informed his colleagues that "a series of accidents too trifling for recital have prevented me from the pleasure of attending the convention according to my serious intention for upwards of a month past. Among the last, let me mention the loss of all my horses. As soon as I can find one of them or purchase another, I shall hasten to the Fishkills [*sic*]."

On December 9, Morris finally returned. As if to atone for his absence, he dutifully attended the interminable committee meetings and drafted a steady stream of official correspondence, from a letter to the Connecticut governor protesting an embargo on New York goods, to a recommendation that capital punishment be meted out to "a gang of villains" who robbed a house in Cortlandt Manor.

Two months later, British advances forced the delegates to move again. They fled Fishkill for Kingston, on the other side of the Hudson, where the redcoats were unlikely to interrupt the New York legislators' most crucial task: drafting a state constitution and bill of rights.

The redcoats still held New York, and the war rumbled in the distance, but Morris would wage his fight for liberty with pen and parchment rather than powder and steel. He was well-prepared for the task, as he had been giving much thought to citizenship and statehood. At some point during 1776, perhaps even during his absence from the Provincial Congress, Morris wrote a series of short essays on government, human happiness, individual liberty, and the importance of protecting people's rights while curbing their worst impulses. He was exploring his ideas and didn't intend for them to be published, judging from the many lines he crossed out and the ones he inserted. But the essays were a window into his fertile mind. "We need not inquire whether mortal beings are capable of absolute felicity," he began, "but it is important to know by what means they may obtain the greatest portion which is compatible with their state of existence." To Morris, the answer was plain: the best route to widespread happiness was virtuous behavior and "obedience to the moral law." There would be less evil in the world, he noted, "if each individual did to others what he would wish from them." And how could government promote virtue and morality? It should "watch over the education of youth," avoid conferring honor and authority on "vicious men," and institute laws that "compel the performance of contracts, give redress for injuries, and punish crimes," thereby protecting property and commerce.

Natural liberty, Morris observed, "implies in every man the right to do what he pleases." Clearly, society could not function if everybody did whatever they wanted, whenever they wanted. Anyone who desired complete freedom had to live alone, apart from society. The best alternative was *political* liberty, which gave men a voice in creating the laws. But it wasn't practical for men to have "the right of assenting to or dissenting from every public act by which a man is to be bound." Some level of political liberty was necessary, but it couldn't be absolute. In those notes lay the seed of the republic's future debates. Freedom, he believed, could not survive without order; passion must be yoked to reason, liberty to law.

Morris's philosophical musings would become political soon enough.

The Ulster County Courthouse in Kingston, which had a jail in the basement, wasn't an ideal site to debate these, or any, ideas. On March 18, 1777, about a week after the convention began drafting a state constitution, Morris proposed that "for the preservation of their health," the delegates should be allowed to smoke during the proceedings to counter the "very nauseous and disagreeable effluvia" that wafted into the meeting room from the unwashed inmates below. The measure passed 14–11. He scored a more significant triumph in an argument with his friend John Jay over religious freedom. Jay, whose Huguenot ancestors had been forced to flee Catholic France, proposed that New York "erect a wall of brass around the country for the exclusion of Catholics." Jay wanted to bar them from voting or owning land until they swore an oath before the state supreme court that "no pope, priest or foreign authority on earth" would supersede their loyalty to the law. When the delegates rejected that motion, Jay proposed a guarantee of religious liberty with the caveat that it "shall not be construed to encourage licentiousness" or "disturb or endanger the safety of the state." But Morris recognized that Jay's vague language could lead to people being prosecuted for their beliefs, not their actions. Instead, Morris proposed that the religious freedom provision prohibit *acts* of licentiousness and *actions* that could threaten public safety. The delegates unanimously approved Morris's amendment.

Morris's proposal for a strong state executive met with less success.

He wanted to give the governor sole authority to veto legislation and appoint state officials, but memories of imperious royal governors were fresh in the delegates' minds, and they balked at concentrating so much power in the hands of one man. As an alternative, they created a council to make appointments. The governor would preside over the panel but would have a single vote, just like the other members.

The delegates had rejected Morris's design for the executive branch, but the conviction behind it endured. Morris believed that liberty without a steady hand at the helm would soon drift into chaos. At the Constitutional Convention a decade later, he would present the same principle on a grander scale, shaping the office of the president with the same arguments that had failed in Kingston.

Morris didn't let the naysayers stop him from sharing other ideas. Two weeks after that setback, he proposed another motion: This son of a slave owner had concluded that slavery was incompatible with the principles of his nascent nation. In his home state, at least, he wanted to put it on a path to extinction. "A regard to the rights of human nature and the principles of our holy religion loudly call upon us to dispense the blessings of freedom to all mankind," he proclaimed. However, "inasmuch as it would at present be productive of great dangers to liberate the slaves within this state, it is therefore most earnestly recommended to the future legislatures of the state of New York to take the most effectual measures consistent with the public safety, and the private property of individuals, for abolishing slavery within the same, so that in future ages, every human being who breathes the air of the state shall enjoy the privileges of a free man." Morris might have envisioned a gradual emancipation law like the one New York eventually enacted in 1799, under which children born to enslaved mothers after July 4 of that year would be free. (Men would be indentured servants until they were twenty-eight, women until they were twenty-five.) A political pragmatist, he knew that immediate abolition was a nonstarter. But there was no mistaking the bold principle behind the cautious language; it was his first attempt to fix the flaw woven into the American fabric.

Jay agreed with Morris on slavery, but he wasn't there to provide support because he had left the convention following the death of his mother. Meanwhile, Morris's friend Robert R. Livingston led the opposition to the idea. The convention at first tabled Morris's measure, then took it up again several days later. At that point, the delegates voted 31 to 5 not to include it in the state constitution. If there was a discussion on its merits, no record of it survives.

Ten years later at the Constitutional Convention in Philadelphia, Morris would again rise to confront the hypocrisy of a nation that proclaimed the sanctity of liberty while tolerating bondage. Of all the Founders, Morris spoke most plainly about slavery—a "nefarious institution," he called it, and a curse that would bring divine judgment upon America.

On April 20, the convention approved the new state constitution with only a single dissenter. It wasn't Morris, who voted in favor despite his reservations, especially, "the want of vigor in the executive," as he put it in a letter to fellow New Yorker Alexander Hamilton. "That there are faults in it is not to be wondered at, for it is the work of men perhaps not the best qualified for such undertakings," Morris quipped.

Now that the state had a constitution, it needed a constitutional government. Livingston and Jay both accepted government posts, but Morris declined. William Smith heard that his old protégé protested that he was still too young and unsettled in life.

But Morris's work for the patriot cause was only beginning. On May 13, the convention elected him to serve as a delegate to the Continental Congress in Philadelphia, the governing body of the new American nation. For the first time, Morris was to step fully onto the national stage, where his pen, his intellect, and his temperament would face tests beyond those he had known at home in New York.

SEVEN

"THE SKELETON OF AN ARMY"

Morris had imagined Philadelphia as a welcome contrast to the dank courthouse in Kingston—a return to bustle, female company, and the civilized rhythms of urban life. Instead, by the time he set out to join the Continental Congress, the war had blocked his path. On September 11, 1777, the British defeated Washington's Continental Army at the Battle of Brandywine Creek and began advancing toward Philadelphia, a mere thirty miles away. "If Congress have not yet left Philadelphia, they ought to do it immediately without fail, for the enemy have the means of throwing a party this night into [*sic*] the city," Hamilton, Washington's aide-de-camp, wrote to John Hancock a week later. The redcoats arrived on September 26 to begin what would be a nine-month occupation. It was a perilous moment for the revolution; would it buckle with the collapse of the capital?

Congress was forced to flee—first to Lancaster, Pennsylvania, for a single, uneasy day, then again across the Susquehanna River to the rural hamlet of York, a hundred miles west of Philadelphia. Here, among muddy lanes, overcrowded lodgings, and a courthouse that reeked of damp wool and overwork, Morris entered national service.

York was a farming community of about eighteen hundred people—nothing like America's major metropolis. "Believe me," North Carolina delegate Cornelius Harnett wrote to a friend back home. "It is the most inhospitable scandalous place I was ever in. If I once more can return to my family, all the devils in hell should not separate us." There were fewer than three hundred houses in the town. The few inns couldn't accommodate all the members of Congress with their aides and servants, so some delegates had to bunk together as guests in some of the larger homes.

At any given time, many of the delegates were absent because they were busy with politics at home, ill, or just fed up with serving. In January 1778, Henry Laurens of South Carolina, who had replaced Hancock as president of Congress, reported that the assembly had "about twenty-one members, often thirteen, sometimes barely nine states on the floor represented by as many persons." The delegates convened early in the morning at the York County Courthouse for several hours of committee meetings and continued their work until eight or nine at night, with breaks that never added up to more than two hours, Laurens said. Not surprisingly, tempers were short. "Devil a foot will I go tonight!" North Carolina delegate Thomas Burke, who was in bed nursing a cold, thundered when Laurens called him back for one late-night session. "It is too late and too unreasonable."

★

Morris, elected in May 1777, didn't show up in York until January 20, because the New York legislature would not release him from state assignments. When he finally did appear, he made an immediate impression. On January 25, Pennsylvania delegate Robert Morris (no relation) wrote that the young man had "first-rate abilities" and predicted that "he will be immensely useful if he pursues his objects steadily (for I have been told his only blemish is being a little too whimsical)." Robert might have been referring to the younger man's high-flown rhetoric, his extended absence from the New York Provincial Congress, or his growing reputation as a lover of wine and women. Whatever their reservations about the newcomer, Gouverneur's congressional elders immediately entrusted him with a vital task: Along with four other delegates, they sent him to Valley Forge, Pennsylvania, to help Washington reorganize the Continental Army, which was in a desperate state. Morris quickly became the committee's driving force.

A few days after Christmas, Laurens had received a letter Washington had written on December 23 from Valley Forge, where the American forces were encamped for the winter. In the courtroom where Congress met, Laurens and Charles Thomson, the congressional secretary, sat at the judge's desk while the delegates sat in rows in front of them, warmed by a huge woodstove with a pipe that stretched to the back wall. Alarmed by the contents of Washington's letter, Laurens handed it to Thomson and asked him to read it aloud:

> I am now convinced beyond a doubt, that unless some great and capital change suddenly takes place . . . this army must inevitably be reduced to one or other of these three things: starve, dissolve or disperse, in order to obtain subsistence in the best manner they can. Rest assured, Sir, this is not an exaggerated picture, and that I have abundant reason to support what I say.

The quartermaster general had not provided supplies since July, Washington explained, and his army was in desperate need of food, clothes, shoes, blankets and other necessities. The general took aim at Pennsylvania state legislators who had criticized him for leading his men into winter quarters—but his words indicted every member of Congress. "I can assure those gentlemen," he wrote, "that it is a much easier and less distressing thing, to draw remonstrances in a comfortable room by a good fireside, than to occupy a cold, bleak hill, and sleep under frost & snow without clothes or blankets." The delegates, cozy by their woodstove, shifted uncomfortably in their seats. "However, although they seem to have little feeling for the naked and distressed soldier, I feel superabundantly for them, and from my soul pity those miseries, which it is neither in my power to relieve or prevent."

Morris arrived at Valley Forge at the end of January to find roughly twelve thousand soldiers huddled on a gusty plateau. The site was about twenty miles from Philadelphia, where the British army was spending the winter. That distance made a redcoat raid unlikely, but if the British dared to attack, they would have to overcome Americans dug into defensive positions on the ridgetops. The site offered other advantages to the patriots: timber for fuel and shelter; clean water from the Schuylkill River and Valley Creek, and nearby farms that could provide food. The soldiers were living in log huts they had constructed in a flurry during the previous month. Per Washington's instructions, each hut was roughly fourteen by sixteen feet, with about six and a half feet of headroom, and was home to up to a dozen men. At first, their spirits were high. "I was there when the army first began to build huts," wrote the political philosopher Thomas Paine. "They appeared to me like a family of beavers: everyone busy, some carrying logs, others mud, and the rest fastening them together."

But conditions quickly deteriorated. As soldiers cut down tens of thousands of trees for fuel and shelter, the camp turned into a sea of mud. Instead of supplying the patriots, local farmers opted to sell their produce to the British troops in Philadelphia, who could pay in solid pounds sterling instead of the rapidly depreciating Continental currency. Food supplies dwindled, forcing the soldiers to subsist on "fire cakes" made of flour and water, cooked on hot stones. The remains of horses, killed by starvation or exhaustion, lay unburied, radiating a rancid stench. It was not a particularly cold winter, but that didn't matter much to soldiers who lacked proper clothes, blankets, or even shoes. Some tried to make their own with canvas strips they tore from tents. Malnourished and exposed to the cold, many soldiers were felled by typhoid fever, dysentery, and other diseases. "There comes a bowl of beef soup—full of burnt leaves and dirt, sickish enough to make a Hector spew—away with it, boys!" Dr. Albigence Waldo, an army surgeon from Connecticut, wrote in his diary on December 14, 1777. "There comes a soldier, his bare feet are seen through his worn-out shoes, his legs nearly naked from the tattered remains of an only pair of stockings, his breeches not sufficient to cover his nakedness, his shirt hanging in strings, his hair disheveled, his face meager, his whole appearance pictures a person forsaken and discouraged." Even Washington's personal attendants didn't have enough to wear. "One of them that attends my person and table is indecently and most shamefully naked," he complained.

A few days after Morris got to Valley Forge, he recorded his first impressions in a letter to John Jay. "Our quartermaster and commissary departments are in a most lamentable situation," he wrote. "Our troops: *Heu miseros*! The skeleton of an army presents itself to our eyes in a naked, starving condition, out of health, out of spirits." But Morris did not believe the situation was hopeless, and he relished the opportunity to participate in so pivotal a moment. "This is the seed time of glory as of freedom," he wrote to Livingston three weeks later.

One of the first people Morris met at Valley Forge was a twenty-year-old French nobleman who had defied his king to fight for the American cause. Marie-Joseph Paul Yves Roch Gilbert du Motier—better known as the Marquis de Lafayette—had crossed the Atlantic about seven months before in a ship called *La Victoire*, which he had loaded with food and munitions for the patriots. Lafayette first learned about the American rebellion in 1775, at a dinner party that included the Duke of Gloucester, King George III's younger brother. The duke was not fond of George, and he told the assembled guests that in his opinion, the colonists had every right to rebel. The teenage Lafayette, who hungered for fame and glory, was riveted. By virtue of his high birth, Lafayette was a captain in the French military. In 1776, an American recruiter, intrigued by Lafayette's wealth, nobility, and connections to the royal court, offered him a commission in the Continental Army. Lafayette embarked on *La Victoire* despite a royal order forbidding him to do so. While onboard, he wrote his wife Adrienne

(Lafayette was just sixteen and Adrienne fourteen when they wed in April 1774—a match arranged by their parents) that he was going "as a friend to offer my services to this most interesting republic. I bring there only my sincerity and my goodwill, and no personal ambition or selfish interest. . . . The welfare of America is intimately connected with the happiness of all mankind; she will become the respectable and safe asylum of virtue, integrity, tolerance, equality and a peaceful liberty."

In fact, Lafayette was highly ambitious, but unlike many other French officers who came to America just to advance their careers, he was a true believer in the ideals of the revolution. Washington was impressed by Lafayette's performance at the Battle of Brandywine Creek in September 1777, where he fought bravely and rushed back into the fray despite being shot in the leg. Tall and thin, with reddish-brown hair already receding at the temples, the nobleman had a boyish enthusiasm that appealed to older men, and by the time Morris arrived at Valley Forge, Washington had taken Lafayette under his wing. Morris also took an immediate liking to the Frenchman. "I am deeply surprised at the mature judgment and solid understanding of this *young* man," he wrote to Henry Laurens soon after arriving at the encampment.

As Morris settled into camp life, his work quickly brought him into Washington's inner circle. Morris likely met with Washington at the Isaac Potts House, where the commander in chief lived and worked with his military "family," which included Hamilton, fellow aide-de-camp John Laurens (son of Henry Laurens), and salaried and enslaved servants. The latter included Hannah Till, a cook who purchased her freedom several months after the army left Valley Forge, but who continued to work for Washington as a salaried employee throughout the war. The general and his wife slept in a bedroom on the second floor of the house. The main room downstairs was an office during the day but doubled as a bedroom at night. On most nights, half a dozen aides slept on the floor after they moved aside the furniture.

Washington huddled with Morris, who was young enough to be his son, next to the fireplace in his private first-floor office, puzzling over the army's supply problems. Gradually, their working relationship blossomed into a friendship. As a product of the New York gentry, Morris had different sensibilities from the Virginia planter, but both men were aristocrats who placed a high premium on self-control, moderation, integrity, and grace. Washington respected Morris's abilities, and Morris grew to venerate Washington, seeing him as a father figure. Together they mapped out a plan.

First, they chose replacements for the quartermaster general (to oversee the delivery of supplies) and commissary general (to procure food). The former had resigned, and the latter was too ill to perform his duties. To address shortages, Morris and his fellow committee members advised Congress to ask the states to provide more provisions. And to improve distribution, they suggested ordering the commissary branches to inventory their supplies, list their personnel, and standardize rules.

To strengthen his army's fighting capacity, Washington also wanted other changes. He recommended drafting infantrymen from state militias and increasing the size of the cavalry. And to improve morale among officers—desertions were a perennial issue—he wanted to guarantee them half pay for life upon retirement and pensions for widows. With Washington's guidance, the committee gave Congress detailed blueprints, written by Morris, to revamp the army's infantry, artillery, cavalry, and corps of engineers.

The commander in chief made another move that winter to bolster his forces that didn't involve Morris, but which the New Yorker, now firmly opposed to slavery, would have supported. In January, Washington granted permission to Brigadier General James Mitchell Varnum of Rhode Island to recruit Black troops by offering them freedom in exchange for serving in an all-Black battalion. Massachusetts soon adopted a similar policy.

Morris and his colleagues finished their work at Valley Forge at the end of March. About two weeks later, Congress began debating Washington's requests, with Morris leading the fight. He wrote at least six letters to Washington in April and May to provide updates, and

Washington wrote to Morris at least four times. The proposal to give officers half pay for life met the most resistance. Opponents argued that Congress had the authority to wage war but not to keep officers on the payroll during peacetime, which amounted to the establishment of a standing army. After a month of debate, Congress approved a compromise: payments for seven years, rather than for life. "It is not what you wished but it may do," Morris wrote Washington when it finally passed. "No measure hath ever been more severely contested."

The compromise, Washington replied, gave him "singular pleasure." It wasn't all he had asked for, he noted, but it was more than he had expected. However, he was worried about reports that the British were preparing to move out of Philadelphia. It was critical that Congress approve the other reforms—and fast. "The sooner, however, the regimental regulations and other arrangements are set about, the sooner they will be finished," he wrote. "And for God's sake, my dear Morris, let me recommend it to you, to urge the absolute necessity of this measure with all your might." Morris told the general not to worry. "We are going on with the regimental arrangements as fast as possible and I think the day begins to appear with respect to this business," he replied. The only reason Congress hadn't approved it already, Morris wrote, was because too many delegates liked to hear themselves talk. "Our superior abilities, or the desire of appearing to possess them, lead us to such exquisite tediousness of debate that the most precious moments pass unheeded away like vulgar things."

On June 4, Morris's confidence was borne out: Congress approved the rest of Washington's reorganization plan. He sent the final documents to Washington on June 9 with a request that the commander in chief let him know if the army needed anything else from Congress.

EIGHT

FRANCE COMES TO THE RESCUE

While Washington's men shivered at Valley Forge, the redcoats in Philadelphia waltzed through candlelit rooms and drank to the king's health. They watched and performed in plays, organized cricket matches, and raced horses. Officers escorted young Loyalist women to dances and concerts. They converted City Tavern, on Second and Walnut Streets, into a casino—except on Thursday nights, when they held a ball there—and convened monthly dining clubs at the Bunch of Grapes and the Indian King taverns. For the intellectually inclined, there were book auctions and lectures. The redcoats drilled and paraded in almost every open space, and regimental bands played on the State House grounds, delighting large crowds of onlookers. For Rebecca Franks, the beautiful eighteen-year-old daughter of a prominent Philadelphia businessman, the British occupation was a social whirlwind. "You can have no idea of the life of continued amusement I live in. I can scarce have a moment to myself," Franks wrote in February 1778 to a girlfriend in Maryland, urging her to visit. "I know you are fond of a gay life as myself—you'd have an opportunity of raking as much as you choose either at plays, balls, concerts or assemblies.

I've been but three evenings alone since we moved to town. I begin now to be almost tired."

The climax was the *Meschianza*, a fête held on May 18, 1778, to honor General William Howe and his brother Admiral Richard Howe as they prepared to return to England. The fair but gusty day began with a two-hour water pageant on the Delaware River, featuring three separate flotillas festooned with bunting, flags, and streamers. Crowds cheered from the wharves and the roofs of houses along the waterfront, and cannons positioned along the route fired salutes as the boats passed by. After the regatta, two groups of British officers, the Knights of the Blended Rose and the Knights of the Burning Mountain, squared off in a mock jousting tournament on open ground between the river and the Walnut Grove mansion, the abandoned country seat of the prominent Wharton family, whose patriarch had died two years earlier. Each team fought for the honor of seven young ladies—Rebecca Franks was one of them—who watched the contest from amphitheaters erected at either end of the field. Each woman wore a "Turkish" costume, which included a white silk gown and a gauze turban spangled with gold and silver and topped with a feather. When the jousting was over, more than four hundred guests passed under two triumphal arches (one for each of the Howe brothers) and between two columns of knights and other British soldiers to enter the mansion. Upstairs in a mirrored hall, they gasped at tables piled high with jellies, cakes, and sweetmeats. Two dozen enslaved servants wearing turbans, blue sashes, and silver jewelry served chicken, lamb, veal, ham, Yorkshire pies, and several kinds of pudding. The celebration concluded with fireworks and dancing until daybreak.

Even as they enjoyed the night, the British, worried the rebels would attack Philadelphia, were making plans to decamp for a more secure base in New York. Exactly one month after the *Meschianza*, ten thousand British and Hessian troops, with a wagon train trailing a dozen miles behind them, marched out of Philadelphia. Their departure meant the Continental Congress could finally come home. Before leaving York, some delegates walked a mile to a nearby farmhouse and celebrated by eating cherries and drinking whiskey.

The patriots' happy homecoming was tempered by what the redcoats had wrought in America's proud metropolis. They had cut down trees, yanked out fences and church pews, and dismantled whole houses for firewood. In the northern section of the city, the few houses left standing were gutted or missing doors, windows, or roofs. Trash and excrement were piled on side streets. In many private homes, soldiers had cut holes in the floor and pushed their garbage and feces into the basement. The filth in the city attracted swarms of flies, "which are here in the greatest possible numbers that one hand is employed in brushing them away while the other is writing," one returning resident observed. An aide to Baron Friedrich Wilhelm von Steuben, the Prussian-born Continental Army general, said he and his boss had a hard time enjoying their tea because "as fast as our cups were filled, myriads of flies took possession of them." The homes of prominent patriots were singled out for particularly rough treatment: Soldiers staying in Benjamin Franklin's house carried away electrical equipment, a printing press, books, and a painting. Perhaps worst of all, the occupiers had befouled the redbrick State House—hallowed site of the signing of the Declaration of Independence—by using the first floor as a barracks and the second floor as a hospital for wounded American prisoners. They heaped the dead bodies of men and horses in a pit just outside the building now known as Independence Hall. It was impossible to convene a sufficient number of delegates before July 7, Henry Laurens wrote, because of "the offensiveness of the air in and around the State House, which the enemy had made a hospital and left in a condition disgraceful to the character of civility. Particularly they had opened a large square pit near the House, a receptable for filth, into which they had also cast dead horses and bodies of men who by the mercy of death had escaped their further cruelties."

Soon after the delegates reconvened in the State House—following a thorough scrubbing and airing out of the building—they received momentous news: A French fleet had landed in Delaware Bay, carrying an emissary from America's new ally. It was the culmination of a process that had begun in Paris in February, when an American delegation led by Franklin signed treaties that formalized France's financial and military support of the patriots. The agreement between "the most Christian King and the United States of North America" stipulated that the United States would come to the aid of France if Britain attacked it. Neither party could make peace with Britain without the formal consent of the other, and France recognized that the goal of the alliance and the war was to secure America's independence.

Even before the treaties, the French had contributed arms and other supplies to the American war effort. In the fall of 1777, their help had been instrumental in the American victory at the Battle of Saratoga, which upended the British plan to cut off New England, the revolutionary stronghold, from the rest of the colonies. This triumph convinced France that America would be a worthwhile ally against its ancient enemy. A formal alliance meant more aid and the participation of the French navy to counter British superiority at sea. The agreement was a "matter for heartfelt joy," Washington wrote to Virginia statesman Richard Henry Lee, "and it must, I should think, chalk out a plain and easy road to independence."

The Continental Congress enthusiastically approved the treaties in early May, after spurning a peace offer from the British, who hastily reached out after hearing about the agreement with France. Washington viewed the British proposal as "diabolical" and so did Congress. The offer "implies a criminality in our justifiable resistance," Congress declared, "and consequently, to treat under it, would be an implied acknowledgment that the inhabitants of these states were what Britain had declared them to be: rebels."

The alliance had scarcely been ratified when diplomacy turned theatrical. Hearing of the arrival of the French ships, Congress scrambled to arrange a suitable welcome for King Louis XVI's minister plenipotentiary, Sieur Conrad Alexandre Gérard de Rayneval. Congress appointed Morris, Samuel Adams, and Richard Henry Lee to invent the protocol for receiving Gérard. The rough-hewn Adams knew he was an odd choice for the job. "Would you think that one so little of the man of the world as I am should be joined in a committee to settle ceremonials?" he wrote. "It is, however, of some importance that we agree upon forms that are adapted to the true republican principles, for this instance may be recurred to as a precedent in futurity." Meanwhile, all of Philadelphia was abuzz. "Who would have thought," the *Pennsylvania Packet* observed, "that the American colonies imperfectly known in Europe a few years ago and claimed by every pettifogging lawyer in the House of Commons, and every cobbler in the beer houses of London, as part of their property, should in the course of three years of a war with Great Britain, receive an ambassador from the most powerful monarchy in Europe!"

On the morning of August 6, 1778, the air was thick with anxiety inside the now immaculate State House. Members of Congress fidgeted in their seats, wool coats clinging to damp shirts, as they waited for the first formal envoy ever to be received by the United States. It was a ceremony no one had ever experienced—how did a republic, sworn to equality, meet the representative of a king?

When the Frenchman appeared in the doorway, plumed hat in hand, the murmurs subsided. Conrad Alexandre Gérard advanced slowly through the crowded room. Henry Laurens rose from his mahogany chair on the dais and the delegates stood as one—some stiff with pride, others overwhelmed by the sheer improbability of the moment. Gérard pulled two letters, addressed to Congress from Louis XVI, from his coat. Charles Thomson, the congressional secretary, read them aloud—first in French, then in English, each syllable formal and strange in this new nation's ears. The fateful words were still vibrating in the air as Gérard bowed deeply, the light catching the braid on his coat. The crowd rose and returned the compliment. Trembling with emotion, Laurens labored through a short speech before he and Gérard exchanged bows, awkward and long, as if diplomacy itself had to be invented in the space between them. Then came a cheer that rippled through the gallery. America, once a collection of colonies, was now a nation among nations. In that humid room, the revolution suddenly felt real—the republic had stepped onto the world stage.

That night, at the City Tavern, the delegates drank twenty-one toasts to the new alliance. Bands played, cannons boomed, and the guests lifted their glasses to the "Most Christian King" of France, his queen, the union of France and America, and the success of their combined arms. Morris, watching Gérard's polite smile over the rim of his wineglass, knew what the alliance meant: not merely more ships and silver, but a validation of what he viewed as "the just cause of all mankind."

He was soon asked to give that cause a voice. When Britain issued a new peace manifesto—offering amnesty, plum government posts, and even cash to the delegates if the colonies would repent their rebellion—Congress turned to Morris to answer. His reply was as defiant as any musket volley. "The towns on [Britain's] coast are at least as defenseless as ours," he warned, "and their citizens, unused to arms, are utterly incapable of repelling an assault." Englishmen "may easily be found in any part of the earth," he continued darkly, "and the dreaded scalping-knife itself may, in the hands of our riflemen, spread horror through their island." In other words: what you have done to us, we can do to you. The threat was not bluster; it was an assertion that Americans had become a match for their old masters. Then, almost in the same breath, Morris elevated his prose from menace to majesty. "The portals of the temple we have raised to freedom shall be thrown wide, as an asylum to mankind," he wrote. "America shall receive to her bosom and comfort and cheer the oppressed, the miserable and the poor of every nation and of every clime."

The two halves of the manifesto—vengeance and vision—were pure Morris: the steel and spirit of revolution joined in one pronouncement. Congress printed thirteen hundred copies, and the words raced through the colonies, proof that the revolution was becoming something larger than a war. It was an idea.

Even as his words echoed through the states, Morris was drowning in work. He chaired the congressional committees that managed everything Washington had argued for at Valley Forge: food, clothing, medicine, and money. He was overseeing the commissary and quartermaster departments, drafting the regulations that would put muscle on the army's bones. He tracked each state's quotas, petitioned for supplies, and devised rules to keep profiteers in check. At the same time, he was busy arguing for a uniform currency, a single treasury, and a national tariff to stabilize the government's finances. His pen was an army of its own, marching from dawn until exhaustion drove him to bed.

He reflected on his suite of responsibilities to Robert R. Livingston that summer: "Let me paint my situation. I am on a committee to arrange the treasury and finances. I am of the medical committee and have to prepare the arrangements of that department. I have the same thing to go through with relative to the commissary's quartermaster and clothier general's departments. . . . These are the leading things, but the everyday minutia are infinite." He added that he never exercised, seldom slept, and was ruining his health. Yet there was no hint of quitting. "This is the seed time of glory as of freedom," he had written months earlier, and he meant it.

Despite the sheer scope of his service, Morris had detractors. They fell into several camps: There were the jealous, who resented his confidence and ease of intellect; the moralists, who admired his talent but were put off by his wit and fondness for wine and women; and the provincial leaders of New York.

While there was no question Morris was considered a leader on the national front, in his very own state there was cause for concern. One irritant was the territory of Vermont, which New York wanted to keep under its jurisdiction instead of allowing it to become an independent state, as it had declared itself to be in January 1777. In Congress, Morris went through the motions of defending his home state's claims, but New York leaders sensed that his heart wasn't in it; privately, he admitted that he favored setting Vermont free. Overall, many New

York state legislators believed, Morris spent too much time defending the interests of the nation and too little defending those of his state.

Furthermore, Morris's talk of centralized finance and a stronger executive smacked, to provincial ears, of aristocracy. It did not go unnoted that several of Morris's relatives were Tories—including his mother. However, the letters he wrote to her during the war—there were only two—made it clear where his loyalties lay. He told her he wanted to be a dutiful son "but a higher duty has bound me to the service of my fellow creatures . . . I know that for such sentiments I am called a rebel, and that such sentiments are not fashionable among the folks you see." Apparently, Morris's mother did not reply. She had reason to be annoyed with Gouverneur and other patriots in the family; because she had rebel relatives, the British had occupied Morrisania. A Loyalist regiment erected seventy huts on the estate and deforested 470 acres for fuel and firewood. The British also quartered dozens of horses there and removed forty-five head of cattle and ninety-four sheep.

In addition to relatives, Morris maintained contact with at least one other Loyalist during the war. Since 1770, his good friend from his legal apprenticeship with William Smith, Peter Van Schaack, had been buffeted by misfortune. Van Schaack had buried his wife, his father, and six of his children. He had become blind in one eye and feared losing his sight entirely. And his refusal to pledge loyalty to the patriot cause had made it difficult for him to earn a living. In July 1778, state leaders banished him from New York. The next month, Van Schaack left his home in Kinderhook, bound for exile in England. "I am now going into the wide world," he wrote in his journal, "without friends, without fortune, with the sad remembrance of past happiness, and the gloomy prospect of future adversity." At least one friend, Morris, wrote to wish him well. "I always have regretted . . . that you did not take part with us in the cause, which, let the success of it be what it may, I cannot but consider as the just cause of all mankind," Morris wrote a week before Van Schaack departed.

Despite some criticism at home, New York Governor George

Clinton assured Morris he was a shoo-in for reelection to Congress. Just to be sure, Morris returned to New York in August 1779 for six weeks to bolster his political prospects. He was right to be worried: in early October, New York state legislators voted him out. Instead of returning to New York, Morris remained in Philadelphia, where he was "daily employed in making oblations to Venus," Jay joked to Livingston in reference to their friend's romantic adventures. No wonder Morris was popular with the ladies: just twenty-seven, he had already played a leading role in his country's affairs, and he was handsome, intelligent, and charming. Meanwhile, his professional reputation as a thinker and administrator was undiminished. In December, his friends in Congress put his name forward to serve as Benjamin Franklin's secretary in Paris—a post that would have placed him at the center of American diplomacy. While it would have been a plum position for the right person, Morris was uncertain whether he even wanted the job, dismissing it in a letter to his cousin as "a thing which I probably shall not get, which I wish I may not get." Morris hesitated at the edge of opportunity. But the question would soon become academic.

★

On May 14, 1780, Morris set out to visit George Plater III, a Maryland planter and congressional delegate, and his wife Elizabeth at their country home outside the city. He climbed onto the seat of his phaeton, grabbed the reins, and in an instant his future changed. His pair of gray horses bolted, causing an accident that might have been regarded as the great physical calamity of his life, had he not already carried the scars of the burns from his youth. This new injury would test him again, in body and spirit, and would shadow him in ways he could not yet imagine.

NINE

THE SCANDAL OF GENIUS

We will never know what caused the horses to bolt, but the damage was traumatic. Morris was pitched off the four-wheel carriage. Tumbling toward the ground, his left leg caught in the spokes of one of the spinning wheels, with gruesome results: the spokes pulverized Morris's leg, shattering several bones and dislocating his ankle.

Morris was carried home, in agonizing pain. With his own physician out of town, several other prominent Philadelphia doctors were summoned to examine his injuries. It didn't take long for them to reach a unanimous, and severe, verdict: the leg would have to be amputated. Morris calmly gazed at the doctors arrayed around him. "Gentlemen, I see around me the eminent men of your profession, all acknowledged competent to the performance of the operation," he said. "You have already secured renown, the capital by which you live. Now the removal of my leg cannot add to your celebrity; is there not one among you younger in your calling who might perform the act, and thus secure the éclat for his benefit?" One of the physicians nominated Dr. James Hutchinson, a surgeon in the Continental Army who was in his mid-twenties. "I will select him," the patient proclaimed. "Let him rise to fame by amputating the leg of Gouverneur Morris." Even in agony, Morris's wit—an irrepressible quality that some admired, and others found a fault—remained intact.

On the day of the operation, Hutchinson likely arrived with various knives, a saw, retractors, a tourniquet, a variety of bandages and compresses, sponges, and a crooked needle and thread. Lorenz Heister, the German surgeon and anatomist whose 1743 surgical manual was widely consulted at the time, recommended six assistants for an amputation—three to hold down the patient, two to help the surgeon, and one to provide help to either the surgeon or the patient. Hutchinson might have given Morris wine or cordial before the operation to prevent him from fainting from the pain. Sometimes opium was administered, but usually afterward because it could produce serious side effects. Hutchinson began the procedure by tying a tourniquet around Morris's upper thigh, over the femoral artery. Then, standing between Morris's legs, the surgeon made a semicircular cut over his left shin. From the end points of the semicircle, he used a double-edged scalpel to cut straight lines leading toward the foot, then made another semicircular cut. Hutchinson separated the muscles from the bone, used the retractors—which might have been made of linen, leather, or iron—to hold back the muscles and skin, and grabbed his saw. Using long and steady strokes, the surgeon cut through the bone while an assistant held the leg securely. Within minutes, Hutchinson had amputated Morris's leg just below the knee. He closed and dressed the wound and put his patient to bed. William Churchill Houston, a member of Congress from New Jersey, reported that Morris "bore the operation with amazing firmness. I have not seen him but am told this morning that though his fever is pretty high, and he has a good deal of pain, he is not in danger of life. The bruises he received in the fall are a great addition to the principal accident."

When Morris's personal physician, Dr. Samuel Jones, returned to

Philadelphia, he questioned the wisdom of amputating the leg. If he had been available, Jones said, he might have saved the limb. Hearing that would drive many others to rage or anguish, but Morris bore his life-altering misfortune "with becoming fortitude," according to Robert R. Livingston. Given his injury, Morris officially withdrew from consideration to be Franklin's secretary.

Philadelphia wags gossiped endlessly about the mishap. Friends joked that he had been fleeing an enraged husband, though Morris denied it. "Let it pass," he told John Jay. "The leg is gone and there is an end of the matter." Convalescing in the Platers' home for six months, he charmed his hostess, Elizabeth Plater, whose beauty and enthusiasm for French fashions captivated the salons of the city—and who was several years older than Gouverneur and more than a dozen years younger than her husband. She nursed him back to health, and when Morris reemerged in society, he did so with the same confidence and flair that had made him notorious before the accident.

The gossip did not end—it mushroomed. There was talk of late-night rides through the countryside, of daring witticisms that scandalized moralists. Morris's wooden leg didn't impede his social life—it added to his charm. Drunk on champagne at an event in nearby Chester, Pennsylvania, Morris rode away with the fetching sixteen-year-old wife of a wealthy merchant. The husband sent a runner to overtake the pair, but when he caught up to the one-passenger sulky, the girl refused to get out. "Madam, it is your husband's command," the messenger implored. The starry-eyed teenager just waved, cracked her whip, and urged the horses on.

To his admirers, Morris embodied the young republic's audacity—he was a man who believed pleasure and intellect need not be enemies. To his critics, he was proof that genius without restraint bordered on vice. John Adams would dismiss him as "a man of wit" who "made pretty verses." Josiah Bartlett of New Hampshire called him "an eternal speaker," with "brass" equal to any man in Congress. Even Henry Laurens warned Lafayette that Morris was "often guardless and incautious." Beneath the jokes about women and wine lay genuine unease. The revolution prided itself on audacity, yes, but also virtue, and Morris, for all his service, did not always fit easily into that mythology.

Yet by this point in the war, his record was formidable. He had helped draft the New York Constitution, rejuvenated Washington's army at Valley Forge, given voice to America's defiance in his manifesto of 1778. He had argued for independence when it was perilous and for unity when it was unpopular. The gossip, though relentless, could not obscure the work.

By 1781—barely a year after his accident—Morris was moving confidently on his oaken leg. Though he was known to tumble on ice or cobblestones, he'd rise with a laugh and a curse. The limb was gone; the swagger remained. Meanwhile, the new nation was bleeding money, and Congress was on the hunt for a solution. Once again, Morris's talents for reason and rhetoric would draw him back into the center of his country's struggle.

TEN

THE POWER OF THE PURSE

In the smoky half-light of their log huts, men wrapped rags around their feet, gnawed at dwindling rations, and wondered whether the cause for which they'd sacrificed so much would survive the winter.

In December 1780, the soldiers of the Continental Army's Pennsylvania Line were wintering at Mount Kemble near Morristown, New Jersey, living in huts like the ones at Valley Forge. Smoke and the smell of damp wool clung to everything; frost feathered their blankets before dawn. They were hardy men, farmers and tradesmen in civilian life, and they were used to rough accommodations. For nearly a year, however, they had subsisted on less than full rations one out of every three days. By December 7, they had been without liquor for two months, except for an eighth of a pint of rum—a single shot—two weeks before. As Congress debated strategy in distant Philadelphia, the pressures of the war were reaching a breaking point at Mount Kemble.

The commander of the Pennsylvania Line, Brigadier General Anthony Wayne, prided himself on the loyalty of his troops. "I know that I have the hearts of the soldiery," he said—and it was true. But hearts could not feed families. By December, the Continental currency had so shrunk in value that the troops' annual salary was worth about a dollar—and they hadn't been paid for close to a year. When darkness fell, the men huddled around their fires and spoke of home, of wages owed, of the promises that seemed to vanish like breath in the cold. In the silence between the gusts of wind and the creak of the frozen trees, discontent grew. "They have now served their country for near five years, poorly clothed, badly fed, and worse paid," Wayne wrote to Joseph Reed, Pennsylvania's chief executive. "Believe me, my dear sir, that if something is not immediately done to give them a local attachment to this country, and to quiet their minds, we have not yet seen the worst side of the picture."

On New Year's Day 1781, officers tried to buy a little peace with celebration: Each man received a half pint of rum. At dusk, songs and shouts rolled through the camp, echoing off the icy hills. By eight o'clock, many of the men were drunk; by ten, their jubilation had soured into rage. Small knots of soldiers whispered between the huts, muskets glinting in the firelight. A skyrocket hissed upward and burst above the trees—a signal, perhaps, because suddenly soldiers were flooding out of their huts toting weapons and knapsacks. Wayne rode into the maelstrom, calling on his men to remember their oaths. Some yelled back that their officers had no power to relieve their suffering, that Congress had cheated them of their due. Shots were fired—a warning, not an attack—but one bullet nearly grazed Wayne's hat. He turned in his saddle, his face hard in the torchlight. "If you mean to kill me," he shouted, tearing open his coat, "then fire here!" The men lowered their weapons. They did not want to kill the commander they still admired, only to make the country hear them. They had fought and bled for independence, but freedom meant little if their families starved. The mutineers rousted more recruits from the huts, seized ammunition, horses, wagons, and tents, and began marching out of camp.

Wayne feared the men intended to defect to the British and wondered whether enemy agents had engineered the mutiny. If he could not stop them from leaving, he hoped to steer them toward Philadelphia, where they might negotiate with Congress and Pennsylvania's leaders, instead of toward the British lines. He made a final appeal to their patriotism, pleading with them not to abandon their country's cause. They told him they were patriots, not traitors, but they would not obey any more orders—even from him—until their demands were met. The mutiny terrified the high command. Washington feared the rebellion would spread through the rest of the army before it could be contained. British agents soon approached the insurgents, offering gold and rations if they would change sides. The soldiers spurned them, marching not toward the enemy but toward Philadelphia, determined to confront the government they served. Wayne shadowed them as they moved south.

It took a week of pleading and negotiation to end the crisis. Reed, who rode out from Philadelphia to meet the mutineers in Princeton, New Jersey, promised them back pay along with new shirts, shoes, and blankets. He had no idea where the money would come from, but his sympathy was enough to quiet the rebellion.

After the mutiny staged by the Pennsylvania Line, and smaller uprisings elsewhere, Congress knew it had to make radical changes. The revolution could not survive on patriotism alone; it required credit, organization, and fiscal discipline. In February 1781, Congress appointed individual executives to oversee the finance, war, foreign affairs, and marine departments, abandoning the unwieldy committees that had blundered since the war began. The most important of these would be the superintendent of finance—more like a president than a minister or secretary, he would be responsible for overseeing the entire federal government.

The choice for the job was unanimous. Congress turned to a man who was both a creature of commerce and a patriot of conviction: Robert Morris, a fabulously wealthy merchant. Robert and Gouverneur, who were not related, had become close friends while serving together in Congress in 1778. For the three and a half years that Robert served as superintendent of finance, they would be inseparable.

Born in Liverpool to a modest tobacco broker, Robert had crossed the Atlantic to Maryland as a boy of thirteen and arrived in Philadelphia at fifteen with little more than nerve and a sharp mind for numbers. Robert showed almost no interest in school, so a family friend got him a seven-year apprenticeship at a shipping firm. It didn't take long for the tall, sandy-haired teenager to graduate from sweeping floors to clerking in the countinghouse. Soon he was sailing to Caribbean ports on his employer's ships, charged with finding the most profitable cargo for the return trip. He had keen business instincts, and in the home office he was a whiz at keeping accounts and tracking currencies. At twenty-one, Robert finished his apprenticeship and became a regular employee. In 1757, he became a vested partner.

Through trade, speculation, and sheer audacity, Robert amassed a fortune and became a member of the Philadelphia elite. In 1769, he married Mary White, the daughter of a prominent lawyer, and the following year he bought a second home located a couple of miles northwest of the city, on a bluff overlooking the Schuylkill River. Robert and Mary liked to host lavish banquets at the two-story mansion they named The Hills—Gouverneur was a frequent guest—and they became widely known for their hospitality and extensive wine cellar. Robert, six feet tall and stout, was wealthy but not ostentatious. Unlike many other rich Philadelphians, he did not wear a wig or powder his hair.

By the eve of the Revolutionary War, he was known as the richest man in America—a self-made merchant prince.

Robert's fortune had bought him comfort but not complacency. In Congress, he argued that a free market was as vital to independence as arms and ammunition. "Commerce ought to be as free as air," he had written, yet he also knew that freedom demanded structure.

When Congress offered to make him superintendent of finance, Robert hesitated for weeks, torn between duty and self-preservation. He realized that taking the job would deal a blow to his wallet—and his reputation. He agonized over balancing his responsibilities as a husband, father, and citizen. Gouverneur pressed him to accept. "You are called on by the public, urged by duty, restrained by inclination," Gouverneur wrote to his friend. In the end, duty prevailed. On February 20, 1781, Robert Morris accepted the post—and immediately sent for Gouverneur to help him design the nation's rescue. "Aided by your talents and abilities, I feel better courage," Robert told him.

It was not an impulsive choice. As colleagues in Congress, the Morrises had helped keep the army alive through the shortages of 1778. Even then, Gouverneur's command of figures and policy distinguished him. He could translate confusion into clarity, and his drafts gave coherence to what others only debated. Robert had recognized in the younger Gouverneur a rare mix of intellect and courage. It was an unlikely partnership, between a self-made man who had mastered finance through trade, and a wealthy aristocrat with a head for economic theory. Yet the Morrises shared a faith in structure over sentiment.

To keep the revolution alive, Robert Morris pledged not the government's credit—it had none—but his own. He borrowed vast sums in his own name, mortgaging his ships, warehouses, and real estate, staking every asset he possessed. His word, once the guarantee of private commerce, became the collateral of a nation.

When cash ran out, he invented his own currency. He printed promissory notes signed in his bold hand—merchants and shopkeepers called them "Morris notes." Some were payable on sight, known on the streets as "short Bobs," while "long Bobs" were redeemable later. These notes circulated like cash throughout the colonies, buying gunpowder, salt, flour, boots, and clothing for the troops. To every man who took one, the signature of Robert Morris meant more than the seal of Congress.

At times Robert advanced money directly from his own accounts, dipping into the fortune he had built over two decades of trade. He paid suppliers, chartered ships, and kept the army clothed and fed. Robert knew what was at stake. If the revolution failed, he would lose his fortune and his good name. His goal was not merely to keep the army alive but to build a system that would outlast him. With Gouverneur at his side, he set out to create a financial framework strong enough to turn promises into power.

They worked out of a house next to Robert's redbrick mansion, on Front Street along the Delaware River, where the air smelled of fish entrails, the rotting carcasses of dead animals, and piles of garbage. Outside, stevedores flung curses at the children who scampered between the crates, barrels, and wagons. From dawn until long after the lamps were lit, the Morrises were bombarded by army officers and sea captains, bakers and butchers, clothiers and drovers—all clutching worthless Continental currency and demanding payment for wartime services or supplies. The superintendent's office must have looked less like a ministry than a warehouse of paper—ledgers stacked high, invoices and vouchers spilling from desks.

Gouverneur was Robert's full financial deputy, drafting policy, designing fiscal mechanisms, and working through accounts himself. Gouverneur thought like a financier as well as a philosopher. He saw that money itself was only a measure of trust, and that a nation's credit reflected its character. His reports on taxation, his plans for federal excise and land taxes, and his call for a decimal currency were not abstractions but blueprints for a self-sustaining republic. Robert told John Jay that he could "do nothing" without Gouverneur, adding later that his young partner "has more virtue than he shows, and more consistency than anybody believes." Robert was alluding to the fact that while both Morrises attracted criticism, many found Gouverneur's youthful self-assurance to be especially galling. "He has talents and much knowledge, but he has not a bit of character," a Dutch visitor observed, adding that Gouverneur was a powerful orator but had an off-putting "air of superiority." A French nobleman offered a slightly kinder appraisal, noting that Gouverneur "appeared to me to possess the most spirit and nerve" of anyone he met in Philadelphia.

The broader economy was healthy, but Congress had no way to tap into that private prosperity. The Morrises' solution was to establish the nation's first bank, a private institution that would be governed by investors who would purchase shares for four hundred dollars apiece. Under a plan drafted by Gouverneur, the new Bank of North America would lend money to and receive deposits from Congress, but its main sustenance would be commercial loans, issued in notes payable on demand. The notes would circulate as independent paper currency, backed by the full faith and credit of the bank, not the government. "The first bank in the country," Gouverneur later recalled with dry satisfaction, "was planned by your humble servant."

Another challenge for the Morrises was the baffling assortment of state-issued bills and coins, which so muddled interstate commerce that "the commonest things become intricate where money has anything to do with them," Robert quipped. To untangle this mess—and braid the states into one country—the Morrises proposed establishing a single national currency. After researching all the currencies in circulation, Gouverneur decided that America's new currency should be built on tens rather than the jumble of pounds, shillings, and pence. There were a hundred pennies to a dollar under Gouverneur's system, so he can fairly be called the inventor of the penny. However, Congress delayed final approval of a national currency until after the war. In 1786, it adopted a slightly different system designed by a committee headed by Thomas Jefferson. That panel decided that Gouverneur's quarter was too small, and instead proposed making the dollar the basic unit, subdivided a hundred times.

★

On August 14, 1781, Washington received word that a French fleet under the command of Admiral François Joseph Paul de Grasse was on its way from the West Indies, bound for Chesapeake Bay. The commander in chief desperately wanted to retake New York, but now his eyes turned south: the arrival of the French fleet would determine whether the alliance that Franklin had forged in Paris could deliver victory.

De Grasse, who had twenty-eight ships and thirty-five hundred troops, was expected to arrive by September 3. Virginia had been spared during the early years of the war, but since June the fighting there had been intense. Troops under Lord Charles Cornwallis had combined with the forces of the American turncoat Benedict Arnold to terrorize Washington's native state, devastating the estates of Revolutionary leaders. The British didn't damage Mount Vernon, but the sloop-of-war *Savage*, after torching homes on the Maryland side of the bay, had threatened Washington's beloved plantation. After casting anchor in the Potomac River, the captain of the *Savage* offered freedom to the enslaved people at Mount Vernon—fourteen men and three women took him up on the offer—and extracted a tribute of sheep, hogs, and other supplies from Lund Washington, a cousin of the general who was serving as caretaker in his absence.

A small force of about forty-five hundred soldiers, under the command of Lafayette, had been harassing Cornwallis, who sought refuge on the eastern tip of a peninsula that protruded into Chesapeake Bay, dividing the York and James Rivers. Cornwallis ordered his men to dig trenches and construct earthworks at a place called Yorktown, a tobacco port town where they would have easy access to the British fleet. Washington recognized, however, that on that narrow neck of land, the normally capable general had blundered into a trap.

Now the Americans and their French allies saw a chance to destroy Cornwallis's army—and perhaps deal a decisive blow to Britain's hopes of winning the war. But to do so, Washington and General Jean-Baptiste-Donatien de Vimeur, Comte de Rochambeau, had to move nearly seven thousand American and French troops from Westchester, New York, to Virginia—and quickly, because de Grasse had been ordered to return to the West Indies in the middle of October. They also had to conceal their destination for as long as possible, so British commanders in New York City wouldn't send reinforcements to bolster Cornwallis. The combined French and American armies began their nearly seven-hundred-mile journey on August 18. To avoid the heat of the day, they often traveled in the middle of the night, in the pitch-dark. Trailed by horses, tormented by mosquitoes, they trundled south, removing obstacles and erecting bridges along the way.

At the end of August, the British received reports that de Grasse was sailing for the Chesapeake, and they dispatched a fleet from the Hudson River to confront him. Admiral Sir Thomas Graves and his nineteen warships rounded the Virginia capes on the morning of September 5, and the Battle of the Chesapeake began. The British and French navies fought to a draw, but many of the British ships were severely damaged, and Graves determined that he could not provide any help to Cornwallis. He lingered for a week before sailing back to New York.

On September 28, the armies of Washington and Rochambeau reached Yorktown. Cornwallis was outnumbered two to one, and he was hemmed in by water, with no navy to save him. Crouched behind their fortifications, the redcoats and their Hessian allies could see American troops and artillery to their left and Frenchmen to their right. There was no mistaking one for the other: the Americans were dressed in rags, while the Frenchmen wore fashionable blue-and-white coats with white underclothes. More than a hundred allied cannon pulverized the British defenses, and every few days the attackers dug trenches closer and closer to the enemy. Cornwallis made a last gasp attempt to save his army on the night of October 16 by sneaking it across the York River, only to be thwarted by a violent storm.

At ten the following morning, a drummer boy appeared before the British fortifications, followed by an officer waving a white flag. The negotiations were brief. On October 19, 1781, Cornwallis surrendered his army—more than seven thousand soldiers—along with their cannons, muskets, and colors. Three hours later, drummers beating a solemn march led the defeated British and Hessian troops through two columns of French and American soldiers. "In passing between the two armies, they showed the greatest scorn for the Americans, who, to tell the truth, were eclipsed by our army in splendor of appearance and dress," Baron Ludwig von Closen, Rochambeau's young aide-de-camp, wrote in his journal. Most of the Americans "were clad in small jackets of white cloth, dirty and ragged, and a number of them were almost barefoot," von Closen observed. The beaten redcoats sullenly surrendered their weapons, pitching them onto a pile in an open field. Meanwhile, according to legend, British fifes and drums played an English ballad called "The World Turned Upside Down."

For once, the music was not ironic.

Officially, the war would drag on for nearly two more years, but the outcome was no longer in doubt: the ragtag American forces, along with their indispensable French allies, had defeated the world's most powerful empire and won their independence.

In Philadelphia, Robert Morris and Gouverneur Morris received the news with more relief than triumph. Their ledgers still lay open, and the numbers were still grim. But the gamble had paid off. Credit, character, and conviction—these were the weapons that had helped secure the victory. A merchant and a philosopher had proved that revolutions are not won by armies alone but by the faith that binds one man's financial promise to another's.

Peace, when it came, would not bring rest. The victory at Yorktown had proved that a republic could fight and survive; the harder test would be whether it could govern itself. In the years to come, Gouverneur Morris would turn his attention from the balance of ledgers to the balance of power. The habits of order and accountability he had forged in the countinghouse would follow him to the Pennsylvania State House, where a new constitution would take shape. The war for independence had been won with courage and credit; the war to define that freedom had only just begun.

ELEVEN

"ALL THAT MEN CAN BEAR"

America's stunning victory at Yorktown did not solve its fiscal problems, which threatened the unity of the new nation and its prospects for long-term survival. As Baron von Closen had noted, American troops were still underclothed, underfed, and underpaid, and the possibility of mutiny remained. The Morrises pushed on.

A critical piece of their overall plan fell into place when the Bank of North America opened on January 7, 1782. Without federal taxing power, however, it was a body without blood; the Morrises' proposals for new, reliable sources of federal revenue still languished in Congress. It didn't take long for aggrieved soldiers to rise again. At the end of 1782, a group of officers from Washington's army—camped for the winter near Newburgh, New York—came to Philadelphia with a familiar demand: they wanted to be paid. They intended to present a petition to Congress, but first they met with the Morrises.

"We have borne all that men can bear," they wrote. "Our property is expended, our private resources are at an end, and our friends are wearied out and disgusted with our incessant applications." Thanks to the contracting reforms the Morrises had pushed through, the troops were better fed and clothed than they had been in winters past. But they still hadn't received their paychecks, and as the end of the war loomed, they feared that Congress would demobilize the army and send them home penniless—while men who had never shouldered a musket grew rich in wartime trade. "The uneasiness of the soldiers for want of pay is dangerous," the petition warned. "Any further experiments on their patience may have fatal effects."

Gouverneur wasn't distressed by the petition; he welcomed it. If it took the threat of armed soldiers to give Congress taxing authority, so be it. Robert saw opportunity, too. On January 24, the day Congress was scheduled to debate the officers' appeal, he issued an ultimatum: unless the delegates made "permanent provision for the public debts of every kind" by May 31, he would resign.

Over the next few weeks, Gouverneur went further—dangerously so. On February 7, he wrote a letter to Major General Henry Knox and on February 13, he wrote one to Major General Nathanael Greene, urging them to use the threat of military force to compel Congress to act. "During the war they find you useful, and after a peace they will wish to get rid of you," he warned Knox. "Then they will see you starve rather than pay you a six-penny tax."

The generals recoiled. "When soldiers advance without authority, who can halt them?" Greene replied. "It is a critical business, and pregnant with dangerous consequences." Knox, more measured, deflected Gouverneur's dangerous logic toward a different kind of rebellion: "As the present constitution is so defective," he wrote, "why do not you great men call the people together and tell them so—that is, to have a convention of the states to form a better constitution?" Several years later, Knox urged Washington to attend a gathering in Philadelphia to do just that.

Still, the embers of mutiny smoldered. Washington soon uncovered a plot by younger officers stirred by anonymous circulars passed through the Newburgh camp. On March 15, he ordered his officers to convene in a wooden building nicknamed the Temple of Virtue, raised the previous month for Sunday services and dances. The commander in chief, who was not expected to attend, entered quietly through a side door, climbed the platform, and drew nine pages from his breast pocket.

Washington began by rebuking the men for trying to meet without his knowledge—"How inconsistent with the rules of propriety! How unmilitary!"—then defended Congress, insisting its efforts to find the money to pay them "have been unwearied, and will not cease until they have succeeded." His voice softened. "As I have never left your side one moment but when called from you on public duty . . . as I have been the constant companion and witness of your distresses and not among the last to feel and acknowledge your merits . . . it can scarcely be supposed, at this late stage of the war, that I am indifferent to [your] interests."

Then, before reading aloud a letter from a Virginia congressman, Washington did something no one had ever seen him do. He reached into his coat and produced a pair of spectacles. "Gentlemen, you must pardon me," he said. "I have grown gray in your service and now find myself growing blind." The simple gesture—the acknowledgment of age, of sacrifice—broke the mutiny in an instant. Hardened men wept.

★

Congress, informed of the near rebellion, acted quickly to pacify the officers. In 1780, it had finally approved half pay for retired soldiers for life, but the states had yet to supply the necessary funds. Now, Congress granted the officers a lump sum of five years' full pay instead. The federal government, not the states, assumed this debt. To the Morrises and their fellow nationalists, this new public debt was the seed of unity—a force that would make a revenue system for the central government inevitable.

A week after Washington's speech at Newburgh, word arrived that a provisional treaty had been signed with Britain. On April 11, 1783, Congress declared an end to hostilities, and the final peace treaty was signed in Paris that September.

The war's heroes had begun to turn into monuments, Washington most of all—his reserve mistaken for divinity, his authority unquestioned. It was that aura, rather than the man himself, that Gouverneur Morris set out—perhaps foolishly—to test. One evening at a dinner table with Washington, or so the story goes, Morris found himself surrounded by Hamilton, Lafayette, Greene, von Steuben, and other men who had faced cannon fire without flinching yet still adjusted their coats and moderated their laughter whenever the commander in chief appeared. Before the dinner, Morris had wagered Hamilton that he could break the spell that Washington cast. After relaying a story to the men gathered around the table, Morris swayed in his chair, clapped Washington on the back, and blurted out, "Wasn't it so, my old boy?" The reaction was instant and wordless. Washington turned. The look that met Morris was not one of anger, nor even surprise, but a kind of majestic astonishment—as if marble itself had come briefly to life to rebuke presumption. In that heartbeat, all of Morris's bravado collapsed. He murmured an apology, his face flushed the color of claret. "I have won the bet but paid dearly for it," a chastised Morris admitted to Hamilton after the meal, "and nothing could induce me to repeat it."

If Robert Morris was embarrassed by his partner's misstep, he could not dwell on it for long. The nation's finances still demanded his attention, and he stayed in office long past his supposed resignation date, finally stepping down in November 1784. For nearly five months after that, he worked on a final "Statement of Accounts," which he submitted to Congress—he had five hundred copies printed—in March 1785. He used it to issue another warning: "No treason has operated, or can operate, so great an injury to America, as must follow from a loss of reputation." Congress was still not ready to hear him. If Europe lost confidence in America's willingness—or ability—to honor its debts, foreign credit would disappear, domestic lenders would balk, trade would contract, and the entire financial scaffolding of the new nation would collapse. By this point, the greatest danger was not an enemy army, but the prospect of the country's public promises going unpaid.

After Robert finally left office, the two Morrises turned to private pursuits, sometimes collaborating on business ventures. Gouverneur occasionally practiced law, lobbied on behalf of merchants and the Bank of North America in the Pennsylvania legislature, and tried to build his fortune. (Philadelphia—not New York—was still the nation's financial capital.) Together, the Morrises sent a partner to Europe to borrow money for land speculation across New York, Pennsylvania, New Jersey, Maryland, and Delaware; backed a Massachusetts merchant's enterprise in ships and naval stores; and invested in a New York mercantile firm. In February 1787, Gouverneur bought shares to support John Fitch's new steamboat, and five months later joined Robert in purchasing one hundred thousand acres along the St. Lawrence River in the far north of New York State near the Canadian border. The same restless ambition that had driven Gouverneur through war now turned to enterprise—less patriotic perhaps, but no less audacious. Some of these postwar ventures—land, banking, shipping—produced handsome profits, giving him enough liquidity to live comfortably.

★

Gouverneur's family was just one of many that had been split between Loyalist sentiment and revolutionary fervor. Another such household was the Chew family, an elite Philadelphia clan whose patriarch, Benjamin Chew, had begun his term as chief justice of the Supreme Court of Pennsylvania before the revolution and whose ties to British officers made the family suspect during the occupation. When peace returned, however, the Chews resumed their place at the center of the city's social life. It was at one such celebration that Peggy Chew, Benjamin's lively twenty-three-year-old daughter, crossed paths with Gouverneur Morris.

Peggy served as a bridesmaid at a wedding in January 1784. In a letter to a friend, she described the festivities: At one of the dinners during the three-day celebration, the bridesmaids sat at their own table in an adjoining room, "to which many gentlemen followed, for the sake of ease and air and, I flatter ourselves, for the sake of our company also. Gouverneur Morris kept us in a continual smile (I dare not say laughter for the world, but you may admit it in the back room)." In Peggy's teasing account, Morris appears as he so often did: the irresistible talker, turning any room into his salon.

After years of deprivation and war, the tone of the new republic was changing; merriment could be found in Philadelphia again, and Morris was once more at its center. Yet even in moments of levity, the nation's unfinished business pressed close. The next storm would rise not from overseas but from within: from states invested in their own advantage rather than the idea of union, from the tension between slaveholding and free, from the question of how to build an executive strong enough to govern yet not as indelibly fixed as a monarch. The fragile republic had won its independence; it had yet to invent its government. And when that reckoning came, Gouverneur Morris would be there, ready to help shape the government that might finally match the nation's ambitions.

TWELVE

"AN ASSEMBLY OF DEMIGODS"

Morris had long predicted that financially aggrieved soldiers would compel Congress to strengthen the central government. In 1786, an uprising in western Massachusetts led by a Continental Army veteran fulfilled that prophecy.

An economic boom that followed the end of the revolution soon fizzled. Merchants who called in the enormous debts they were owed and demanded cash for further purchases deepened the downturn by creating a shortage of hard currency. Farmers—many of them veterans still owed payment for their military service—began to lose their land and property to debt collectors. In Connecticut, Maryland, New Hampshire, Pennsylvania, South Carolina, Vermont, and Virginia, farmers' frustrations flared into violence. The most serious outburst erupted in August 1786 in western Massachusetts, where mobs led by a veteran named Daniel Shays halted foreclosures by using the threat of violence to shut down the civil courts.

The Massachusetts uprising rang alarm bells in every state. Henry Knox, now the secretary of war, told Washington that while high taxes were the "ostensible cause of the commotions," the underlying issue was the rebels' confidence that neither the state nor the federal government had the power to stop them. "What is to afford us security against the violence of lawless men?" Knox wrote in October. "Our government must be braced, changed, or altered to secure our lives and property."

By early 1787, Shays and his followers had organized into regiments and expanded their ambitions beyond closing the courts; now they aimed to topple the state government in Boston. To do that, they needed more weapons and ammunition, and the federal armory in Springfield—which held seven thousand muskets with bayonets, thirteen hundred barrels of powder, and large amounts of shot and shell—was a tempting target. After raiding the armory, Shays vowed, the insurgents would march to Boston to vanquish the "nest of devils" responsible for their financial misfortunes and burn the state capital to the ground. On January 25, 1787, Shays led about fifteen hundred men in an attack on the arsenal. After firing warning shots, the defenders of the armory bludgeoned the insurgents with artillery fire, killing four and wounding twenty more. The rebels retreated over the blood-stained snow and disappeared into the countryside. Eventually, many of them were captured though most, including Shays, received pardons.

Washington, and many others, feared the country was on the edge of anarchy. "No morn ever dawned more favorable than ours did—and no day was ever more clouded than the present!" he had written to James Madison the previous November, as the Massachusetts uprising was gaining strength. "Without some alteration in our political creed, the superstructure we have been seven years raising at the expense of much blood and treasure, must fall." The retired general predicted that "thirteen sovereignties pulling against each other, and all tugging at the federal head will soon bring ruin on the whole."

Individual states issued their own currencies, pursued separate trade deals, even conducted their own foreign policy. Georgia was waging war against the Creek Indians; Virginia ratified a separate peace treaty with Britain and granted preferential trade access to French wines and brandy, defying a national pact with the Dutch; and Maryland parleyed directly with the British to recover its stock in the Bank of England. Nine states claimed to have their own navies, and those with bustling ports levied their own duties on cargo. Regional interests diverged so dramatically that some Southern newspapers were chewing over the idea of creating four new countries rather than preserving the current one.

On February 21, 1787, Congress endorsed a convention of the states in Philadelphia to discuss the nation's future. It was time to determine how a republic of thirteen quarrelsome states would be governed. Should sovereignty rest with the people themselves, or with the individual states claiming to represent them? How much authority should a national legislature have, and who would choose it? Could a single executive lead a free people without becoming their monarch? What, finally, was to be done about slavery, the contradiction beating at the heart of their revolution?

The meeting that became known as the Constitutional Convention was the opportunity that Morris and other proponents of a stronger central government had been waiting for. "Never, in the flow of time was there a moment so propitious as that in which the convention assembled," he later reflected. "The states had been convinced, by melancholy experience, how inadequate they were to the management of our national concerns." Though Morris was a native New Yorker, Pennsylvania legislators elected the Philadelphia resident to the state's eight-member delegation. Morris was surprised to be chosen and somewhat reluctant to accept, since he wanted to concentrate on Morrisania and his business ventures. Furthermore, it wasn't clear the delegates would be permitted to make wholesale changes; Congress had instructed them to gather "for the sole and express purpose of revising the Articles of Confederation," which had governed relations between the states since 1781.

If the scope of the mission was uncertain, there was no doubt about the men chosen to carry it out; Thomas Jefferson called them "an assembly of demigods." Among the fifty-five representatives were two future presidents, a future vice president, five future Supreme Court justices, a future secretary of state, and a future secretary of the treasury. Eight delegates had signed the Declaration of Independence, and fifteen had helped draft their state constitutions. Twenty-five served in the Continental Congress during the revolution. Jefferson and John Adams, who were serving as envoys to France and Britain, respectively, were absent. But Washington, Franklin, Madison, and Hamilton were there, as was Robert Morris.

Gouverneur, by many accounts, outshined them all.

At thirty-five, he was one of the youngest delegates, but he took the floor one hundred and seventy-three times—more than anybody else. He scathingly denounced slavery and called for its extinction, even as other abolitionists sat silent. He argued successfully for a strong chief executive and was a stalwart defender of civil liberties. And he used his pen to shape the final document in ways that have echoed through the ages. "Gouverneur Morris was probably the most brilliant member of the Pennsylvania delegation"—a group that included Franklin—"and of the convention as well," according to Max Farrand, the Yale historian whose three-volume collection of the convention records, published in 1911, is the seminal account. Farrand described Morris as "sharp-witted, clever, startling in his audacity, and with a wonderful command of language." Morris's fellow delegates were dazzled by his eloquence and erudition. To William Pierce of Georgia, Morris was "one of those geniuses" who "winds through all the mazes of rhetoric, and throws around him such a glare that he charms, captivates, and leads away the senses of all who hear him." Pierce concluded that "no man has more wit—nor can anyone engage the attention more than Mr. Morris."

Morris's coldly realistic view of human nature rankled more idealistic delegates. Madison knocked him for harping on "the political depravity of men, and the necessity of checking one vice and interest by opposing them to another vice and interest." James Wilson, another

Pennsylvania delegate, who often spoke for the ailing eighty-one-year-old Franklin, was miffed by Morris's relentless emphasis on protecting private property. Years later, however, Madison praised Morris for his open-mindedness to opposing arguments, noting that "to the brilliancy of his genius, he added what is too rare, a candid surrender of his opinions when the lights of discussion satisfied him." Madison also credited Morris with "a readiness to aid in making the best of measures in which he had been overruled."

To Pierce and many others, that flexibility was a fault. Morris was "fickle and inconstant, never pursuing one train of thinking, nor ever regular," the Georgian wrote. Farrand echoed that criticism, writing that Morris "was admired more than he was trusted, for he was inconsistent, and he was suspected of being lax in morals as well as lacking in principles." That criticism rings hollow today. On the question that left a moral stain on the convention and doomed the country to a bloody civil war seventy-four years later, Morris was more principled and unwavering than anybody else.

★

Madison arrived in Philadelphia on May 3, eleven days before the convention was supposed to begin, and ten days earlier than any other delegate traveling from outside Pennsylvania. The thirty-six-year-old Virginian, who represented his state in Congress, was unmarried—he didn't meet his future wife, Dolley, until 1794. He was short and weighed barely a hundred pounds, with hair he brushed forward to conceal his receding hairline. He usually wore black and was reluctant to do or say anything that might call attention to himself. Madison quietly moved into Mary House's boardinghouse on Fifth and Market Streets, where visiting Virginia officials often stayed, and prepared to advance ideas he had been mulling over for months. He had already compiled a memorandum outlining eleven "vices of the political system of the United States." Among them: the states' refusal to comply with international treaties; the states' insistence on advancing their own financial and commercial interests to the detriment of other states; insufficient safeguards against internal violence and sedition; and conflicting state laws. Madison also criticized the "injustice" of various state laws, specifically their failure to protect the rights of the minority and individuals. All societies were divided into different interests and factions, Madison wrote, citing as examples creditors and debtors, the rich and the poor, merchants and manufacturers, and people of different religions. Surely the majority should rule in a republic, he wrote, but "what is to restrain them from unjust violations of the rights and interests of the minority, or of individuals?"

Washington arrived in Chester, about twenty miles from Philadelphia, on Sunday, May 13. At midday he dined with some former army colleagues at Mrs. Withy's Inn. His entrance into the city that afternoon befitted his Olympian stature: After the meal, a parade of dignitaries and the First Troop Philadelphia City Cavalry, sporting black and silver hats, white breeches, and high boots, escorted the great man into the metropolis. Church bells pealed and an artillery company fired a thirteen-gun salute, one blast for each of the states. Despite the rainy weather, the streets were lined with cheering residents.

Like Madison, Washington planned to lodge at Mary House's boardinghouse. But Robert and Mary Morris intercepted him there, prevented him from unloading his baggage, and insisted he stay with them. Washington had declined a written invitation from the Morrises, but he could not refuse them in person. After settling in at their three-story brick mansion, the general walked four blocks down Market Street to Franklin's home, pumping many outstretched hands along the way. Even Washington felt duty-bound to pay his respects to the legendary philosopher, scientist, and statesman, who received him in his dining room with a cask of dark beer. The Morrises proudly introduced their houseguest to Philadelphia society. Ten days after arriving, Washington recorded in his diary that he drank tea "in a very large circle of ladies" at the town house of Benjamin Chew, the former chief justice of the Pennsylvania Supreme Court. The circle likely included Chew's daughter Peggy, the bridesmaid who had raved about Gouverneur's charm at her friend's wedding; she had just become a bride herself.

Washington had left Martha at Mount Vernon, but he didn't arrive in Philadelphia alone: He was accompanied by three of the men he enslaved—Giles, Paris, and William Lee, often called Billy. Shortly after he got to town Washington purchased soap powder, a puff, and a black silk handkerchief for Lee, later supplementing them with two pairs of stockings and a pair of breeches. On many mornings during the convention the general rose early to ride with Giles, his coachman. Just a year earlier, he had written to Robert Morris on behalf of a Virginia slave owner who was involved in a lawsuit with Philadelphia Quakers who were trying to liberate his slave. "I hope it will not be conceived from these observations, that it is my wish to hold the unhappy people who are the subject of this letter, in slavery," Washington explained. "I can only say that there is not a man living who wishes more sincerely than I do, to see a plan adopted for the abolition of it." But, he continued, when slaves "are happy and content to remain with their present masters," persuading them to pursue freedom "introduces more evils than it can cure."

At least a third of the delegates were slave owners, and on the eve of the convention, about one-sixth of the American population—nearly seven hundred thousand people—lived in bondage. The percentage was much higher in Virginia, where slaves constituted almost a third of the population. In 1787, only a single state—Massachusetts—had banned slavery, though Connecticut, New Hampshire, Pennsylvania, and Rhode Island had gradual emancipation laws that provided for the eventual freedom of people newly born into slavery. More than two thousand free Black people lived in Philadelphia, more than anywhere else. Many worshiped at St. George's, a Methodist church close to the State House.

The delegates did not relish a debate on slavery, which was not mentioned in Congress's call for the convention nor in the resolutions the states adopted to guide their delegations. Like Washington, several of the Virginia delegates were conflicted. They recognized that slavery was incompatible with their republican principles and hoped it would fade away. But all of them owned slaves and dreaded the financial consequences of parting with them. Only one, George Wythe, would emancipate his slaves during his lifetime.

The tension in Madison's mind was evident in a letter he wrote to his father in 1783, explaining why he didn't intend to punish Billey, an enslaved man who had been recaptured after he fled into Philadelphia while Madison was serving in Congress. Madison wrote that he wouldn't send Billey back to Montpelier, his Virginia plantation, because "I am persuaded his mind is too thoroughly tainted to be a fit companion for fellow slaves in Virginia." Billey had been infected, that is, by what he had heard in Philadelphia about democracy, freedom, and inalienable rights. "The laws here [in Philadelphia] do not admit of his being sold for more than seven years," Madison lamented. "I do not expect to get near the worth of him, but cannot think of punishing him by transportation merely for coveting that liberty for which we have paid the price of so much blood, and have proclaimed so often to be the right, and worthy the pursuit, of every human being." Four years later, Madison harbored the same doubts. "Where slavery exists, the republican theory becomes still more fallacious," he wrote in his preconvention memorandum.

Virginia delegate George Mason, Washington's Fairfax County neighbor, described slavery as "that slow poison, which is daily contaminating the minds and morals of our people." Mason believed that a man became "a petty tyrant" when he owned slaves. Two years after the convention, Virginia delegate Edmund Randolph mused to Madison that he might move to Philadelphia to seek medical care for his wife, who was ill with cancer. "In that case a new revolution will take place with me," Randolph wrote. "For if I found I could live there, I should emancipate my slaves and thus ending my days, without undergoing any anxiety about the injustice of holding them."

The members of the South Carolina delegation, the most vehement defenders of slavery at the convention, had no such compunctions.

Their leader was John Rutledge of Charleston, a forty-seven-year-old trial lawyer who had been governor of South Carolina—some likened him to a dictator—during the revolution. Rutledge was tall and dignified, with long powdered hair and dark, piercing eyes. A French commentator described him as "the most eloquent man in the United States, but also the proudest and most imperious." Upon meeting him before the war, John Adams said Rutledge had "an air of reserve, design and cunning."

Rutledge was joined by a pair of cousins, General Charles Cotesworth Pinckney, forty-three, and twenty-nine-year-old Charles Pinckney. Both Pinckneys were lawyers and planters. The elder, who had been captured by the British during the war, mainly spoke up during the convention to defend slavery. The younger, known as "Blackguard Charlie" for his aggressive manner, dove into a variety of topics. He lied about his age so he could have the distinction of being the youngest delegate; in fact, that title belonged to Jonathan Dayton of New Jersey, who was only twenty-six. The fourth and final member of the South Carolina delegation was Pierce Butler, a forty-three-year-old planter. All the South Carolina delegates owned slaves.

Along with the Virginians and the South Carolinians, Morris and his fellow Pennsylvania delegates had the greatest impact on the proceedings.

The dean of the Pennsylvania delegation was Franklin, the only American whose stature rivaled Washington's. "Dr. Franklin is well known to be the greatest philosopher of the present age," William Pierce wrote. "All the operations of nature he seems to understand. The very heavens obey him, and the clouds yield up their lightning to be imprisoned in his rod." Pierce added that Franklin, who had returned to America in 1785 after nearly a decade as a diplomat in France, "possesses an activity of mind equal to a youth of twenty-five years of age." Franklin's election as president of Pennsylvania, akin to the governorship, had not diminished his passion for inventing and experimenting. In his newly renovated home on Market Street, the library occupied the entire second floor, and it was filled with wonders. They included a glass machine that mimicked the circulation of blood through the human body, and a rocking chair with an overhead fan, operated by a foot pedal, that Franklin had fashioned to fend off heat and flies. He invented a rolling press to copy documents, and a long, mechanical arm to retrieve books from high shelves.

Franklin had been feted in the courts of Europe, but he was neither imperial nor unapproachable. Short and heavyset, with a bald pate ringed by short white locks, he favored plain Quaker clothes. He warmly welcomed visitors to the shade of the mulberry tree in his garden, where his daughter laid out a tea table and the conversation flowed freely. "When I entered his house, I felt as if I was going to be introduced to the presence of a European monarch," recalled Manasseh Cutler, a Massachusetts clergyman who visited that summer. Instead, when Cutler was brought to the mulberry tree, Franklin stood up, took his guest by the hand, welcomed him to Philadelphia, and invited him to sit next to him. Speaking softly, with an open and frank expression on his face, Franklin proudly showed the clergyman a vial containing a two-headed snake—he had just received it from a friend—and took him on a tour of his library. There were several delegates under the mulberry tree that day; Franklin's garden was just a few hundred yards from the State House, and it was an oasis for delegates seeking respite from the debates. The amiable old man was a calming influence, and his tales and aphorisms often nudged the younger delegates toward compromise.

Franklin suffered from gout and kidney stones, and on some days he had to be carried to the State House in a glass-windowed sedan chair he had brought from Paris, borne aloft by four beefy prisoners from the Walnut Street Jail. When Franklin wanted to contribute but didn't feel well enough to deliver a speech, he relied on fellow Pennsylvania delegate James Wilson as a spokesman. Tall with auburn hair, Wilson was a stern-looking lawyer who spoke with the burr of his native Scotland. More than a mouthpiece, he would help steer the debates over representation and slavery.

Franklin had recently accepted the presidency of the Pennsylvania Abolition Society, but earlier in his life he had owned enslaved people and carried advertisements for the sale of slaves in his newspaper, *The Pennsylvania Gazette.* Wilson still owned a slave, who worked primarily in his kitchen. He didn't free the man until he married a Quaker woman in 1793.

★

Though the convention was supposed to begin on May 14, there were only enough delegates to form quorums for Virginia and Pennsylvania. Finally, on Friday, May 25, there were sufficient numbers from a majority of the states to begin the official proceedings. A steady rain was falling as the twenty-nine men, representing nine states, made their way to the State House. On Chestnut Street, in front of the building, the city had scattered dirt and gravel over the cobblestones to muffle the din of the carriages and horses passing by. Delegates approaching from the rear had to scurry past the Walnut Street Jail, where the inmates poked long poles with caps of cloth through the bars of their cells to beg for a few coins—spitting profanities at passersby who refused. Brushing the rain off their coats, the delegates gathered in the East Room, the same chamber where the Second Continental Congress had signed the Declaration of Independence. There were thirteen tables, one for each state, covered in green baize and arranged in a semicircle around a raised platform with a high-backed chair.

The first order of business was to elect a presiding officer to occupy that chair, which had the top half of a sun—with facial features and hairlike beams—carved into the wood. Only two men were judged worthy of the honor: Franklin and Washington. Franklin, perhaps not feeling well or unwilling to brave the rain, was absent. But he had asked Robert Morris to nominate Washington, and the delegates elected him unanimously. Robert and Rutledge escorted the general, who wore his old Continental Army uniform, to the platform. Madison followed the trio to the front of the room and took a seat in front of Washington, facing the rest of the delegates. For the duration of the convention Madison sat there taking notes, never missing a day or leaving the chamber for more than a few minutes. His colleagues trusted him to keep an accurate record of the proceedings—to a point. A handful, including Franklin, preferred to give Madison written texts of their speeches, to ensure that he was faithful to what they had said.

On the following Monday, the delegates adopted rules. As in Congress, each state would have a single vote, decided by a majority of its delegates. If a state had an even number of delegates present and they were split on a question, the state could not cast a vote. Only New York required all its delegates (it had three) to be present to vote. They often weren't. That fact, combined with New Hampshire's frequent absences and Rhode Island's refusal to participate (it wanted to continue to issue its own currency) gave Southern states disproportionate power.

The delegates also approved a rule allowing reconsideration of any matter, even after a vote. This gave them an unlimited ability to rethink and revise their positions, and to rework seemingly settled provisions. To protect this messy process from public scrutiny, they voted to cloak the proceedings in a blanket of secrecy; nothing discussed in the chamber would be shared with the outside world. George Mason called the secrecy rule "a necessary precaution to prevent misrepresentations or mistakes." There was a big difference, he noted, "between the appearance of a subject in its first crude and undigested shape, and after it shall have been properly matured and arranged." To protect their privacy, the delegates posted sentries outside the chamber and kept the windows shut—no matter how hot it got inside. On one occasion, William Pierce recalled, somebody found a document a delegate had inadvertently left outside the chamber. Washington was incensed. "Gentlemen, I am sorry to find that some one member of this body has been so neglectful of the secrets of the convention as to drop in the State House a copy of their proceedings, which by accident was picked up and delivered to me this morning." He flung the paper onto his desk. "I do not know whose paper it is, but there it is—let him who owns it take it." Washington put on his hat and stormed out of the room. Unable to locate his own copy of the document, Pierce slinked to the platform, peeked at the paper, and exhaled—thankfully, it was not his. Fearing Washington's wrath, nobody dared claim it.

★

In the predawn darkness of May 30, Philadelphians of every station and color streamed toward Market Street. It was Wednesday, a market day, and under a covered structure that extended for nearly half a mile, vendors were laying out their wares. Women, some of them holding infants in their arms, were arranging fruit. The meat on offer included raccoon, opossum, and bear's foot, and fishmongers worked the area closest to the river. As more customers trooped in, the sellers appealed to them quietly, without shouting; only a low murmur of voices buzzed under the patter of a steady rain.

Meanwhile, inside the State House, the delegates were wrestling with a fundamental question: What were they doing there?

The day before, Edmund Randolph of Virginia had submitted what became known as the Virginia Plan. The fifteen-point proposal envisioned a bicameral legislature—with one house popularly elected and the second chosen by the first—that could declare state laws unconstitutional; a chief executive, selected by the legislature, who would serve for a fixed term and could not run for reelection; and a council, including the executive and several national judges, that would be empowered to veto legislation.

It was a lot for the delegates to digest, but one thing was immediately clear: this wasn't a revision of the Articles of Confederation—it was the framework for a whole new government.

The first of Randolph's fifteen points was that the Articles of Confederation had to be "corrected and enlarged" to ensure the states' "common defense, security of liberty and general welfare." This statement corresponded with what Congress had asked the delegates to do: revise the Articles of Confederation. The rest of the plan went far beyond that, so Gouverneur Morris suggested that Randolph replace his fifteen points with three new resolutions. First, that a loose union of states, like the Articles of Confederation, could not guarantee the common defense, liberty, and the general welfare. Second, that a treaty or treaties among sovereign states would not be enough, either. And third, that "a national government ought to be established, consisting of a supreme legislature, executive and judiciary."

There was a pause in the proceedings as the delegates considered these three points. Then South Carolinian Charles Cotesworth Pinckney rose to speak. If the purpose of the convention was to revise the Articles of Confederation, Pinckney asserted, then flatly stating that they could *not* be revised, which is what Morris's first two resolutions did, meant the convention had concluded its business and it was time to go home. The delegates admitted that Pinckney had a point. To skirt that issue, they dropped the first two resolutions and took up Morris's third one, which led to the first substantive discussion of the convention: What did the words *national* and *supreme* mean? And would an all-powerful national government "annihilate" the states?

Morris seized this opportunity to explain why the country needed a stronger central government. "We are not now under a federal government," he said, because "a federal government is that which has a right to compel every part to do its duty." The bottom line, he argued, was that it wouldn't be possible to fulfill the mission Congress had given the convention—to ensure the common defense, liberty, and the general welfare—without making the national government the supreme authority over the states. "I cannot conceive of a government in which there can exist two supremes. A federal agreement which each party may violate at pleasure cannot answer the purpose," he said. "We had better take a supreme government now, than a despot twenty years hence—for come he must."

Morris's view carried the day. The convention endorsed a new "national government" made up of a "supreme legislature, executive and judiciary." It was a straightforward statement that changed everything:

The delegates would scrap the Articles of Confederation and organize the states into a whole new government, one where the parts were subservient to the whole.

★

Three days later, the Pennsylvania Abolition Society adopted its own resolution: an appeal to the delegates to end the slave trade. "In vain will be their pretentions to a love of liberty or a regard for national character, while they share in the profits of a commerce that can only be conducted upon rivers of human tears and blood." The members of the society were making their appeal, they said, in the name of a God "offended by this inhuman traffic" and in fear of "the certainty of the great and awful day of retribution." They gave the address to Franklin, their president, and asked him to present it and other documents to the convention. Franklin declined to do so, explaining that he "had thought it advisable to let them lie over for the present."

The delegates were apprehensive about discussing slavery, but they couldn't let it "lie over" for long.

THIRTEEN

NEITHER PEOPLE NOR PROPERTY

As soon as the delegates began debating how many seats each state would get in Congress, the slavery question barreled into the East Room like an uninvited guest.

Under the Virginia Plan, large states would get more congressional seats than small states—and small states hated the idea. Delaware, for one, had ordered its delegates to leave the convention if the plan won approval. Bridging this gap, if it could be bridged, meant answering a question the delegates dreaded: Were slaves, who comprised much of the population and wealth of the Southern states, people or property?

The delegates tussled over representation for most of June—without Gouverneur Morris. On May 31, Morris left the convention and returned to New York for a month to oversee repairs and renovations at Morrisania. His mother had died eighteen months earlier, and under Lewis Morris's will, the portion of the estate Sarah had inherited upon her husband's death passed to Staats Long Morris, the second eldest son. But Staats Long had long since moved to England, where he had become a lieutenant general in the British army and a member of Parliament, so he agreed to sell his fourteen hundred acres of Morrisania to Gouverneur. After taking possession of the property a few months before the convention started, Gouverneur hired an overseer and a large group of laborers to refurbish the buildings and plant trees and crops, and he wanted to be on hand to supervise their work.

Given the stakes in Philadelphia—no less than "the happiness or misery of millions yet unborn," as George Mason put it—it is hard to understand how Morris could have missed so much of the convention. But his absence was not unusual: Only thirty delegates were there for the entire four months, and on most days, there were no more than thirty-five men in the East Room. At no point were all fifty-five delegates present. Rhode Island maintained its boycott throughout the summer, and New Hampshire's delegation didn't arrive until late July. Alexander Hamilton was absent for two months. Hamilton's two New York colleagues, far less enamored of a strong central government than he was, left in a huff at the end of July. Their departure deprived New York of a quorum, so Hamilton was unable to cast an official vote on behalf of his state.

Meanwhile, in Morris's absence, the delegates moved forward. In early June, they decided—at least for the time being—that citizens would elect the lower house of the legislature, while state legislators would elect the upper house. But they were still wrestling with how many seats each state would get. On June 9, that question flared into a conflict between large and small states, leading to a strange alliance that brought slavery to the fore.

Irish-born William Paterson of New Jersey struck the first blow. Short, deliberate, and respected for his calm intelligence, the forty-two-year-old lawyer warned that giving the largest states—Massachusetts, Pennsylvania, and Virginia—more votes than the smaller ones would destroy the balance of the Union. "Give the large states an influence in proportion to their magnitude," he said, "and their ambition will be proportionally increased." The small states, he argued, "will have everything to fear." New Jersey, he declared, would sooner submit to a monarch than be "swallowed up" by its larger neighbors.

Across the aisle, James Wilson of Pennsylvania, peering through his spectacles "like a surveyor through a compass," rose to answer him. New Jersey and Delaware had hinted they might walk out rather than yield power, but Wilson refused to be cowed. Referring to the smaller New Jersey, he asked if it should have "the same right or influence in the councils of the nation with Pennsylvania? I say no! It is unjust—I never will confederate on this plan."

Wilson's reasoning was hard to refute: If laws were to apply to people, not states, representation should reflect the number of people in each state. The large states believed this was fair: they had supplied more soldiers and money to win America's independence, and they expected a proportionate voice in the national government. The small states saw a trap. Under proportional representation, they feared, their interests would be crushed beneath the weight of the larger states. They preferred to keep the system of equal votes under the old Articles of Confederation, where every state—big or small—had a single vote. Each side believed the survival of the republic depended on its view. They appeared to be at an impasse.

Searching for a way to break the deadlock, Wilson turned south. The Carolinas and Georgia were sparsely populated for the moment but growing fast. In time, proportional representation—allocating legislative seats by population—would favor them, too. Their delegates were wary but pragmatic. The Southern economy, built on enslaved labor, faced scrutiny from the North, where abolitionist sentiment was rising. If Wilson and his allies would agree to count enslaved people in the population totals, the South might back the proportional system Wilson championed. It was a brutal calculus: human bondage turned into a bargaining chip.

When the delegates reconvened Monday morning, the tone and tempo of the debate had shifted; it seemed the delegates had reached some sort of understanding outside the hall. Indeed, over the Sunday recess, factions had splintered off to bargain privately—testing compromises before they risked them in debate. One such compromise, whispered in tavern rooms and boardinghouses, would shake the convention to its foundations.

Lanky, sixty-six-year-old Roger Sherman of Connecticut had immense hands and feet, a sharp nose, and dark hair cut straight across his forehead. Thomas Jefferson once remarked that the former shoemaker turned statesman "never said a foolish thing in his life." On June 11, this awkward but clear-minded man rose to propose an elegant compromise: that the legislature be divided into two chambers: a lower house, where representation would be apportioned by population (what would become the House of Representatives), and an upper house (the future Senate), where every state would have an equal number of votes. Debate broke out immediately. John Rutledge of South Carolina, cool in his linen suit despite the heat in the airless chamber, argued that representation should not depend on population at all, but on wealth and what each state paid into the public treasury. Power, he said flatly, should follow money. Wilson, joined by Rufus King of Massachusetts, countered that representation must rest on "some equitable ratio," whether by population or wealth. And to lend the argument moral weight, Wilson tapped a formidable ally: Franklin, who had been scribbling at his seat. The inventor handed the speech he had prepared to Wilson. Franklin had hoped that members of the new legislature would consider themselves Americans rather than representatives of their states, it said, "but as I find this is not to be expected, I now think the number of representatives should bear some proportion to the number of the represented." The question remained: Would the number be calculated according to population or wealth?

Pennsylvania's Wilson had an answer ready, one almost certainly shaped during a Sunday of quiet negotiation with the South Carolina delegates. Representation, he proposed, should be based on "the whole number of white and other free citizens," plus "three-fifths of all other persons not comprehended in the foregoing description."

Thus emerged the formula that would darken the Constitution. The Three-Fifths Clause categorized enslaved people as something between human beings and property, acknowledging their existence only to enlarge the political power of those who enslaved them. It gave the South more seats in the lower house without granting its slaves citizenship. Because counting enslaved people—even partially—increased Southern population totals, the South joined the larger Northern states in supporting population-based representation, securing the votes needed to pass the measure.

Elbridge Gerry of Massachusetts, slight and almost birdlike, rose to protest. Gerry stammered and had an unnerving habit of squinting and widening his eyes as he spoke. He hailed from a populous state, but he also was a corresponding member of the Pennsylvania Abolition Society, and he homed in on the contradiction in the Three-Fifths Clause. In the South, slaves were treated as property. Why then, he asked, "should they be in the rule of representation more than the cattle and horses of the North?" His question hung unanswered in the humid air.

When the roll was called, nine states voted in favor, while only Delaware and New Jersey voted against. The Three-Fifths Clause stood, at least for now. Under the convention rules, it could be revisited later. Few doubted it would return to the floor before summer's end, as the delegates reconsidered every major issue in search of a final compromise.

Morris didn't miss any final decisions during his monthlong absence. What he missed was a dramatic change in the climate; the amity that prevailed at the beginning of the convention evaporated as the temperature climbed.

Two days before Morris returned, on Saturday, June 30, Gunning Bedford Jr. of Delaware gave voice to the small states' anger in a speech that scorched the chamber. Bedford, a stocky, sharp-tongued lawyer, accused the large states and their Southern partners of putting their own interests ahead of the country's. "Even the diminutive state of Georgia," he thundered, "has an eye to her future wealth and greatness. South Carolina, puffed up with the possession of her wealth and Negroes, and North Carolina, are all, from different views, united with the great states." He turned to face all of them. "I do not, gentlemen, trust you." It was an extraordinary outburst—part warning, part plea. Bedford concluded by going even further, implying that Delaware would rather seek protection from abroad than submit to domination at home.

The room went still. Bedford's words sounded treasonous to men who had lost comrades in the fight against foreign domination. King tried to defuse the situation, pointing to the union of England and Scotland as an example of a smaller state thriving in concert with a larger one. "Since I am up, I am concerned for what fell from the gentleman from Delaware," King added. "Take a foreign power by the hand! I am sorry he mentioned it, and I hope he is able to excuse it to himself on the score of passion."

By Monday, when Morris returned from New York, tempers had cooled, but the fault lines were plain. Questions of representation and slavery had become inseparable, and unity was splintering under the weight of ambition and fear. The small states clung to their bid for equality; the South demanded recognition for its enslaved population; the large states, eager for progress, were losing patience.

On July 11, the matter arose again when the delegates discussed the census that would determine future representation. Beneath the bureaucratic wrangling ran a deeper current. The South's enslaved population was growing, and new states would soon rise in the western territories. Would they join as free or slave? The answer could determine the balance of power in Congress for generations.

Morris saw the danger immediately. Ever the realist, he approached the subject obliquely, avoiding open talk of slavery but making his meaning plain. The western settlers, he argued, were unfit to wield equal power with the established states. "It must be apparent," he said coolly, that "they would not be able to furnish men equally enlightened to share in the administration of our common interests." Surely, the "busy haunts of men," not the wilderness, were the "proper school of political talents." Then, almost as an afterthought, he struck at the heart of the compromise itself. Including enslaved people in the census, he said, would make the free citizens of Pennsylvania revolt. "They would reject any plan that was to have such an effect." He was not expressing sympathy with racial prejudice but rather delivering a stark warning: Pennsylvania would never accept a system that rewarded slave states with greater power.

James Wilson—the same man who had proposed the three-fifths formula—admitted that even he could not justify it logically. "Are [enslaved people] admitted as citizens?" he asked. "Then why are they not admitted on an equality with white citizens? Are they admitted as property? Then why is not other property admitted into the computation?" Still, he concluded, the inconsistency "must be overruled by the necessity of compromise."

Morris's reply stripped away the pretense. "I am compelled," he said, "to declare myself reduced to the dilemma of doing injustice to the Southern states or to human nature—and I must therefore do it to the former." He vowed that he would "never agree to give such encouragement to the slave trade as would be given by allowing them a representation for their Negroes." In other words, he would sooner risk dividing the Union than enshrine injustice as its foundation.

The effect was electric. His speech came at the end of the day, but its echo carried into every tavern and boardinghouse that night. The next morning, Charles Cotesworth Pinckney of South Carolina rose at once. "I was alarmed," he said, "at what was said yesterday concerning the Negroes." Moments later, William Davie of North Carolina, who had barely spoken all summer, stood to deliver his first major statement. It was "high time now to speak out," he proclaimed. It was clear, he said, that "some gentlemen"—meaning Morris—"intend to deprive the Southern states of any share of representation for their Blacks." If the eastern states persisted, Davie warned, "the business is at an end." North Carolina would never join the Union on such terms.

Morris did not flinch. "It has been said that it is high time to speak out," he replied, so he would be candid too. He had come to "form a compact for the good of America," but if some states were unwilling to unite, the others would unite without them.

The elder Pinckney from South Carolina countered immediately that any government that respected private property must protect the property rights of slave owners. Edmund Randolph of Virginia, sensing disaster, tried to douse the fire, urging "express security" that enslaved people would continue to count toward representation—though he "lamented that such a species of property existed." Wilson again reached for compromise, suggesting that representation be tied to each state's taxes, and *that* figure would be based on the white population and three-fifths of the enslaved population.

But South Carolina's younger Pinckney closed the day by laying bare the South's position. If representation was to be based on people, he said, then let enslaved people count equally with whites—not because they were equal, but because a one-to-one ratio would maximize the political power of their enslavers. Only South Carolina and Georgia voted for his motion.

The sparring spilled into the next day. "The Southern gentlemen," Morris observed, "will not be satisfied unless they see the way open to their gaining a majority in the public councils." If the South would not yield, he said, "let us at once take friendly leave of each other."

That remark drew a furious outburst from Pierce Butler of South Carolina, who accused Morris and the Northern delegates of conspiring to abolish slavery altogether. "The security the Southern states want," Butler snapped, "is that their Negroes may not be taken from them, which some gentlemen—within or without doors—have a very good mind to do."

The line was drawn. What began as a debate involving arithmetic had become a contest for the nation's soul.

★

Just as the dispute over slavery threatened to tear the convention apart, the delegates laid it aside to turn to another fundamental question: How should the new nation be led?

They had agreed there would be a single executive, but little else. How much authority should he wield? Who would choose him—and for how long would he serve? Could a president govern a free people without becoming their master?

On these questions, Gouverneur Morris was as firm as he had been about slavery. He had long believed the young republic needed a vigorous executive, not a feeble figurehead bound by the legislature. He had argued this before—at New York's Provincial Congress in 1777 and as a member of Congress in 1778—insisting that a weak executive invited chaos. To him, the executive was the vital force of government and the most likely defender of the people's interests. But many in the chamber quailed at that idea. Memories of King George III were too fresh; even the word *executive* carried a whiff of tyranny.

On July 17, Morris rose to answer them. A president chosen by Congress, he argued, would be "the mere creature of the legislature." He would spend his term courting its favor, not protecting the people's liberty. If the people were empowered to pick their president, he said, they would reliably choose an accomplished person of character. If it were left to Congress, the selection would be based on pure politics. It was a radical notion for the time: a chief executive chosen by the people. Even delegates who admired Morris's reasoning hesitated at his conclusion. A popular election seemed impossible in a country so vast and unconnected. The roads were rough, the distances immense, and few citizens knew much of men beyond their own borders. The skeptics suspected that people would always favor candidates from their own state, or that residents of the most populous states would unite to ensure that one of their own would always win the presidency. Allowing the people to pick their president, Mason said, would be like asking a blind man to judge colors.

Morris saw further. He imagined the presidency as an office large enough to attract a man of Washington's character—and enduring enough to outlast him. The president, he said, "should be the guardian of the people—even of the lower classes—against legislative tyranny, against the great and the wealthy who in the course of things will necessarily compose the legislative body." He wanted an executive strong enough to check corruption and ambition—and one who could run for a second term, because the prospect of reelection would be an incentive for him to behave honorably. A one-term president, he warned, might loot the office for personal gain before returning to private life.

When the debate turned to impeachment, however, Morris hesitated. At first, he opposed it, believing that a president chosen by the people should answer to them alone. But as Madison and Mason described the dangers of corruption, incapacity, or treason, Morris's position evolved. "Corruption and some few other offenses" should be impeachable, he conceded, though he thought such cases "ought to be enumerated and defined." It was a moment of rare humility from a man known for his self-assurance, and it demonstrated his capacity to yield when the logic of liberty demanded it.

On July 26, the convention adjourned for ten days so that a Committee of Detail—which included Wilson, Rutledge, and Randolph—could draft the first version of the Constitution. The delegates, exhausted, gratefully spilled into the streets. For once, even Gouverneur Morris put down his pen.

That Monday, Washington's enslaved coachman hitched his horses to Morris's phaeton, and the two men drove into the countryside to fish for trout in the cool waters of Montgomery County, Pennsylvania. The next day, Washington rode on to Valley Forge, to visit the ruins of the encampment where he and Morris had cemented their friendship. There were plowed fields between the old earthworks, and the once muddy slopes were dry and dusty. A decade earlier, in that place of hunger and resolve, Washington had faced a crucible of scarcity and discipline—one that Morris had helped him overcome. On August 3, the two men joined Robert and Mary Morris for another outing. This time they went fishing for perch in the Delaware River near Trenton and spent the night with Gouverneur's sister Euphemia and her husband, Samuel Ogden. It was a temporary respite from the storm that awaited them.

When the delegates reconvened on August 6, they found copies of the first printed draft of the Constitution on their tables—seven pages in elegant type, wide margins set for notes. After the secretary read the draft aloud, the delegates adjourned for the rest of the day so each man could study the new text in peace. The next morning, as the broiling sun burned away the fog, they reconvened to pick it apart.

They moved briskly through the first three articles. Then Morris stopped them cold. The fourth article stated that citizens who met their state's voting requirements could vote in federal elections, too. In practice, that meant the franchise would vary wildly from state to state. In most states, free Black men who owned property could vote; in Georgia, South Carolina, and Virginia, they could not. Women were excluded everywhere but New Jersey. Morris thought the rule too loose—and too dangerous. He argued that the vote should be tied to property, not to citizenship alone. "Give the votes to people who have no property," he warned, "and they will sell them to the rich, who will be able to buy them."

In arguing for a popularly elected president, he had placed faith in the people's judgment. But when it came to the franchise, his faith faltered. "The time is not distant," he said, "when this country will abound with mechanics and manufacturers who will receive their bread from their employers. Will such men be the secure and faithful guardians of liberty?"

It was a paradox that defined him—the democrat who feared too much democracy. There had to be an equilibrium between freedom and order.

The delegates disagreed but did not condemn him. Property requirements, after all, were the norm across the states. Madison, for one, called landowners "the safest depositories of republican liberty." However, they ultimately decided to leave voting requirements up to the states. The last state to drop its property-owning requirement, North Carolina, ditched it in 1856. Pennsylvania and Rhode Island retained their tax-paying requirements into the twentieth century.

★

On July 11, Morris had referred to slavery as an injustice against human nature. Otherwise, he had couched his opposition to it in coldly political terms; he objected to the Three-Fifths Clause and opposed the easy admission of western states because he didn't want to give the South disproportionate political power. He had even suggested that white Pennsylvanians would object to being put on an equal plane with enslaved Black people.

That all changed on August 8.

FOURTEEN

"THE MOST SACRED LAWS OF HUMANITY"

The delegates had already debated slavery and approved the Three-Fifths Clause, but Rufus King of Massachusetts could not let the matter rest—and under the convention rules, he didn't have to. Because every matter could be reopened, he seized the moment when the delegates took up how to adjust representation for population growth.

The Three-Fifths Clause, King said, was "a most grating circumstance to his mind," and he warned that many Americans would feel the same. The new draft, he argued, not only preserved the slave trade but also forbade export taxes—two decisions that would increase Southern power while denying the North the means to counter it. Allowing the importation of slaves, King noted, would swell the South's representation in Congress and, by increasing the number of slaves, heighten the risk of an insurrection. "Either slaves should not be represented, or exports should be taxable," he concluded.

Roger Sherman of Connecticut shared King's distaste for slavery but urged restraint. The trade was "iniquitous," he admitted, yet the delegates had already agreed to the Three-Fifths Clause; reopening the issue now would jeopardize the fragile progress they had made. Madison tried to steer the conversation elsewhere, arguing that a rapidly growing nation might soon find its legislature unwieldy. Nathaniel Gorham, a forty-nine-year-old businessman from Massachusetts, brushed the problem aside. "Can it be supposed," he asked, "that this vast country, including the Western territory, will 150 years hence remain one nation?"

While others deflected, Gouverneur Morris could not. Watching from his seat, he braced a hand on the table and rose once more on his wooden leg. He proposed inserting the word *free* before *inhabitants*—in effect, scrapping the Three-Fifths Clause altogether. Slavery, he declared, was a "nefarious institution" and "the curse of Heaven on the states where it prevailed."

"Upon what principle," he demanded:

> is it that the slaves shall be computed in the representation? Are they men? Then make them citizens and let them vote. Are they property? Why then is no other property included? The houses in this city are worth more than all the wretched slaves which cover the rice swamps of South Carolina. The admission of slaves into the representation, when fairly explained, comes to this: that the inhabitant of Georgia and South Carolina who goes to the coast of Africa and, in defiance of the most sacred laws of humanity, tears away his fellow creatures from their dearest connections and damns them to the most cruel bondages, shall have more votes in a government instituted for protection of the rights of mankind, than the citizen of Pennsylvania or New Jersey who views with a laudable horror so nefarious a practice.

The delegates sat in stunned silence. By now they were used to hearing Morris speak—frequently, at great length, and in perfectly formed paragraphs. But they had not heard him speak with such passion—and he wasn't done.

He had often been accused of being an aristocrat, he thundered, but the protection of slavery was the most aristocratic feature of the Constitution. In exchange for "a sacrifice of every principle of right, of every impulse of humanity," the Northern states would be bound to help the South when enslaved people inevitably rose up. Meanwhile, the Southern states could continue to import slaves, increasing the likelihood of rebellion. In fact, this draft *encouraged* the South to import more slaves to enlarge its representation in Congress. He would "sooner submit himself to a tax for paying for all the Negroes in the United States," Morris declared, "than saddle posterity with such a constitution."

At a different time, under different circumstances, his eloquence might have moved the room. But only the youngest man present, Jonathan Dayton of New Jersey, met the moment. Dayton seconded the motion, he said, so that "his sentiments on the subject might appear, whatever might be the fate of the amendment." He surely knew that fate: The vote was ten to one against, with only New Jersey in support. It was the last serious threat to the Three-Fifths Clause, which stained the Constitution until its repeal by the Fourteenth Amendment in 1868.

★

The slave trade, however, was still unresolved. On August 21, Luther Martin, Maryland's formidable but disheveled attorney general, rose to speak. Martin was slovenly, vulgar, and "seemed to take pleasure in showing his utter disregard of good taste and refinement," noted one observer. A fellow delegate described him as so long-winded that "he never spoke without tiring the patience of all who heard him." Yet on this day, Martin went straight to the point: the delegates must either tax the slave trade or abolish it. The Three-Fifths Clause, he argued, was an incentive for the South to import more slaves, making insurrection more likely. The slave trade "weakened one part of the Union which the other parts were bound to protect," and it was "inconsistent with the principles of the Revolution and dishonorable to the American character."

The debate continued the next day. Sherman counseled neutrality—better, he said, not to judge whether the slave trade was right or wrong. If the Southern states insisted on importing slaves as the price of union, he believed, the others should accept it.

But abolitionists found an unlikely ally in George Mason of Virginia. At Gunston Hall, Mason's plantation, hundreds of enslaved people worked the fields and tended the house, yet he denounced the trade with unexpected fervor. "This infernal traffic originated in the avarice of British merchants," he said. "The Western people are already calling out for slaves for their new lands, and will fill that country with slaves if they can be got through South Carolina and Georgia." By "Western people," he meant settlers in the new territories stretching beyond the Appalachians—what would soon become Kentucky and Tennessee. Then his tone hardened. "Every master of slaves is born a petty tyrant," Mason said. "They bring the judgment of Heaven on a country. . . . Providence punishes national sins by national calamities." The federal government, he concluded, must have the "power to prevent the increase of slavery."

It was a stirring appeal, but Oliver Ellsworth of Connecticut could not resist exposing Mason's hypocrisy. Never having enslaved anyone himself, Ellsworth said tartly, he could not judge the institution's effects on one's character. But if the delegates were going to stand on morality, then why not abolish slavery itself? Virginians, he added, could afford morality on the question of the slave trade only because slavery had already become self-sustaining there. "They multiply so fast in Virginia and Maryland," he observed, "that it is cheaper to raise than import them, whilst in the sickly rice swamps [of the Deep South], foreign supplies are necessary." Ellsworth believed slavery would die out naturally. "Let us not intermeddle," he said. "As population increases, poor laborers will be so plenty as to render slaves useless. Slavery in time will not be a speck in our country." It was a prediction born of Northern optimism—and one that, within a generation, would prove tragically wrong.

The South Carolinians bristled. "If slavery be wrong, it is justified by the example of all the world," protested the younger Charles Pinckney. "In all ages, one half of mankind have been slaves." His cousin, Charles Cotesworth Pinckney, was even blunter: "South Carolina and Georgia cannot do without slaves. As to Virginia, she will gain by stopping the importations. Her slaves will rise in value, and she has more than she wants." John Rutledge warned that if the convention thought the Carolinas or Georgia would sign a constitution restricting the trade, "the expectation is vain."

If the South Carolinians were bluffing, no one called them on it. On August 25, the convention voted to forbid Congress from ending the slave trade before 1808. For the next twenty years, Africans could be trafficked into the United States—a compromise written into the nation's charter. In that span, some 170,000 human beings were brought to America in chains.

Morris, perhaps realizing he had already alienated the Deep South, held his tongue through this debate. Yet he didn't want there to be any doubt about what the delegates had done, and who had made them do it. The current draft stated that Congress would not prohibit "the migration or importation of such persons as the several states now existing shall think proper to admit." Morris proposed replacing that euphemism with the plain truth: "the importation of slaves into North Carolina, South Carolina, and Georgia." His motion failed. The delegates preferred their disguise.

Three days later, the convention approved one final proslavery measure: the Fugitive Slave Clause. Adapted from the Northwest Ordinance, the law that provided a path to statehood for the territories northwest of the Ohio River, the clause required that enslaved people who fled to free states be returned to their enslavers.

★

On September 8, the convention appointed a five-member Committee of Style and Arrangement—Morris, Madison, Hamilton, King, and

William Samuel Johnson of Connecticut—to refine the final draft. Johnson, a respected jurist with an even temper, would serve as chair.

More than his wit, Morris had wielded moral clarity, eloquence, and persistence in his fight against slavery. Though defeated, later generations recognized his integrity. Abraham Lincoln called him one of "the most noted antislavery men of those times," while Theodore Roosevelt praised his audacity in making the moral argument against slavery. Others who shared Morris's views lacked his nerve: Franklin and Hamilton sat silently during the debates over slavery, having advised their abolitionist friends that it would be pointless to push their views inside the East Room. "The position of the Southerners was ridiculous: he tore their arguments to shreds," Roosevelt wrote in his 1888 biography of Morris, "but he was powerless to alter the fact that they were doggedly determined to carry their point, while most of the Northern members cared comparatively little about it."

Morris scored more than a moral victory when it came to shaping other parts of the Constitution, especially the presidency. Largely because of him, the country would have a vigorous chief executive who could run for reelection, veto legislation, form a cabinet, make treaties, and appoint Supreme Court justices. Morris was also a stout defender of civil liberties—speaking out against bills of attainder, religious tests for public office, and the suspension of the writ of habeas corpus. Despite missing a month of the convention, he gave more speeches than any other delegate, offered the most motions (thirty-nine), and had the most adopted (twenty-two).

Now it was up to the Committee of Style and Arrangement to stitch the messy motions adopted by the convention into a harmonious whole. The members recognized that Morris was the best writer, so after creating an outline they handed him the quill. "The *finish* given to the style and arrangement of the Constitution fairly belongs to the pen of Mr. Morris," Madison later recalled. "A better choice could not have been made, as the performance of the task proved." Hamilton was so impressed by Morris's work that he invited Morris to join him and John Jay in writing *The Federalist Papers*. Morris declined, forcing Hamilton and Jay to go with their second choice: Madison.

In writing the final draft, Morris made dozens of refinements. He tightened language and elevated rhythm, but he also made subtle changes to wording and punctuation that altered the very meaning of the document, without the other delegates noticing what he had done. Most importantly, Morris used the power of his pen to make sure that if the Constitution did not abolish slavery, at least it would not bless it.

The draft handed to him did not mention the words *slave* or *slavery*—a reflection of the Framers' discomfort with it—but the Fugitive Slave Clause did infer that slavery was morally right. The original phrasing read: "If any person bound to service or labor in any of the United States shall escape into another state, he or she shall not be discharged from such service or labor in consequence of any regulations subsisting in the state to which they escape; but shall be delivered up to the person *justly* claiming their service or labor." Morris struck out "justly," so that the clause would instead read: "shall be delivered up on claim of the party to whom such service or labor may be due." As historian Sean Wilentz has written, that one deletion—removing the word *justly*—"removed the possible implication that there was justice in slavery."

By using a semicolon rather than a comma, Morris also tried to block the looming admission of new slave states Kentucky (formed out of Virginia) and Tennessee (formed out of North Carolina). The original draft read: "New States may be admitted by the Legislature into this Union; but no new State shall be hereafter formed or erected within the jurisdiction of any of the present States, without the consent of the Legislature of such State as well as of the general Legislature. Nor shall any State be formed by the junction of two or more States or parts thereof without the consent of the Legislatures of such States as well as of the Legislature of the United States." Morris tightened the language by combining the two sentences into one and deleting "without the consent of the Legislature of such State as well as of the general Legislature," in what had been the first sentence.

On their own, those changes wouldn't have altered the meaning of the provision—it still would have said that new states, whatever their origin, couldn't be admitted without the approval of Congress and the state legislatures involved. Morris changed the meaning, however, by using a *semicolon*, rather than a *comma*, after the phrase "no new State shall be formed or erected within the Jurisdiction of any other State." As a result, the stipulation that new states could be admitted to the Union with the permission of state legislators and Congress no longer applied to new states carved out of existing ones. Instead, such states could *never* be admitted to the Union, full stop. It was a quiet effort to restrain the creation of future slave states with nothing more than a change of punctuation.

As it turned out, despite Morris's best efforts, nobody raised constitutional objections when Kentucky was admitted in 1792, and North Carolina skirted the issue by ceding the land that became Tennessee to the United States, which governed it as a territory for seven years before admitting it as a state in 1796.

With slight changes to wording and punctuation, Morris also bolstered the executive and judiciary branches; laid the foundation for judicial review; strengthened protections for private property; and crafted a more expansive framework for impeachment.

Despite these victories, the Constitution protected liberty in principle but tolerated bondage in practice.

In the decades to come, this prompted many abolitionists to condemn the document. On July 4, 1854, William Lloyd Garrison burned a copy in front of a crowd in Framingham, Massachusetts, denouncing it as "a covenant with death and an agreement with hell." But others, including Frederick Douglass, leaned on the fact that it did not mention, let alone endorse, slavery. "In *that* instrument I hold there is neither warrant, license, nor sanction of the hateful thing; but interpreted, as it *ought* to be interpreted, the Constitution is a *glorious liberty document*," he proclaimed. For Douglass, the genius of the Constitution lay in its silences—its refusal to name slavery, to enshrine it in the nation's sacred text.

Morris's final and most enduring contribution was to transform the Preamble from a clunky compact of states into a declaration of nationhood and a soaring statement of purpose.

The original version read like the introduction to a contract: "We the People of the States of New-Hampshire, Massachusetts, Rhode-Island and Providence Plantations, Connecticut, New-York, New-Jersey, Pennsylvania, Delaware, Maryland, Virginia, North-Carolina, South-Carolina, and Georgia, do ordain, declare and establish the following Constitution for the government of Ourselves and our Posterity." In fifty-two words, Morris reframed the Constitution as a blueprint for a new nation. "We the People of the United States, in Order to form a more perfect Union, establish Justice, insure domestic Tranquility, provide for the common defense, promote the general Welfare, and secure the Blessings of Liberty to ourselves and our Posterity, do ordain and establish this Constitution for the United States of America."

The distinction was profound. No longer *We the People of the States*, but *We the People.*

Skeptics of a stronger central government noticed the difference. "Who authorized them to speak the language of, 'We, the people,' instead of 'We, the states'? Patrick Henry complained during Virginia's debate over ratification. "The people gave them no power to use their name."

To later generations, however, Morris's Preamble was an inspiration, a reminder that the country was on an endless quest to extend the blessings of liberty to *all* its inhabitants.

"It was 'We, the people,' not 'We, the white male citizens'; nor yet 'We, the male citizens,' but 'We, the whole people' who formed the Union," suffragist leader Susan B. Anthony said in 1872. During the depths of the Great Depression, Franklin D. Roosevelt urged Americans to "read and reread" the Preamble, which made it clear that the

Constitution should "be used as an instrument of progress, and not as a device for prevention of action." And in 1963, Martin Luther King Jr. called for "the resumption of that noble journey toward the goals reflected in the Preamble to the Constitution."

The convention approved Morris's draft with little debate and only slight revisions. As the delegates signed their names, Franklin took a last look at the carving of the sun on the back of Washington's chair. "I have often and often in the course of the session . . . looked at that behind the President without being able to tell whether it was rising or setting," he remarked to another delegate. "But now at length I have the happiness to know that it is a rising and not a setting sun."

FIFTEEN

TWO AMERICANS IN PARIS

With the Constitution signed, it was time for Morris to move on, both metaphorically and literally. Just months after the ink dried, he prepared to cross the Atlantic—the journey he had once imagined as a young man but set aside as he plunged into revolution and nation-building.

When Washington learned of Morris's travel plans, he asked him for a favor and granted him another. Washington wanted a gold watch from Paris—not a trifling ornament, he emphasized, but a large, flat watch "well executed in point of workmanship," just like the one Jefferson, the American minister to France, had procured for Madison. Washington, soon to be inaugurated as the country's first president, handed Morris twenty-five guineas and urged him to consult Jefferson when he arrived in the French capital. "Should the expense be greater (for I wish to have a good watch)," he added, "I will take care to reimburse it to you."

The favor Washington granted in return was infinitely more valuable: letters of introduction from him that would open doors across Europe. With those in hand, Morris boarded the *Henrietta* in Philadelphia on December 18, 1788, bound for France. Along with the letters and a long-deferred desire to taste the pleasures of Europe, Morris carried with him a variety of schemes to make money: He wanted to complete a tobacco deal for Robert Morris, find buyers for real estate in New York, and advance Robert's plan to purchase America's $34 million debt to France and resell it, at a profit, to Dutch investors. The letters from Washington, along with ones he had gotten from Franklin, would ease every negotiation.

The forty-day winter passage was brutal. When Morris couldn't sleep in his storm-tossed cabin, he wrote a three-thousand-word essay on America's finances. At last, on January 27, 1789, the battered *Henrietta* reached Le Havre. Belatedly, Morris was beginning the European adventure he had long imagined, one that would mix commerce with diplomacy and test his republican convictions in another nation on the brink of revolution. His efforts to moderate that revolution would earn him enmity and mistrust—and hand ammunition to rivals whose criticisms did lasting damage to his historical standing.

★

Morris arrived to find France in crisis. Hail had flattened wheat, vegetable, and fruit crops the previous summer; drought followed, then the hardest winter in living memory. Many rivers froze, mills stopped turning, and boats could not deliver flour. Warmer weather, when it finally came, just created more affliction; once the Loire River thawed in mid-January, the floodwaters inundated fields and pastures and surged into city streets.

Bread prices soared—from eight sous to fifteen for a four-pound loaf—a cost that nearly consumed laborers' daily wages. In the countryside, small farmers lost their land, defeated by ruined crops, high taxes, and crushing debt along with the high price of food and firewood. People begged for bread and milk at the churches or streamed into larger towns and cities, where conditions were just as dire. In Paris alone more than a hundred thousand people—a fifth of the population—lived on public relief. Families warmed themselves by street fires. The rumors that nobles were hoarding grain were more plentiful than bread itself.

Meanwhile, France's monarchy staggered under immense debts, much of it incurred helping the Americans win their own liberty. The American Revolution also contributed to the social unrest by giving the French people an example: a republic of laws, not kings. Its existence showed the French that they, too, could be citizens with equal rights, and not just subjects with obligations imposed on them by an absolute monarch.

Ten days after his arrival, Morris called on Jefferson at the elegant Hôtel de Langeac, the envoy's two-story town house on the Champs-Élysées. It boasted two dozen rooms, a walled garden where Jefferson grew American corn and grapes, and even an indoor toilet—a Parisian rarity. Almost forty-five, Jefferson was nearly a decade Morris's senior, his red hair fading to sand. He was also a widower, still marked by the grief of losing his wife Martha in the fall of 1782. For three weeks after her death, he had refused to leave his bedroom, sleeping on the floor. He destroyed all Martha's letters, and when he finally mustered the will to leave his house at Monticello, the Founding Father known for his incredible array of interests and talents spent countless hours on his horse, riding randomly around the countryside. "The only circumstance which could have brought me to Europe," he would later say, was her death.

Jefferson had been living in Paris with his daughter Martha (known as Patsy) since August 1784, later joined by his younger daughter Maria (Polly) in July 1787. The Jeffersons were attended by the enslaved Hemings siblings, James and fifteen-year-old Sally. Under French law, both could have claimed their freedom; Jefferson did not tell them so. Sally would become his concubine and later bear at least six of his children. Morris, a close observer of character, soon realized that Jefferson's devotion to liberty had its limits.

The evening of Morris's visit, Jefferson hosted a small dinner. The table was set in Parisian style, with individual side tables, so servants need not intrude. Jefferson spoke easily of politics, architecture, and wine. Morris admired the simplicity of his dark suit—republican in taste, if not price—but found his host solemn. Quick with a jest, Morris tried several risqué stories; Jefferson blushed crimson. Their temperaments diverged. Jefferson judged individuals sharply but believed mankind perfectible. Morris trusted individuals but feared the crowd. That difference would define—and strain—their friendship in the years to come.

The two spent many hours together exploring the city, by carriage and on foot, undeterred by Morris's wooden leg. Jefferson, who was captivated by architecture, enjoyed lecturing Morris on the buildings and bridges—perhaps not realizing that the younger man did not share his enthusiasm. One day, Jefferson pointed to the fifteen-year-old Pont de Neuilly spanning the river Seine and rhapsodized about its graceful stone arches, suggesting that it might be the most beautiful bridge in the world. Morris had crossed it four times without noticing it.

Beyond Jefferson's town house, Paris teemed. The city's streets, which had no sidewalks, were dirtier and more crowded than those in London, with mud a foot deep. Young men of fashion raced around the city in one-horse cabriolets, spattering so much mud on pedestrians that people who could not afford to travel by coach had to wear dark clothing, and black stockings, to hide the filth. And yet, even an English visitor had to admit that between the coffeehouses on the boulevards, the music and the noise and "*filles* without end," Paris had everything "but scavengers and lamps."

The Palais-Royal, a section of the city owned by the liberal Duc d'Orléans, had become a sovereign enclave where the police did not patrol. Its arcades overflowed with wigmakers, lace sellers, lemonade hawkers, gamblers, poets, prostitutes, and pamphleteers. A guitar-playing abbé sang bawdy songs while speakers denounced the Crown to roars of approval. Writers paid by the Duc distributed subversive newspapers by torchlight. Visitors marveled that the authorities tolerated "such nests and hotbeds of sedition and revolt."

Morris, who had known New York taverns and Philadelphia clubs, had never seen anything like it. Soldiers strutted beside clerks, nobles minced through mud in high-heeled shoes and powdered wigs, and women—from courtesans to duchesses—spoke freely of politics, scandal, and philosophy. "The city," he wrote, "is a sort of whirlwind which turns a man round so fast that he can see nothing." Yet he looked all the same. He bought a notebook, bound in apple-green vellum, and began recording everything: the elegance of salons, the filth of alleys, the restless energy of a people who wanted change but didn't know what form it should take.

Invitations poured in. To the French elite, Morris was a curiosity: the American who had helped frame the Constitution, a financial mind of the first order, and a man endorsed by Washington and Franklin—the two Americans France admired most. His wit, charisma, and striking appearance made him welcome everywhere; his wooden leg only heightened the effect. But his rudimentary French hindered him. "Not being perfectly master of the language, most of the jests escape me," he complained after one dinner with a circle of poets. "I take my leave immediately after the coffee."

Women in Paris also startled him. Unlike in American society, where women were discouraged from engaging in political talk, Parisian women participated vigorously in political debates. Morris found their insight sharp—far sharper than Jefferson did. Jefferson thought Frenchwomen's access to public officials was a main source of the country's political corruption. "The manners of the nation allow them to visit, alone, all persons in office, to solicit the affairs of the husband, family, or friends," Jefferson huffed in a 1788 letter to Washington. Jefferson wrote in a similar vein to his friend Angelica Church. "The tender breasts of ladies were not formed for political convulsion," he told her, "and the French ladies miscalculate much their own happiness when they wander from the true field of their influence into that of politics."

Morris disagreed. He admired the political acumen of Madame de Staël ("a woman of wonderful wit"), the Comtesse de Ségur ("very sensible and indeed a lovely woman"), and the Duchesse d'Orléans, who confided in him about her husband's frequent indiscretions—and liked to remove her glove and touch her face so onlookers could admire "perhaps the handsomest arm in France." But one woman soon eclipsed all others.

SIXTEEN

FRANCE IN CRISIS

Morris socialized with an upper-class crowd, but he encountered Paris's poor every time he stepped into the street. At first, he had scant sympathy for the beggars who accosted him for bread, believing that what they really wanted was wine, or stronger stuff. But Morris's attitude softened. Visiting the Hôtel des Invalides, the home for elderly and disabled soldiers, he was deeply depressed by the sight of "mutilated" veterans on their knees in the chapel, men with "no hope this side of the grave." As Morris shambled among the old soldiers, his companion heard several of the veterans, who assumed their visitor's missing leg was a war injury, remark that it was a pity that "so fine a man" as Morris should have lost his leg in battle. The companion did not realize that Gouverneur had been surreptitiously handing them coins along the way.

France's economic agony soon ignited political revolt. On April 26, 1789, a rumor that wallpaper manufacturer Jean-Baptiste Réveillon had called for wage cuts sparked mass fury. In truth, Réveillon had urged lower bread prices, not lower pay, but the nuance was lost in the hungry streets. Thousands of workers—brewers, tanners, stevedores—stormed his mansion and gutted his factory. When troops arrived and were pelted with stones and tiles, they opened fire. Several hundred were killed.

Witnessing the chaos, Morris felt renewed gratitude for America. "Oh, my country! How infinitely preferable that equal partition of fortune's gifts which you enjoy!" he wrote. "Where none are vassals, none are lords, but all are men." He respected the French people's desire for change but doubted they were ready for republican government. In a letter to Washington he wrote on the day the Réveillon riots began, he lamented that the nobles clung to "the dear privileges of centuries long elapsed," while the common people had "no religion but their priests, no law but their superiors, no moral but their interest." Reform, he believed, was possible; revolution was perilous.

France's political future came sharply into focus when the Estates General convened on May 5, 1789—the first such gathering in 175 years. Jacques Necker, the Swiss banker serving as Louis XVI's finance minister, had convinced the king to convoke the Estates General to address the country's fiscal woes, after the nobles had resisted his unilateral efforts to raise taxes. Many observers, including Jefferson, thought the deputies would adopt a declaration of rights and a written constitution that would give Frenchmen at least some of the rights that Americans enjoyed. Before the year was out, Jefferson predicted, France would "have as full a portion of liberty dealt out to them as the nation can bear at present, considering how uninformed the mass of their people is."

The ceremonial opening of the Estates General, a procession to the church of Saint-Louis in Versailles, dazzled Morris and other spectators: Swiss Guards in embroidered coats, royal falconers with hooded birds, deputies in robes of scarlet, white, gold, or plain black, depending on their order. Yet Morris was most struck by what he did not see: enthusiasm for the queen. Louis XVI was cheered repeatedly, but Vienna-born Marie Antoinette—blamed for extravagance, foreign influence, and rumored indifference to the people's suffering—received only cold silence. She gazed at the crowd with contempt, but Morris, more chivalrous than many in the crowd, pitied her. "It seems unmanly," he wrote, "to break a woman with unkindness."

The next day, Morris attended the first meeting of the assembly at the Salles des Menus-Plaisirs, its walls decorated with vibrant tapestries from the famous Gobelins factory in Paris. Louis XVI, wearing a round beaver-fur hat ornamented with white plumes and a large diamond, read a short speech. "Long live the king!" the crowd shouted. The delegates' enthusiasm for their sovereign moved Morris to tears. Marie Antoinette was quietly weeping, too—but not at this expression of love for her husband. Like the day before, there was no cheering for her. When, to Morris's great relief, one kind soul faintly cried, "Long live the queen!" Marie Antoinette made a low curtsy before following her husband out of the hall.

By the middle of June, the rifts in the Estates General were evident. The Third Estate—the 621 representatives of the common people, more than twenty-five million strong—insisted that all deputies vote as individuals, not as estates. The 593 clergymen and nobles of the First and Second Estates—representing a mere half million people—resisted, fearing loss of their privileges. When compromise failed, the Third Estate, emboldened by defecting parish priests, declared itself the National Assembly on June 17. Then, in a direct challenge to royal authority, the new body declared that existing taxes were illegal because the people had not consented to them, an echo of the argument made by the American colonists. Three days later, the king locked their hall, prompting the deputies to gather in a nearby indoor tennis court, where they swore not to disband until they drafted a constitution—the famous Tennis Court Oath.

Louis XVI, grieving the death of his seven-year-old son and pulled between Necker's pleas for constitutional compromise and Marie Antoinette's insistence on firmness, hesitated for days. At last, on June 23, he convened a *séance royale* to reassert control. He offered a few concessions—that new taxes and loans would require the deputies' consent, that reforms to arbitrary royal orders and press restrictions might be considered—but insisted that the estates, not the National Assembly, remained the legal foundation of government. Their self-declared National Assembly, he proclaimed, was "illegal and unconstitutional." He ordered them to disperse.

After the king's departure, the nobles and clergy rose and filed out of the hall. The Third Estate remained seated. Carpenters began dismantling the royal dais, and still they sat.

When the master of ceremonies repeated the king's command, Honoré Gabriel Riqueti, comte de Mirabeau—enormous of head, scarred by smallpox, and possessing the most commanding voice in France—rose. "Go tell those who have sent you," he roared, "that we are here by the will of the people and that we will not be dispersed except at the point of bayonets." The chastened official withdrew.

That evening, Morris dined in Versailles beside the young Marquis de Lafayette—the same Lafayette who had crossed the Atlantic as a volunteer to fight for American independence and now served as a noble deputy in France's Second Estate. Lafayette defended the Assembly's defiance. Morris, who had voiced his apprehensions openly in salons and private letters, was quoted everywhere as a skeptical foreign sage. "You are continually quoted against the good party," Lafayette complained. Morris warned that the French were rushing headlong toward bloodshed, trying to impose a system "inconsistent with the materials of which it is composed." Lafayette, flush with revolutionary zeal, declared that if violence came, he would die with his party. Morris replied dryly that it would be better to bring them to their senses and live with them.

★

While France wrestled with the shape of its future, Morris was undergoing a quieter, more intimate upheaval of his own. In the salons and apartments of Paris—where wit was valued as highly as noble blood—he found himself drawn into the orbit of Adélaïde Filleul, comtesse de Flahaut.

Adèle was nearly ten years his junior, raised in the half-shadowed world of Versailles intrigue. Her father had been a royal secretary; her mother, a mistress of Louis XV. Orphaned at six years old, Adèle grew up in a convent under the tutelage of an English nun and spoke English fluently. At eighteen she married the aging keeper of the king's gardens, thirty-five years her senior. Her true partner, however, was Charles-Maurice de Talleyrand-Périgord, the ambitious and irreligious bishop of Autun—one of the most influential, and famously slippery, statesmen of his time—with whom she had a long-running affair and a young son. Adèle and her elderly husband lived in an apartment in the Louvre, the former fortress and royal palace, but they slept separately.

The doe-eyed, chestnut-haired Adèle was shapely, sharp-witted, and self-reliant. She entertained lovers whenever she pleased and was secretly writing a novel (one that featured a free-willed protagonist named Adèle). With Talleyrand's help, she established a salon that had become one of Paris's liveliest: mathematicians, courtiers, scientists, writers, and deputies passed through her rooms, drawn by her intelligence, her warmth, and her unorthodox independence. Morris quickly recognized that she was not a "sworn enemy to intrigue," as he put it—a sly assessment that she was both politically astute and romantically willing.

From their first meeting at Versailles on March 21, 1789, he was captivated. Eight days later, Morris ran into Adèle in the Tuileries, and the two strolled together. Two days after that, he called on her at the Louvre for the first time. Throughout the spring, Gouverneur didn't go more than a few days without seeing Adèle, or trying to. Seeing the attraction, their mutual friend Madame de Corny arranged to put them together at a dinner party. Morris recorded every moment in his diary: the wit in her eyes, the fluency of her English, the quick assessment she made of any man who approached her.

But the path was not smooth. On one planned visit to view the Louvre's sculptures and paintings with Adèle, her husband unexpectedly accompanied them, leaving Morris to record with irritation that "a scene which imagination painted very well turns out good for nothing." Worse still was Talleyrand, whom Morris encountered twice in her apartment—once tolerably, once intolerably, as the club-footed bishop lectured pompously about noble privilege until Morris, half out of boredom and half out of rivalry, "very uncivilly fell asleep."

Adèle's interest sharpened under this competition. One afternoon she delicately asked Morris about his past "affairs of gallantry." Caught off guard, he insisted the stories were unworthy of credit and that he always retained "perfect respect" for any woman who had once been dear to him. She probed further: What, precisely, did he mean by "respect"? His answer—that affection never erased esteem—pleased him immensely. "This idea will dwell on her mind," he wrote that night, congratulating himself.

Through riots, breadlines, and the first tremors of revolution, Morris's pursuit of Adèle became a stabilizing thread, a human connection in a society poised on the edge of upheaval.

SEVENTEEN

"GRACIOUS GOD, WHAT A PEOPLE!"

By July 1789, Paris was a city ready to detonate. Months of ruined harvests had left bread scarce and tempers raw. To a great degree, the people's fragile hope rested on one man: Jacques Necker, the finance minister. Necker had called for fiscal transparency, published the kingdom's accounts, and promised reform—rare honesty in a court of excess. To common Parisians he seemed the one minister who spoke their language, a figure of near-saintly virtue. His portrait hung in cafés and shop windows; the Palais-Royal, that city within a city where pamphleteers and speakers had already made sedition fashionable, buzzed daily with talk of him. When a woman was caught spitting on his likeness there, the crowd forced her to her knees and spanked her.

So when word spread on July 12 that the king had dismissed Necker, Paris erupted. Crowds surged from the Palais-Royal into the boulevards, crying *"Aux armes!"* Shops slammed shut, bells clanged from every steeple, and foreign mercenaries—German dragoons and Swiss Guards—marched into the streets.

That afternoon, Morris, on his way to call on Jefferson, nearly collided with a detachment of German cavalry. The Germans, sabers drawn, were facing off against a mob that hurled stones and curses. Morris's carriage veered aside; he watched, appalled, as the line of soldiers fell back before a tide of citizens armed with paving stones and fury. On his way home, he saw rioters smashing the windows of gunsmiths' shops, looting muskets and powder.

During the night of the thirteenth, rumors rippled through the cafés that troops from Sèvres and Saint-Denis—less than ten miles away—were marching to crush the uprising. The next morning, throngs of Parisians headed toward a hulking medieval fortress that loomed over the eastern quarter of the city.

Built in the fourteenth century to defend the capital from English attack, the Bastille had long since become a prison for the king's enemies—seditious writers, religious renegades, and others unlucky enough to be condemned by a *lettre de cachet*, a royal letter, signed by the king, ordering imprisonment without trial. Its thick walls symbolized everything the French people detested about absolute monarchy. In truth, the Bastille's cells now held only seven prisoners: four forgers, two madmen, and one aging nobleman. Even the notorious Marquis de Sade, who had furnished his cell with tapestries, books, and velvet cushions, was gone—moved just days before for shouting obscenities through a megaphone fashioned from his chamber pot. But the Bastille's name had become shorthand for tyranny, and the people wanted its gunpowder, its arms, and its fall.

By late morning nearly a thousand Parisians had gathered before its outer gate. Inside, the governor, Bernard-René de Launay—born within those very walls and heir to his father's post—refused to surrender without orders from Versailles. Negotiations dragged on in the heat until the crowd, weary of talk, forced the issue. A group climbed onto the roof of a perfume shop beside the gate, hacked through the drawbridge chains, and dropped it with a crash. The fighting commenced.

Gunfire thundered; smoke and stone filled the air. For nearly four hours the Bastille was a battlefield—the defenders Swiss Guards and a handful of elderly and disabled French soldiers, versus the attackers, a motley army of clerks, craftsmen, and ex-soldiers. At last, outnumbered and lacking enough food for a prolonged siege, de Launay raised a white handkerchief from a tower window.

The gates swung open. The mob flooded in, seized the gunpowder, and freed the bewildered prisoners. They dragged de Launay into the street, beating him as they went, until they reached the Hôtel de Ville, the city hall. There, amid jeers and argument, someone proposed tying him to a horse's tail and dragging him over the cobblestones. Desperate, de Launay kicked a pastry cook named Desnot in the groin and cried, "Let me die!" The crowd obliged. They stabbed him, shot him, and when he fell, Desnot sawed off his head with a pocketknife. Moments later the city's provost, Jacques de Flesselles, who was accused of deceiving citizens about where arms were hidden, was shot on the steps of the Hôtel de Ville. The two men's heads, impaled on pikes, bobbed through the streets as the mob marched past cafés and storefronts. The Bastille had fallen. Paris was drunk on victory—and blood.

Morris, nursing a fever and a headache, was in a banker's office when a messenger rushed in to deliver the news. Soon word had reached every salon and countinghouse: the fortress was taken, the governor slain. "Yesterday it was the fashion at Versailles not to believe that there were any disturbances at Paris," Morris wrote wryly in his journal. "I presume that this day's transactions will induce a conviction that all is not perfectly quiet."

He saw Adèle every day the week after the fortress fell. When he had arrived in France, he was certain that "an engagement in which the heart can take any share [was] out of the question." But when the two of them were alone in her apartment on July 20, he handed her some verses and confessed that he was in love with her. Trying to maintain his "infinite coolness and seriousness," he told her he could no longer be just friends. For now, he was "perfectly my own master," but he couldn't hold out much longer. "I know it to be wrong, but cannot help it." Adèle was taken aback by this "very strange conversation" and wouldn't commit to an affair with the dashing American, though Gouverneur was confident she would come around. "I am much mistaken if it does not make an impression much greater on reflection than at the first moment."

The next day, having procured a special pass from Lafayette, Gouverneur and Adèle toured the Bastille with the architect tasked with demolishing the fortress. The stench in the former prison was overpowering.

★

Paris did not rest after the fall of the Bastille. The king hesitated, his court in disbelief, as vengeance reigned in the streets. Lafayette, newly appointed commander of the National Guard, a Parisian militia formed to guard the National Assembly, rode out each morning to restore calm. "The people, in their enthusiastic delirium, can only be moderated by me," he boasted to his mistress, claiming to have saved the lives of six people who were about to be lynched. But Lafayette's powers of persuasion were ebbing. On July 22, the people's fury found new prey. Joseph-François Foullon de Doué, Necker's replacement, supposedly snickered that "the people will be happy if we give them hay to eat" when informed that Parisians were starving. Foullon's son-in-law, Louis Bénigne François Bertier de Sauvigny, the leader of the royal authorities in the city, was accused of using his office to make a fortune in grain speculation. Both had fled the capital when the fighting began. They were caught, dragged back to Paris, and brought before a wrathful crowd outside the Hôtel de Ville. Lafayette was summoned to calm the mob. "You want to kill this man without judgment!" he cried. "That is an injustice which dishonors you and tarnishes all my efforts for liberty." But the crowd was beyond persuasion. A rope thrown over a lamppost to hang the seventy-four-year-old Foullon snapped under his weight. After several unsuccessful attempts, the mob rushed forward with knives and bayonets, stabbing him until he collapsed.

They severed his head, stuck it on a pike, and stuffed his mouth with hay, grass, and manure. When they spotted the cart that was carrying Bertier de Sauvigny to prison, they waggled the severed head of his father-in-law in his face. "Kiss papa!" they jeered before they snatched him from the wagon, killed him, and mounted his head on a pike, too.

That evening, Morris dined at a *table d'hôte*—a shared public table—near the Palais-Royal. When the meal ended, he stepped outside to wait for his carriage. Down the arcade came the procession: men spattered with blood, carrying Foullon's head aloft and dragging his naked body behind them. "This mutilated form of an old man," Morris later wrote, "was shown to Bertier, and afterwards he also is put to death and cut to pieces, the populace carrying about the mangled fragments with a savage joy. Gracious God, what a people!"

He did not sleep that night. At dawn he began a long letter to Mary Morris, Robert's wife, written in shock and disbelief. "I was never until now fully apprised of the mildness of American character," he wrote. "We know not what it is to slay the defenseless victim who is in our power. We cannot parade the heads of our fellow citizens and drag the mangled carcasses through the streets." He ended with a shudder of self-knowledge. "That these people were tyrannical I shall agree, though I do not know it. But to be executed without trial, without being heard, and then with such a horrid spectacle!"

It was a moment of moral clarity—though a partial one. Morris was appalled by the mob's barbarity yet never paused to consider how violence and dispossession had already marked the young republic he had helped build. Even a man of conscience, who had done his utmost to banish slavery from his native land, could be selective in his sympathies.

Over the next days he met repeatedly with Jefferson, who seemed unfazed by the bloodshed. "The cutting off heads is become so much à la mode," Jefferson joked in a letter, "that one is apt to feel of a morning whether their own is on their shoulders." Morris, still haunted by the image of the pikes, would have found the levity chilling.

A day after the bloody episode in the Palais-Royal, Gouverneur was back at the Louvre to continue his pursuit of Adèle. She remained coy, claiming to have a "marriage of the heart" with one of her lovers—presumably Talleyrand—that she could not betray. But they were drawing closer.

On July 27, Gouverneur awoke with a hangover from drinking "rather too much Bordeaux" the night before. At five in the evening, he had a date with Adèle at her home in the Louvre. When he arrived, she was sitting at her vanity, wearing only a shift. Her husband arrived and "with perfect decency," she finished getting dressed in front of the two men. Finally, Flahaut departed, leaving Gouverneur and Adèle alone. Rain pattering against the window, they sat down to work on a translation. It was a raw evening, and in the gloom of the apartment they drew closer—too close to resist each other any longer. For the first time, they made love.

Just as their affair was starting, Morris had to pause it to travel to London for six weeks to conduct business for Robert Morris. Saying goodbye to Adèle was harder than he had anticipated, but he congratulated himself on managing a "perfectly platonic" farewell.

Two days later, Morris wrote a letter to Washington from Dieppe as he waited to cross the English Channel. His old friend was now president, and Morris wanted to give him an assessment of the situation in France. He described Louis XVI as "a well-meaning man but extremely weak," and dismissed the leaders of the National Assembly as inexperienced and foolhardy. Morris's overall conclusion was that France was headed for disaster. "They have all that romantic spirit, and all those romantic ideas of government which, happily for America, we were cured of before it was too late."

Morris's six-week sojourn in England was a whirlwind of business meetings, social engagements, and sightseeing. He received at least one letter from Adèle while he was away, but their separation cooled his ardor. Her husband was elderly and wouldn't be around forever, but when a London hostess asked Morris whether he would ever marry, he said it wasn't likely.

On September 10, Morris set sail for France in a smuggler's cutter, the cheapest ride he could find. When darkness fell, he laid out a blanket on the floor of his cabin and tried to sleep, but the rats wouldn't leave him alone. He was back on deck at midnight when the cutter sailed past the moonlight-painted cliffs of Calais, and by two in the morning he was tucked into his boardinghouse bed, grateful to be between clean sheets.

Morris finally reached the gates of Paris at seven in the evening on September 13. When he arrived home, the first thing he did was take a bath; the next thing he did was send a message to Adèle. When he learned she was out of town, he sought solace in seven bottles of Hungarian wine he shared with two Frenchmen and a Polish colonel. About a week later, he finally heard from his absent lover, who had rushed back to Paris as quickly as she could after receiving Gouverneur's note, braving "a feeble health, a wretched carriage, a bad road, and worse weather."

Finally reunited, the couple met at the Louvre almost every day—and made love nearly every time they met. Gouverneur recorded each of their encounters, seemingly challenging himself to come up with a fresh euphemism every time. In his diary entries the lovers "celebrate the Cyprian mystery," "satisfy the sentiment," and "perform the part of the first pair."

Two weeks after his return to Paris, Gouverneur and Adèle discussed candidates for various government posts, an exchange that demonstrated how close the American was to the seat of power. The lovers mused that if the king made Talleyrand minister of finance, the two of them could help steer the ship of state. "Finally, my friend, you and I will govern France," Adèle said. That would be "an odd combination," Gouverneur thought, "but the kingdom is actually in much worse hands."

★

By the fall of 1789, France had changed beyond recognition. The king had been forced to recognize the National Assembly, the body formed when the deputies of the Third Estate—and many from the clergy and nobility—declared themselves the sole representatives of the French people. Lafayette's National Guard was outfitted in blue coats and tricolor cockades—the red and blue of Paris combined with the king's white, symbolizing the unity of the Crown and the people. But by early October, any remaining unity was fast dissolving. Bread was still scarce, and the poor were starving. Women, who bore the daily burden of feeding their families, felt the deprivation most acutely. On October 4—less than three months after the fall of the Bastille—a baker ran out of bread and was strung up by a mob.

At dawn the next day, the women who went to the market of Les Halles discovered that once again the bread stalls were empty. By eight in the morning, thousands of *poissardes*—fishwives and market women—had gathered in front of the Hôtel de Ville, demanding bread. Hearing nothing from city officials to satisfy them, they decided to appeal directly to the king. Shouting, singing, and brandishing pikes and muskets, they began marching toward Versailles through the cold autumn rain.

When Lafayette heard that his troops were preparing to follow the women, he rushed to the Hôtel de Ville to stop them. His guardsmen adored their commander but trusted neither him nor the king. If he refused to lead them, they threatened to hang him from the nearest lamppost. Lafayette saw no choice. He mounted his emblematic white horse and led them onward. "He has marched by compulsion," Morris recorded that night, "guarded by his own troops who suspect and threaten him."

It took six hours for the bedraggled, rain-soaked *poissardes* to reach Versailles. Officials greeted the women with speeches and wine; Louis XVI, summoned back from one of his hunting trips, agreed to meet with their leaders. The king's humanity briefly calmed them. When Pierrette Chabry, a seventeen-year-old flower girl chosen to speak for the marchers, fainted with nerves, Louis offered her smelling salts and comforted her—a small gesture that momentarily softened their fury.

He ordered the royal bakeries to work through the night to produce bread for the people, and directed that grain stalled outside Paris be brought into the city immediately.

The National Guard—at least fifteen thousand men—reached Versailles shortly before midnight, but unlike the women who had set out that morning, they arrived not in a rage but in exhaustion. Hours of slogging through rain and mud, combined with Lafayette's steadying hand, had cooled their earlier passions. Their purpose was firmer, more disciplined: to guarantee the king delivered the bread he had promised and, if necessary, escort him to Paris. To signal peaceful intent, Lafayette dismounted and entered the palace grounds alone. Ushered into the king's apartments, the mud-spattered commander assured Louis that he had come to protect him, not unseat him.

"I have come to die at the feet of Your Majesty," Lafayette declared. He urged the king to accept the protection of the National Guard, promise to feed Paris, and consent to live in the city. Louis agreed to the first two conditions and pledged to discuss the third request with Marie Antoinette. Confident that he'd ended the crisis, Lafayette delivered the good news to the National Assembly and his troops and retired to his grandfather's house, which was nearby, for some well-deserved rest.

Before dawn, believing the worst had passed, the palace guards relaxed their vigilance. Just after sunrise, some women discovered that a side gate to the courtyard was unlocked, and thousands of armed protesters surged into the courtyard. The guards, under orders not to fire, were overrun. Two were killed outside Marie Antoinette's apartments. The queen, barefoot and clutching her slippers, fled through a secret passageway to her husband's room, crying, "My friends, my friends, save me and my children!" The king's door was locked—he had gone to look for their children. Frantically, the queen pounded on it as the mob rampaged through the Hall of Mirrors, howling for her head. After about ten minutes, Louis returned, and the royal family was reunited. When Lafayette burst in minutes later, he found the royal family huddled together, expecting death.

The National Guard evicted the mob from the palace, but Lafayette told the royal couple he could not protect them if they remained at Versailles; they had to relocate to Paris. Outside, the mob clamored for the king to appear. "The king to Paris! The king to the balcony!" they shouted. Louis stepped forward and announced that he would return to the city, moved by "the love of my good and faithful subjects." The courtyard erupted in cheers. But then came the cry: "The queen! The queen to the balcony!"

Marie Antoinette hesitated. The foreign-born queen, cursed in the streets of Paris as "the Austrian whore," was suspected of consorting with France's enemies. Many blamed the national deficit on her lavish spending and accused her of being sexually promiscuous. "I know the fate that awaits me," she told Lafayette. "I am ready to die at the feet of my king in the arms of my children." Lafayette extended his arm. "Come with me," he said. Marie Antoinette was incredulous. "What? Alone on the balcony?" "Yes, madame. Let us go." He led her out onto the balcony as curses rose from below. Then, in a gesture he later claimed was spontaneous, he bowed deeply and kissed her hand. The effect was electric. *"Vive la reine!"* the crowd roared, joined by cries of *"Vive Lafayette!"*

Three hours later, as many as sixty thousand people—market women, guardsmen, and members of the Assembly—set out for Paris, some in carriages, others trudging beside wagons of flour from the royal stores. Lafayette rode beside the royal carriage; on two of the pikes above the crowd bobbed the severed heads of the queen's guards.

The royal family never returned to Versailles.

The king and queen were now captives in the Tuileries, their Paris palace, the Assembly governing in their name but subject to the will of France's new rulers: the people.

★

Adèle was shaken by the events of October 5 and 6. The mobs that had seized the king and queen could just as easily turn on nobles like her.

On October 5, she confessed to Gouverneur that she no longer trusted Talleyrand. Brilliant but mercurial, he had a gift for surviving upheaval by shedding attachments as easily as ideals. With the revolution gathering force, she feared he would soon discard her too, along with anyone who might threaten his rise. What she craved now was not safety in politics but constancy in love, and she turned to the American whose calm seemed to steady every storm.

What should I do? she asked.

Whatever you think best, he replied nonchalantly.

The composure that had charmed her in easier times now cut like indifference. Wounded, Adèle pressed harder, promising to give up Talleyrand and be his alone. The next day, October 6, she went further still—proposing marriage, though she already had a husband. When Gouverneur demurred, she faltered. Did he think her despicable for taking Talleyrand as a lover?

No, he told her gently—he did not. Her mood brightened, then clouded again. She wanted a promise, a token to prove that his affection was not a passing amusement. "With all the arts of [a] wily woman," he wrote later, "working to her purpose."

He tried to reason with her. It was foolish to speak of marriage when she was somebody else's wife, when France was on fire. There would be "time enough to talk of that matter when we are both free." But Adèle began to cry. Had he courted her merely for pleasure—for "a vacant hour," as she put it? "I am not wicked enough," she whispered, "to enjoy pleasures which violate the principles of honor."

He took her in his arms. The quarrel dissolved in the oldest reconciliation known to lovers.

Afterward, she asked again: Would he marry her if the world allowed it? Would he buy her a plain gold ring as "a token of our engagement"? He promised he would, though he could not wear one himself—at present, that privilege belonged to Talleyrand.

I will be yours, she whispered. Wherever you go.

"Will you go to England next Monday?" he teased, reminding

her—lightly, almost daringly—that he was about to cross the Channel again on business for Robert Morris.

"I do not think you capable of ruining me," she said. "But if you command, I obey. I am yours."

Two days later, he bought her a ring.

EIGHTEEN

A MISSION FOR THE PRESIDENT

At the end of 1789, Gouverneur Morris stood between two revolutions—one raging in the streets of Paris, the other still defining itself across the Atlantic. In France, monarchy was giving way to chaos; in America, a republic struggled to prove that liberty could coexist with order. He watched both with the same instruments: his wit, his reason, and a heart too susceptible to charm.

Morris knew he was clever. He had raced through King's College, revamped the Continental Army, put the nation on solid financial footing, and helped shape the Constitution. Yet beside Adèle de Flahaut, he sometimes felt outmatched. On a visit to the Louvre in early October, she showed him a letter she had written to Talleyrand, advising the bishop-turned-statesman on how to navigate the volatile National Assembly. The letter astonished him. It revealed, he marveled, "a deep knowledge of human character . . . enforced by the tenderness of female friendship." Morris, who prided himself on intellect, had more than met his match. "I thought well of myself," he confessed, "but I submit frankly to a superiority which I feel."

Their relationship was one of the soul and one of the mind. He teased her to mask the depth of his feeling; she met his teasing with her own. "She says we must be chaste," he recorded in his diary, "which I agree to. After dinner we chat and laugh but approach a breach of her orders . . . She insists I leave her at five. I put on a decent share of coldness and oblige her to solicit embraces which I refuse." The next day she rebuked him sharply. "I tell you that I love you because I love you. If I did not, it would be very easy to get rid of you." Their rivalry of minds and tempers only deepened their romance.

The upheaval in Paris continued, though it wasn't evident from the idle flirtations in its salons. At one dinner, Morris sat beside Madame de Staël, who flirted openly in English while her husband, who did not speak the language, looked on in helpless despair. "He loves you distractedly," Morris told her. "I know," she replied, "and it makes me miserable." Later, her husband sought him out, lamenting that in France "the women are greater whores with their hearts and minds than with their persons." Morris pitied him. He told himself he would resist such entanglements—though his diary suggests otherwise.

When he returned to Adèle a few days later, she greeted him from her bathtub, entirely at ease. She assured him that Parisian women often received visitors while bathing—and besides, she had mixed milk with the water, "so the parts immersed are invisible." When she emerged, shivering, he wrote that he administered "a cordial and restorative medicine which has been in great repute ever since the days of Adam." Beneath the playfulness ran genuine respect. Adèle was as independent, volatile, and as given to appetite as he was.

It was in that state of divided purpose—half lover, half observer—that Morris received two letters from George Washington in January 1790. The first was domestic, almost tender: Washington thanked Morris for "the pains you have taken to procure me a watch," and made a modest request for tableware. He wanted a *surtout de table*—a mirrored centerpiece expandable for large dinners—but cautioned Morris "to avoid extravagance." The new president understood he was setting a republican tone for a monarchy-weary people.

1

2

Left: Lewis Morris, Gouverneur's grandfather, was an odd man who constructed a sloop in the middle of a New Jersey forest, but he contributed to an early victory for the freedom of the press, inspiring his grandson.

Right: Lewis Morris Jr., Gouverneur's father, wanted him to "have the best education that is to be had in Europe or America"—as long as he didn't go to Yale.

3

4

Left: Broad-shouldered, with light-brown hair, blue eyes fringed with long lashes, and an aquiline nose, the young Gouverneur Morris charmed many women—and inspired jealousy in many men.

Right: As a young attorney, Morris joined John Jay (depicted here) and Robert R. Livingston in the Moot, a lawyers' club that met at King's Arms Tavern to debate law, politics, and philosophy.

5

6

Left: Staats Long Morris, Gouverneur's half brother, lived in England, was married to a duchess, and was an officer in the British army.

Right: Morris's old friend Robert R. Livingston lamented his extended absence from the New York Provincial Congress.

7

Robert Morris (right), known as the financier of the Revolutionary War, said he could "do nothing" without Gouverneur (left). His young partner, he said, "has more virtue than he shows, and more consistency than anybody believes."

We the People of the United States, in Order to form a more perfect Union, establish Justice, insure domestic Tranquility, provide for the common defence, promote the general Welfare, and secure the Blessings of Liberty to ourselves and our Posterity, do ordain and establish this Constitution for the United States of America.

Article. I.

Section. 1. All legislative Powers herein granted shall be vested in a Congress of the United States, which shall consist of a Senate and House of Representatives.

Section. 2. The House of Representatives shall be composed of Members chosen every second Year by the People of the several States, and the Electors in each State shall have the Qualifications requisite for Electors of the most numerous Branch of the State Legislature.

No Person shall be a Representative who shall not have attained to the Age of twenty five Years, and been seven Years a Citizen of the United States, and who shall not, when elected, be an Inhabitant of that State in which he shall be chosen.

Representatives and direct Taxes shall be apportioned among the several States which may be included within this Union, according to their respective Numbers, which shall be determined by adding to the whole Number of free Persons, including those bound to Service for a Term of Years, and excluding Indians not taxed, three fifths of all other Persons. The actual Enumeration shall be made within three Years after the first Meeting of the Congress of the United States, and within every subsequent Term of ten Years, in such Manner as they shall by Law direct. The Number of Representatives shall not exceed one for every thirty Thousand, but each State shall have at Least one Representative; and until such enumeration shall be made, the State of New Hampshire shall be entitled to chuse three, Massachusetts eight, Rhode-Island and Providence Plantations one, Connecticut five, New-York six, New Jersey four, Pennsylvania eight, Delaware one, Maryland six, Virginia ten, North Carolina five, South Carolina five, and Georgia three.

When vacancies happen in the Representation from any State, the Executive Authority thereof shall issue Writs of Election to fill such Vacancies.

The House of Representatives shall chuse their Speaker and other Officers; and shall have the sole Power of Impeachment.

Section. 3. The Senate of the United States shall be composed of two Senators from each State, chosen by the Legislature thereof for six Years; and each Senator shall have one Vote.

Immediately after they shall be assembled in Consequence of the first Election, they shall be divided as equally as may be into three Classes. The Seats of the Senators of the first Class shall be vacated at the Expiration of the second Year, of the second Class at the Expiration of the fourth Year, and of the third Class at the Expiration of the sixth Year, so that one third may be chosen every second Year; and if Vacancies happen by Resignation, or otherwise, during the Recess of the Legislature of any State, the Executive thereof may make temporary Appointments until the next Meeting of the Legislature, which shall then fill such Vacancies.

No Person shall be a Senator who shall not have attained to the Age of thirty Years, and been nine Years a Citizen of the United States, and who shall not, when elected, be an Inhabitant of that State for which he shall be chosen.

The Vice President of the United States shall be President of the Senate, but shall have no Vote, unless they be equally divided.

The Senate shall chuse their other Officers, and also a President pro tempore, in the Absence of the Vice President, or when he shall exercise the Office of President of the United States.

The Senate shall have the sole Power to try all Impeachments. When sitting for that Purpose, they shall be on Oath or Affirmation. When the President of the United States is tried, the Chief Justice shall preside: And no Person shall be convicted without the Concurrence of two thirds of the Members present.

Judgment in Cases of Impeachment shall not extend further than to removal from Office, and disqualification to hold and enjoy any Office of honor, Trust or Profit under the United States: but the Party convicted shall nevertheless be liable and subject to Indictment, Trial, Judgment and Punishment, according to Law.

Section. 4. The Times, Places and Manner of holding Elections for Senators and Representatives, shall be prescribed in each State by the Legislature thereof; but the Congress may at any time by Law make or alter such Regulations, except as to the Places of chusing Senators.

The Congress shall assemble at least once in every Year, and such Meeting shall be on the first Monday in December, unless they shall by Law appoint a different Day.

Section. 5. Each House shall be the Judge of the Elections, Returns and Qualifications of its own Members, and a Majority of each shall constitute a Quorum to do Business; but a smaller Number may adjourn from day to day, and may be authorized to compel the Attendance of absent Members, in such Manner, and under such Penalties as each House may provide.

Each House may determine the Rules of its Proceedings, punish its Members for disorderly Behaviour, and, with the Concurrence of two thirds, expel a Member.

Each House shall keep a Journal of its Proceedings, and from time to time publish the same, excepting such Parts as may in their Judgment require Secrecy; and the Yeas and Nays of the Members of either House on any question shall, at the Desire of one fifth of those Present, be entered on the Journal.

Neither House, during the Session of Congress, shall, without the Consent of the other, adjourn for more than three days, nor to any other Place than that in which the two Houses shall be sitting.

Section. 6. The Senators and Representatives shall receive a Compensation for their Services, to be ascertained by Law, and paid out of the Treasury of the United States. They shall in all Cases, except Treason, Felony and Breach of the Peace, be privileged from Arrest during their Attendance at the Session of their respective Houses, and in going to and returning from the same; and for any Speech or Debate in either House, they shall not be questioned in any other Place.

No Senator or Representative shall, during the Time for which he was elected, be appointed to any civil Office under the Authority of the United States, which shall have been created, or the Emoluments whereof shall have been encreased during such time; and no Person holding any Office under the United States, shall be a Member of either House during his Continuance in Office.

Section. 7. All Bills for raising Revenue shall originate in the House of Representatives; but the Senate may propose or concur with Amendments as on other Bills.

Every Bill which shall have passed the House of Representatives and the Senate, shall, before it become a Law, be presented to the President of the

Morris's most enduring contribution at the Constitutional Convention was to transform the Preamble from a clunky compact of states into a declaration of nationhood and a soaring statement of purpose.

9

A portrait of Morris painted during his time in France. His efforts to moderate the French Revolution prompted charges that he was a monarchist.

10

Morris quickly recognized that the shapely, sharp-witted Adèle Filleul was not a "sworn enemy to intrigue"—whether political or romantic.

11

Morris had been impressed with the Marquis de Lafayette when he met him at Valley Forge, but the "hero of two worlds" couldn't prevent France's plunge into the Reign of Terror.

12

Though it held just a handful of prisoners, the Bastille became a symbol of everything the French people hated about the monarchy.

13

The executioners of Louis XVI were so eager to complete the job, Morris told Thomas Jefferson, they "let fall the axe before his neck was properly placed, so that he was mangled."

14

After a decade in Europe, Morris was gratified to return to "a pretty good house . . . on the foundation of that in which I was born, and in which my parents died." Pictured here around 1900, the mansion was demolished several years later by the railroad that purchased it.

15

16

Left: Morris's relationship with his old Paris companion Jefferson frayed under the strain of American democracy.

Right: Both New Yorkers and graduates of King's College, Morris and Alexander Hamilton had long been intellectual kin, bound by their shared belief in order and energy in a strong central government. Hamilton's widow told Morris he had been her husband's best friend; Morris agonized over how to eulogize him.

17 

18 

Left: Morris finally found love with Nancy Randolph—a woman the world had cast aside.

Right: In his second inaugural address, James Madison declared the War of 1812 to be "just . . . necessary and noble"—a statement so detached from reality that Morris wondered whether the president was "out of his senses."

19 

Morris thought the Hartford Convention might be "the day-spring of freedom and glory" and that the participants might "be hailed thereafter as patriots and sages of their day and generation." But this contemporary cartoon depicts the leaders of the convention as traitors jumping into the arms of King George III.

20

21

Left: Morris's fellow canal commissioner DeWitt Clinton often gets the credit, but Morris was the visionary behind the Erie Canal.

Right: The English painter James Sharples completed this portrait of the fifty-eight-year-old Morris in 1810. Morris experienced marriage and fatherhood late in life. After decades of amorous adventures, he cherished his time as a family man.

22

For decades, Morris insisted that a waterway linking the Hudson River to the Great Lakes would transform the young nation.

The second letter was weightier. Washington, anxious to steady relations with the world's great powers, needed a trusted but unofficial hand to probe Britain's intentions. There were a number of unresolved issues more than six years after the Treaty of Paris had ended the Revolutionary War. Washington wanted soft intelligence before risking embarrassment by sending an official envoy. He consulted Hamilton, Jay, and Madison on possible candidates. Morris is the man, Hamilton advised. Madison cautioned that Morris's "imagination sometimes outruns his judgment," but Washington chose him anyway. It is "very important," he wrote to Morris, "that the business be so managed as that it may receive every advantage which abilities, address, and delicacy can promise and afford."

Morris accepted at once. Paris—and Adèle—would have to wait. She was increasingly distraught as he prepared to leave, unmoved by his assurances that he would not be gone for that long. "Not long for a husband because a wife can follow him," she sobbed, "but very long for a lover because I may be detained." He would be away for nearly nine months.

★

Morris knew the mission's peril as well as its promise: Britain still regarded the United States as an unruly experiment, and many Americans still feared their former ruler. If Morris failed, he might embarrass the president he revered. If he succeeded, he might help define America's place in the world.

The stakes reached back to the Treaty of Paris, which had formally ended the war but left a web of grievances unresolved. The British claimed the Americans had not fulfilled promises to repay prewar debts to Loyalists, and they retained a chain of forts along the Great Lakes—Detroit, Niagara, Michilimackinac, and others. More than mere outposts, the forts were conduits through which Britain supplied Native nations resisting American settlement. At the same time, American merchants chafed under British trade restrictions, and Southern slaveholders demanded compensation for the thousands of enslaved people who had escaped to freedom behind British lines during the war. The peace was fragile—signed but never settled.

In a letter to Washington on January 22, Morris promised to set off for London as soon as he could. In a second letter written on the same date, Morris shared concerns about "our friend Lafayette." At a dinner party, Lafayette had told Morris that he expected the National Assembly to appoint him France's supreme leader—and Morris could see in the Frenchman's face that he relished the prospect. He cautioned America's old ally that he should be focused on the loyalty of his troops. When the next crisis arose, would they obey him? Yes, of course, Lafayette replied dismissively, turning to talk to another guest. "He left America, you know, when his education was but half-finished," Morris told the president. "What he learned there he knows well, but he did not learn to be a government maker."

★

Morris stopped first in Amsterdam, the world's banking center, to pursue the speculative plan he and Robert Morris had conceived—to purchase America's debt to France and resell it to Dutch investors. He negotiated by day and charmed by night, filling his diary with accounts of dinners where the clink of glasses concealed the calculations of profit. Dining at the home of a prominent Jewish banker, he simultaneously chatted up the man's daughter and her sister-in-law. "Madame Sara seems to have more understanding than her sister-in-law," he recounted in his diary. "She is equally beautiful though in a different style and has an air *moins lubrique* [less wanton], but her eyes speak the language of that sentiment which warms and melts the heart."

In late March, he boarded a packet for England. Within hours of arriving at Froome's Hotel in Covent Garden, he sought out his half brother Staats Long Morris, still serving in the British Army. Staats Long, loyal to the Crown but proud of his half brother's achievements, received Gouverneur as kin, not traitor. They dined in perfect amity, as if a revolution had never torn their world—and their family—apart.

Then Morris's real work began. After calling on the French ambassador to get the latest news from Paris, Morris went to Whitehall, the heart of the British government in London, to request an audience with Francis Osborne, Duke of Leeds, His Majesty's Foreign Secretary. The reception clerks eyed the wooden-legged American in plain clothes with curiosity. When finally admitted, Morris handed Leeds Washington's letter laying out America's concerns.

"I am very happy, Mr. Morris," the duke said, glancing at the signature, "to see this under the President's own hand. It is very much my wish to cultivate a friendly intercourse between our nations."

"I am happy, my Lord," Morris replied evenly, "for we are too near neighbors not to be either good friends or dangerous enemies."

They spoke with the elaborate courtesy of men who distrusted each other's governments but respected each other's intelligence. Leeds was gracious but cagey, offering compliments in place of commitments. Beneath the civility lay unease. Britain's empire was stretched thin—its navy guarding trade routes from the Caribbean to the Pacific, its diplomats watching the shifting balance of power in Europe with growing apprehension. Leeds wanted calm in the Atlantic—though not enough to risk any concession. For now, he preferred delay: to watch, calculate, and see whether the new republic could hold itself together.

So, when Morris pressed the minister to honor Britain's promises under the treaty, Leeds deflected—first to procedural questions, then to timing. When Morris remarked on Britain's failure to send an ambassador to the United States—"a little circumstance which had operated very disagreeably upon the feelings of America"—Leeds claimed it had been a challenge to find a suitable candidate. Morris didn't buy it and said so.

When Leeds once again tried to change the subject, the American lost his patience. "As it was not worthwhile to discuss the winds and the weather, I observed that as he might probably choose to consider the matter a little and to read again the treaty and compare it with the American Constitution." The duke promised that he would, whereupon Morris told him he would be "glad to receive his answer as speedily as may be."

Weeks passed with nothing but silence. Morris sent polite reminders; the Foreign Office offered nothing in return. He saw plainly what Washington had feared: the British had no intention of yielding the forts or compensating former slaveholders. Britain, rich and wary, still regarded the United States as an experiment unlikely to last.

When the duke finally responded, it was with a "confusion of language which resembles the stammering of one who endeavors to excuse a misdeed which he resolves to commit," Morris told Washington. "It appears clearly that the favorable moment for us to treat is not yet come." Thus far, the mission to London had been a failure. But after reading Morris's letters describing the lack of progress, Washington reassured the envoy that he had acted appropriately.

It was the clearest report the president could have hoped for—measured, candid, and exact. Yet even as Morris earned Washington's trust, forces at home were shifting against him. Abroad, too, the balance was changing.

★

By late spring 1790, the Nootka Sound crisis—a dispute between Britain and Spain over trading rights off the coast of Vancouver Island—threatened to bring the two nations to war. France, bound to Spain by the old Bourbon alliance, was expected to intervene. With revolution already destabilizing Paris, the last thing London wanted was another conflict with the republic across the Atlantic. For His Majesty's Government, peace with the United States was not a matter of friendship but of realpolitik.

That urgency softened the British tone. After weeks of delay, Leeds invited Morris back to Whitehall on May 20. The foreign secretary, once evasive, now greeted him with cordiality. He even acknowledged, somewhat sheepishly, that British captains had impressed, or abducted, American sailors into the Royal Navy—claiming, as they often did, that they had mistaken them for deserters. It was merely a matter of misidentification, he said. Morris, seizing the moment, proposed that the United States issue formal certificates of citizenship to its seamen, protecting them from future abductions.

The two men met again the next day, this time with Prime Minister William Pitt himself. All polish and calculation, Pitt declared that Morris had been mistaken in assuming that Britain wasn't interested in a treaty of commerce. To this Morris replied, with a diplomat's smile and a lawyer's precision, "It is easy, sir, to rectify the mistake—but it appeared idle to form a new treaty until both parties should be thoroughly satisfied with that already existing," referring to the Treaty of Paris and its unfulfilled promises.

Moving through the familiar catalog of grievances, they parried over the compensation supposedly owed to British property owners and American slaveholders before landing on the thorniest issue: the forts, a visible reminder that Britain did not yet treat the United States as an equal.

"I suppose, therefore, you wish to retain those posts," Morris said evenly.

"Why—perhaps we may," Pitt replied, meeting courtesy with irony.

"They are not worth the keeping, for it must cost you a great deal of money and produce no benefit."

"If you consider these posts as a trivial object," Pitt returned, "there is the less reason for requiring them."

"Pardon me, sir." Morris said. "I only state the retaining them as *useless to you*. . . . Near neighbors are seldom good ones, for the quarrels among borderers frequently bring on wars. It is therefore essential for both parties that you should give them up; but as to us it is of particular importance, because our national honor is interested."

The exchange was pure theater—each man performing for history as much as for the other. Pitt wanted calm seas until the European crisis passed; Morris wanted an honest reckoning between former enemies. Only Pitt got what he wanted.

By the end of the summer, it was clear that France would not fight for Spain. The Nootka dispute eased into negotiation; the threat of war vanished. With it went Britain's incentive to please America. Leeds once again became elusive. The ministry "would have agreed to comply with the treaty of peace had they found themselves engaged in a war," Morris wrote to Washington in the middle of August. Perhaps thinking of Adèle, he added that he had "many private reasons" for returning to France, "but as I did believe that by being on the spot, I might be useful . . . I thought it my duty to stay."

He lingered through the damp summer, often ill and confined to his rooms, writing dispatches by candlelight. "Those who pursuing the true interests of Great Britain wish to be on the best terms with America," he observed, are "outnumbered by those whose sour prejudices and hot resentments render them averse to every intercourse except that which may immediately subserve a selfish policy. These men do not yet know America. Perhaps America does not yet know herself."

Morris believed the "sour prejudices and hot resentment" of people inside the British government had doomed his mission. He didn't know that back at home, he was being undermined by an American patriot: his old friend Alexander Hamilton.

Hamilton, who wanted America to forge closer ties to Britain, refused to accept that the former mother country wasn't interested in a warmer relationship. To advance his goals, Hamilton told Washington and Jefferson, who had returned to America in the fall of 1789 and was now secretary of state, that Morris was misrepresenting the British viewpoint. He intimated that Morris's friendship with the French ambassador to England made him overly sympathetic to the French, and even planted rumors that Morris had offended his British hosts. Washington was troubled by what Hamilton told him, but he remained loyal to Morris. Jefferson, after reviewing Morris's account of his contentious meeting with Leeds and Pitt, endorsed his tough approach.

Morris's letters in July, August, and September convinced Washington and Jefferson that there was nothing more the envoy could do, and that further attempts to broker a deal might make things worse. In a December letter, they directed Morris to conclude his mission. By the time Morris received it, he had already left London, having departed the city on September 24. He had little to show for six months of work but a Newfoundland dog—a gift for the Duchesse d'Orléans—and a clearer sense of how hard it was for a republic to be taken seriously in a world still ruled by kings.

After a six-week detour through Belgium and Prussia, during which he tried to find buyers for some of the land that Robert Morris owned in upstate New York, Morris finally returned to France in November. Waiting in Paris was Adèle. She had weathered his absence with her usual blend of resilience and caprice, but their reunion was not the idyll he had imagined. During his long stay in London, she had taken up with another man—Lord Henry Wycombe, a handsome and well-connected twenty-four-year-old English aristocrat who had made himself a fixture in her salon. Morris, confident in his own magnetism, was unprepared for the sting of jealousy. He masked his hurt with irony, noting in his diary that Wycombe was "a little nestled in here" and that they would see—"*nous verrons*"—how things unfolded.

When they met again, affection gave way to argument. He sought tenderness; she offered deflection. "At the Louvre denied," he wrote, underlining the word as though it were an act of moral courage. But as so often between them, a quarrel was only the prelude to reconciliation. Within days, Adèle sent a note summoning him to her apartment. Her elderly husband lingered inconveniently, but when he left, words turned to touches.

That night, she confessed that she had again seen her old lover Talleyrand, newly indispensable to the revolutionaries dismantling the power of the Church. Just a few days ago, she said, she would have slept with the bishop if Flahaut hadn't suddenly appeared. Instead of cooling their passion, this revelation inflamed it. "She says I may if I please possess her," Morris recorded that night. "I agree to do so *pour la dernière fois* [for the last time]." It was not.

She had once begged him for a ring, a simple token of fidelity; he had promised one and delivered it. But both knew that their affair, like the revolution outside their doors, obeyed no fixed laws.

In mid-November, Gouverneur took Adèle to visit her beloved English nun. On a previous visit to see the nun, they had coupled in the carriage on the way to the convent; this time, they made love *in* the convent. "While [the nun] is sent for we sacrifice to the Cyprian Queen in the retreat consecrated to chastity," he wrote giddily in his diary. The lovers found it hard to keep their hands off each other whenever they were alone—and even sometimes when they weren't. On one unseasonably warm mid-December afternoon, Gouverneur dined with Adèle and her niece at the Louvre. The niece was extremely near-sighted, and after the meal the couple nearly had intercourse as the unsuspecting girl played the fortepiano for them.

As 1791 dawned, the National Assembly was stripping the clergy of wealth and influence, while the king and queen were virtual prisoners in their palace. Morris, who moved easily between salons and ministries, sensed that nobody in France—not Louis, not Lafayette, and certainly not the legislators in the Assembly—were equipped to steer the country down a moderate path. "There is not a man among them fitted for the great tasks in which they are engaged," he wrote to Washington. Lafayette, once the bright hope of both nations, seemed to him "so elated by power, already too great for the measure of his abilities, that he looks into the clouds and grasps at the Supreme." He also told Washington that revolutionaries might try to capture the king and queen.

He was right. On April 18, 1791, a mob blocked Louis XVI and Marie Antoinette from departing the Tuileries Palace to spend Holy Week in the suburb of Saint-Cloud, halfway to Versailles. The National Guard disobeyed Lafayette's order to let the royal carriage through. Two months later, disguised as servants, the royal family fled Paris at midnight, hoping to reach the royalist garrison town of Montmédy, near the border with the Austrian Netherlands, where Marie Antoinette's brother reigned and international forces were mobilizing against revolutionary France. But local officials in Varennes-en-Argonne, alerted by a postmaster who recognized the king at a previous stop, arrested the family. Six thousand armed peasants and guardsmen brought them back to Paris.

Morris observed the revolution's descent from idealism into fear. His preference for order, his belief that liberty required restraint, would earn him the charge of being a monarchist. But Morris's conservatism was less about kings than about character. He feared not freedom, but frenzy, not democracy, but demagoguery.

NINETEEN

THE AMBASSADOR

Lafayette met the procession at the edge of the city and ushered Louis and Marie Antoinette back to the Tuileries Palace. The crowds along the route were dumbstruck—or perhaps just cowed by signs warning that "anyone who cheers the king will be beaten; anyone who insults him will be hanged." It had been five days since the royal family's midnight flight. Lafayette's job was to keep them in Paris, yet they had managed to escape. Was he incompetent, or had he been part of the plot? "You, Monsieur Lafayette, will answer to the Assembly on the fate of the king with your head," the radical Jacobin leader Maximilien de Robespierre snarled at the commander before the retrieval of the royal couple.

A week later, Gouverneur Morris called at Lafayette's house and found his wife "half wild" with fear. He wrote to Robert Morris that the king's flight had been "very foolish," and that Lafayette's reputation had fallen with the Crown's. In October, the general resigned his command of the National Guard and retreated to his estate in Auvergne, where he began maneuvering for another post to restore his name.

The Crown fared no better. Marie Antoinette's physician told

Morris that the ordeal had turned the thirty-six-year-old queen's hair gray. The failed flight branded Louis as a monarch who had plotted with foreign powers—above all with Austria—to crush his own people. He still wore the crown, but his aura of sanctity was gone.

France's absolute monarchy was no more; the question now was what would replace it. Moderates in the Assembly, soon called the Feuillants, sought to preserve a constitutional king; the Girondins, a bloc of provincial lawyers and merchants, pressed for broader democracy and a more aggressive foreign policy, aiming to spread revolutionary ideals throughout Europe; and the Jacobins, under Robespierre, demanded a republic. As someone who had helped shape the Constitution, Morris was drawn into these discussions—not officially, but as a trusted foreign observer. He believed that American ideals—liberty, equality, and self-government—were universal, but he didn't think America's political system suited every nation. He feared the French lacked the "education and habit" to govern themselves in a republic, and were so used to overbearing authority—and so desperate to shake it off—that they didn't fully appreciate the dangers of anarchy. His own proposed framework for a French constitution, essentially a memorandum he prepared at the request of several moderate nobles, steered between two ideas. France would be a constitutional monarchy, with the king as a chief executive who could veto legislation, conduct foreign policy, and command the military, but his power would be balanced by a representative legislature with real authority. Morris's ideas circulated among moderates and royal advisers but went unadopted.

Finally, on September 18, 1791, a hot-air balloon trailing tricolor ribbons drifted along above the Champs-Élysées to mark Louis XVI's acceptance of the Assembly's new constitution. It retained the monarchy, as Morris had hoped, but gave the newly created Legislative Assembly far superior powers. Morris doubted it would last. "It is a general and almost universal conviction that this constitution is inexecutable," he wrote to Washington. Louis had to cultivate goodwill "to make himself popular; indeed, his life and crown depend upon it."

The thirty-seven-year-old king, stout and awkward, was ill-equipped for popularity. He was nimble on horseback—hunting was his favorite activity—but ungainly everywhere else. He often holed up in his private study to pore over hand-colored maps and tinker with telescopes, sextants, and locks he designed and made himself. Morris called Louis a "miserable creature," but preferred him to a tyrant from one of the Assembly's revolutionary factions. In a September letter to the king, he advised him to distribute bread to the poor. "The French nation," he observed, "seldom notices the good but goes into ecstasies over the beautiful." Louis did nothing, and the Assembly continued to drift leftward, pulled by the passions of the streets.

★

Since Jefferson's departure from France in September 1789, Washington had lacked a permanent envoy in Paris, a minister plenipotentiary empowered to speak in his name. At the end of 1791, he finally nominated a replacement: Gouverneur Morris. The choice was an expression of Washington's trust, but it exposed Morris to the everlasting enmity of a man who denigrated him behind his back, and whose unfounded criticisms had lasting consequences on his historical reputation.

William Short had been Jefferson's private secretary in Paris, and the two Virginians were distant relatives by marriage. Jefferson had overseen Short's legal education and considered him to be his "adoptive son." When Jefferson left Paris, he designated his then-thirty-year-old protégé as chargés d'affaires, tasked with managing relations with France until Washington appointed a new ambassador. Jefferson repeatedly told Short that he was only an interim representative, but as the months and years went by without a replacement being named, Short held out hope that he would be appointed permanently.

Several months before Washington nominated Morris, a French newspaper predicted that he was the front-runner for the post.

Alarmed, Short began working to undermine him. Short dashed off a letter to Jefferson denouncing Morris's "aristocratical principles," his "contempt of the French revolution and the French nation," and his "dogmatizing manner." Short wrote many more such letters, even after Morris's appointment was official, poisoning Jefferson's perception of his old Paris companion and harming Morris's reputation among historians who accepted Short's diatribes at face value.

Jealousy played its part. At Madame de Staël's salon, Lady Sutherland, wife of the British ambassador, had invited only Morris to dine, ignoring Short at his elbow. "Thus, he will go home with ill will rankling in his heart against me," Morris noted in his diary. "This is hard, but this is human nature." Short never forgave him. Later he grumbled that Gouverneur was "one of those privileged geniuses who possesses by intuition all the knowledge he has occasion for . . . everything is so easy to Mr. Morris in conversation—every obstacle is got over with so much facility in his plausible language." Morris, he muttered, "levels mountains and fills valleys with a few phrases."

The Senate debate over Morris's nomination showed that Hamilton's fabricated account of Morris's actions in London had blemished his reputation, but also that Short's efforts and Morris's bold behavior in the Continental Congress and at the Constitutional Convention had chafed many of his colleagues. James Monroe, senator from Virginia, branded him "a monarchy man." Roger Sherman of Connecticut, the former shoemaker turned statesman who served with Morris at the Constitutional Convention, admitted he had "a sprightly mind" and "can write a good letter," but called him "irreligious and profane." Aaron Burr repeated Hamilton's canard that Morris had offended British ministers so deeply they refused further talks. Despite the sniping, the Senate confirmed him by a narrow vote of 16 to 11 on January 12, 1792.

Morris's main champion during the debate was Rufus King, who had represented Massachusetts at the Constitutional Convention but was now a senator from New York. "I think if you and I should chance to grow old and converse together, it will be no small consolation to reflect that those measures which have rendered our country great and happy were carried in spite of the opposition of our enemies," Gouverneur wrote to King, his ally in the fight against the Three-Fifths Clause.

Washington stood by his choice but warned his friend to tread carefully. Senators "praised your abilities," he wrote, "but you were charged, on the other hand, with levity, and imprudence of conversation and conduct." Critics also highlighted "a hauteur disgusting to those who happen to differ from you in sentiment," according to the president. He said Morris's critics accused him of being "a favorer of aristocracy" in France, and of wrecking his mission to England by sharing too much information with the French ambassador. Washington admonished Morris that he would have to be more careful in his new role and expressed confidence that he would take the criticisms to heart. "In this statement you have the pros and the cons," the president wrote, "by reciting them, I give you a proof of my friendship."

Morris thanked him and promised "that circumspection of conduct which has hitherto . . . formed no part of my character." Now, for the first time, Morris would observe—and take part in—the French Revolution as an official representative of the United States.

On June 3, 1792, in the state rooms of the Tuileries Palace, Gouverneur Morris—excused from wearing a ceremonial sword because of his wooden leg—presented his credentials to the king and queen. Louis took the papers awkwardly. "It is from the United States," he murmured. "Yes, Sire," Morris replied, "and they have charged me to express to Your Majesty their attachment to her and to the French nation." Marie Antoinette smiled faintly, drawing forward their seven-year-old son. "He's not big yet," she said. "I hope, madam, that he will be very large and truly great," Morris offered. "We're working on it, sir," she replied. Three years later, the boy would be dead, felled by tuberculosis in a filthy prison cell.

★

Paris remained combustible. On June 20, a crowd furious at the king's vetoes of measures against nobles and "refractory" clergy—priests who refused to swear loyalty to the state—breached the gates of the Tuileries and stormed inside. They found Louis in the opulent Salon de l'Oeil-de-Boeuf, the "bull's-eye" antechamber named for its large oval window. The intruders pushed the king against a window, brandishing sabers and pikes and holding aloft a calf's heart as "the heart of an aristocrat." Uncharacteristically calm, Louis raised a glass, toasted "the nation," and donned a red liberty cap. By nightfall, the mayor had dispersed the crowd, but Morris saw what the reprieve meant. "The constitution," he wrote, referring to the one the country had just adopted a few months earlier, "has this day, I think, given its last groan."

The king's supporters looked for a way to shift the balance of power. In late June, Morris met in secret with Armand-Marc, comte de Montmorin, France's former foreign minister, and royalist allies Bertrand de Molleville and Pierre Victor, baron Malouet. Given all that had happened, Morris told the men, it would take bold action to preserve the monarchy. "In order to see what stuff they are made of, I tell them what measures would put an end to all troubles, but these measures are deep and dangerous," Morris recalled. Montmorin was so shaken he became physically ill, but Molleville was already working on an audacious plan, and he invited Morris to help: together with other plotters, including Lafayette, they were scheming to spring the king from Paris.

Lafayette now commanded an army on the French frontier, charged with defending the country from the Austrians, Prussians, and royalist French émigrés who wanted to crush the revolution. He could move troops toward the royal château at Compiègne under legitimate orders. The king, still permitted limited travel, would go there under guard—beyond Paris's mobs but within the law—and from that refuge reassert constitutional authority. Louis hesitated but saw the plan's merits; Marie Antoinette, mistrusting Lafayette and still dreaming of foreign intervention to restore the ancien régime, stalled.

On June 29, Morris pressed Lafayette to act. "Fight for a good constitution," he said, or be saddled with "that wretched piece of paper that bears [your] name." Lafayette, skeptical, asked if by a "good" constitution he meant an aristocratic one. "Yes," Morris replied, "I presume you have lived long enough in the present style to see that a popular government is good for nothing in France." Lafayette countered that he wanted something like the American model but with a hereditary executive. Morris warned that such an executive would need a counterweight: a hereditary senate, an upper chamber of stability against the storms of democracy.

Louis was to make his final decision on July 10. "This day the king will commence a new career," Morris hinted to Jefferson. But when the hour came, Louis's courage failed; the plan collapsed, and his ministers resigned. "Their Majesties flashed in the pan," Morris wrote. "There is a want of mettle which will ever prevent them from being truly royal." Two weeks later, the king entrusted Morris with his private funds, which the beleaguered monarch thought he might use to raise an army loyal to him. It was an extraordinary act of confidence and a grave risk for an American envoy. It tied Morris to a monarch whom many in Paris now regarded as a traitor. Morris accepted, though perhaps to protect Washington, he never divulged what he'd done. He was convinced that the move made sense, for reasons of honor and strategy. France, America's first ally, must not sink into anarchy.

Many Americans, including the president, wanted the king and queen to survive. In a letter to Louis earlier that year, Washington had addressed him as our "very great, good, and dear friend and ally." Americans, the president wrote, viewed the events in France "with the feelings natural to those who have themselves passed through like perils," and saw Louis's acceptance of the constitution as proof that he was, for "a second time, the friend and patron of the rights of mankind." Thomas Waters Griffith, a twenty-five-year-old Baltimorean who was traveling in France during the summer of 1792, was struck by the contrast between French views of the king and the prevailing sentiment at home. The French were fed up with their sovereigns, Griffith observed, while Americans thought "tenderly" of the king because "he had secured the independence of our country, after having impoverished his treasury and risked his future in our cause."

Many historians have looked askance at Morris's actions, but not his biographer Theodore Roosevelt. "The whole crisis was one so completely without precedent that it is impossible to blame Morris for what he did," the future president wrote. The threats to Louis and Marie Antoinette, Roosevelt observed, "roused his gallantry and blinded him to the risk he himself ran, as well as to the hazard to which he put his country's interests."

In any case, events soon overtook all prudence. On July 25, Charles William Ferdinand, the Duke of Brunswick-Lüneburg and the commander of the Austro-Prussian forces massed on the French border, issued what became known as the Brunswick Manifesto. Distributed throughout Paris, it proclaimed that the allied armies did not wish to conquer France, but rather to "put an end to the anarchy" and "to restore to the king the security and the liberty of which he is now deprived." The manifesto concluded with a chilling warning: If the revolutionaries dared to attack the Tuileries or harm the royal family, Paris would face "military execution and complete destruction." Austria and Prussia had issued the threat to protect the monarchy and deter the revolution from spreading not only within France but also across Europe, but it backfired. Parisians armed themselves for the showdown to come.

★

On August 10, 1792, some two thousand soldiers—half of them the king's personal Swiss Guards—were deployed at the Tuileries. Antoine Galiot Mandat de Grancey, who had succeeded Lafayette as commander of the Paris National Guard, had blocked the bridges across the Seine to repulse any attackers. Just after dawn, Louis put on his sword and descended to the courtyard to review his troops. Since Lafayette's departure, the makeup of the National Guard had been transformed by the addition of thousands of *fédérés*, provincial volunteers who largely sympathized with the radical legislators. The Swiss Guards applauded the king when he appeared, but the National Guardsmen greeted him with shouts of *"Vive la nation!"*—an ominous sign.

Advised to seek protection with the Legislative Assembly, the king balked, then relented as armed citizens poured into the streets. With Marie Antoinette, their children, and his sister Élisabeth, he crossed to the Salle du Manège, where the Assembly met, and was ushered into the press gallery, a cubby hole behind the protection of an iron grille.

Meanwhile, radicals in Paris seized the Hôtel de Ville, toppling the city's government and proclaiming a new Paris Commune, a revolutionary council that instantly rivaled the Assembly in power and boldness. Mandat, the commander of the National Guard, was summoned to answer for himself and was cut down on the steps, a grim signal of where authority now lay. By midmorning, tens of thousands of armed militants and provincial volunteers were flooding toward the Tuileries. Leaderless guardsmen deployed to protect the palace peeled away, leaving it exposed as the tide of revolution swept in.

Antoine-Marie-René Terrier de Monciel, the former interior minister, visited Morris to deliver a "tranquilizing"—and erroneous—assessment of the situation. "Shortly after he leaves me the cannon begin," Morris wrote, "and musketry mingled with them announces a warm day." The Swiss Guards, loyal to the end, stood and fired but the crowd kept coming, surging through the smoke. Guards who surrendered were slaughtered in the courtyards; those who witnessed the slayings dropped their weapons and fled, shedding their uniforms and cartridge belts as they ran. Some defenders jumped out of the upper windows of the palace to the flagstones below. In the frenzy, *fédérés* in red coats were mistaken for Swiss and butchered as well. Louis-Sébastien Mercier, journalist and playwright, wrote of corpses stripped, limbs piled on carts, and "women, veritable furies." By afternoon, nearly a thousand lay dead. Crunching over shattered mirrors, looters raced through the palace halls, scouring every room for gold and silver, watches, jewels, and other valuables. "One butcher played the violin among the corpses," Mercier wrote, and the queen's bedchamber "became the rendezvous of the vilest prostitutes, and one saw scoundrels belching on the bosoms of their mistresses."

Over the next several days, the Legislative Assembly divested Louis XVI of his remaining powers and transferred power to an emergency government, which arrested the royal family and moved them to the Temple, a medieval fortress on the northeast fringes of Paris that had been converted into a prison.

As the fury spread, Adèle de Flahaut and her young son sought refuge in Morris's house on the Rue de la Planche. Others followed, including the Comte d'Estaing, an admiral who had commanded a French fleet during the American Revolution. Providing shelter was a risk. If the new authorities learned that the American envoy harbored royalists, it could jeopardize his mission and his life. Griffith, the young traveler from Baltimore, stumbled onto the scene; Morris, worried the story might circulate, drew him aside. "The persons you have seen consider themselves in danger and have taken refuge in my house," he said quietly. "If my protection of these persons should become a matter of reproach to me . . . let the consequences be what they may." Griffith assured the minister plenipotentiary that he considered his actions "fully justified as much by patriotism as by private feeling." In his official letter to Jefferson about a week later, Morris mentioned none of it.

In the aftermath of the Tuileries massacre, the Paris Commune became the true government of France. On August 17, heeding the Commune's order, legislators declared priests who refused to take an oath of loyalty to the state to be criminals. On the same day, the revolutionary leader Georges Danton signed an arrest warrant for Lafayette, accusing him of treason. Over the next couple of weeks, the revolutionary authorities arrested hundreds of refractory priests and royalist editors and printers. They also jailed members of the royal court, including Marie-Thérèse Louise of Savoy, Princesse de Lamballe. The princess, an old friend of Marie Antoinette's and mistress of her household, was often depicted by the pornographic press as the queen's lesbian lover. In total, more than a thousand people were taken into custody.

On the night of August 19, Lafayette fled across enemy lines into the Austrian Netherlands. The so-called hero of two worlds thought the Austrians would welcome him as they had many other French émigré officers. Instead, they arrested him and offered him a deal: They would allow him to leave, but only if he disclosed French military secrets. Lafayette refused to betray his country and instead appealed to William Short, now the US ambassador to the Netherlands, for help. Short and other American diplomats, including Morris, were wary. The new French government viewed Lafayette as a deserter, and America was neutral in the war between France and the allies. They did not want to antagonize the Austrians and Prussians. "He has spent his fortune on a revolution," Morris wrote to Jefferson, "and is now crushed by the wheel which he put in motion."

On the day Lafayette defected, Austrian and Prussian forces crossed into France. The Commune, fearing that hidden saboteurs were preparing to aid the invaders, erected a guillotine on the Place du Carrousel, in front of the Tuileries Palace, sometime during the third week of August. On August 28, Danton authorized raids on private homes to search for suspects, firearms, and incriminating documents. The next day, militants showed up on Morris's doorstep, the result of "a denunciation made by some blockhead or rascal that I had arms concealed in my house," he reported to Jefferson. Morris kept his cool, protecting the people he was sheltering inside.

One of the Commune's great fears was that Swiss Guards, priests, and royalist writers swept up in the mass arrests would recruit common criminals to the counterrevolutionary cause and lead a mass escape from Paris prisons. On September 2 outside the Abbaye prison, militants slaughtered nineteen priests with knives, axes, and sabers. A few hours later, they murdered more than a hundred clergymen who were being held at a Carmelite convent.

The Princesse de Lamballe was imprisoned at La Force prison. Dragged before an improvised tribunal, her accusers ordered her to swear an oath of loyalty to liberty and equality, which she did. But when they instructed her to denounce her friend the queen, she refused. She was pulled into an adjoining alley, where men armed with axes and pikes butchered her, stripped the clothes from her corpse, and stuck her head on a pike. They marched with it to the Temple, where they demanded that Marie Antoinette come to the window to see what had become of her friend. The queen fainted before she laid eyes on their bloody trophy.

Adèle, who had lived close to the court, understood what came next. Her sixty-six-year-old husband had fought with the royal forces defending the Tuileries and afterward found refuge in the home of a friend. Shortly after the sacking of the palace, he wrote to Adèle, asking her to procure passports for them by bribing the assistant secretary of the Commune. When she arrived at the official's home, he was in his dressing gown, arranging his hair. She requested passports, but he rebuffed her, saying he did not wish to risk his life to help the king's garden keeper escape retribution. Then he got up and went into the next room to finish getting dressed. Noticing a stack of passports on the table, Adèle grabbed a handful, but the official had watched her through a glass door. Showing mercy, he said she could take one with his signature, along with a few blank ones, if she promised to return the signed one the following day. The implication was that she would forge his signature on the blank passports, which she did.

At the end of September, Adèle fled with her son to England, while her husband decided to remain in France, hiding near Boulogne. There was a large émigré community in London; she placed her son, Charles, in an English school and settled in as best she could. But her former lover Talleyrand, who was also in London, refused to provide any financial help. Within four months, she was contemplating a risky return to France. In January 1793, she wrote to Morris: "Not a line from you, and yet I write, and will even always write. Soon I shall be arriving, however, for my mind is made up and the end of next week will not see me in London."

"Goodbye, my dear and good friend," she concluded. "I am in the best of spirits at the thought of seeing you soon."

TWENTY

"TERROR IS THE ORDER OF THE DAY"

After the fall of the monarchy in August 1792, Louis XVI had been moved from the Tuileries into far harsher confinement. At the fortress-prison known as the Temple, the towers were sealed, the gates guarded, and members of the royal family were treated not as sovereigns but as state prisoners awaiting judgment. What had begun as protective custody hardened into imprisonment; what had been imprisonment soon edged toward something even darker. In the days after Louis XVI's sentencing, Paris froze under a hard winter sky. Horses slipped and fell on the ice-glazed streets as if the city itself recoiled from what had been done. Under the constitution approved in 1791, the worst penalty that could be imposed on the king was removal from the throne. But the National Convention, the successor to the Legislative Assembly, put Louis on trial for trying to thwart the revolution. In mid-December, the deputies hauled him out of prison to interrogate him. "The French people accuse you of having committed a multitude of crimes in order to establish your tyranny by destroying its liberty,"

Bertrand Barère, the president of the convention, declared. The former king, now known as Citizen Louis Capet, responded calmly, acknowledging that while he may have erred, he never conspired against the French people. His denial wasn't enough. On January 15, the deputies rendered a unanimous verdict: guilty. Two days later, they sentenced Louis to death by guillotine, to be carried out on January 21.

★

Drums, beating from every part of the city, broke the dawn on the day of the execution. Just as Louis had calmly denied being guilty of tyranny, he was placid in the face of the guillotine. After he attended Mass, he removed his wedding ring and asked that it be delivered to Marie Antoinette; he'd said goodbye to her, and his children, the night before. He reacted serenely when a commotion in the Temple signaled that troops were preparing to take him to the execution site at the Place de la Révolution—formerly known as the Place Louis XV, in honor of his grandfather. "It's probably the National Guard beginning to assemble," he remarked lightly to his confessor, an Irish abbé named Henry Essex Edgeworth. Soon the two men heard the voices of officers and the tramping of horses as the cavalry entered the courtyard of the Temple. "They seem to be approaching," Louis said.

As he was led from the prison, Louis turned toward the tower where his family was being held. Two gendarmes opened the door of a covered carriage, and one of them climbed inside as the ex-king approached. Louis stepped in, beckoning the abbé to sit beside him. Then the second gendarme entered and closed the door. The clergyman handed his breviary to Louis and selected a few relevant psalms, which they recited together. Troops surrounded the carriage and drummers preceded it, to drown out any murmurs of support for the deposed monarch. It took nearly two hours for the procession to wend its way through the crowded streets. Thousands of Parisians, many armed with pikes and guns, watched it go by.

The carriage finally stopped in the middle of a large space surrounded by cannons and an armed multitude stretching into the distance. "We are arrived, if I mistake not," Louis whispered to the abbé. As he alighted, three gendarmes seized him. Louis haughtily repelled their attempts to untie his neckcloth and open his shirt, but they came at him again, this time to bind his hands.

"What are you attempting?"

"To bind you."

"To bind *me*? No! I shall never consent to that. Do what you have been ordered, but you shall never bind me."

As the guards shouted for reinforcements, the abbé spoke quietly to the condemned man.

"Sire, in this new insult, I only see another trait of resemblance between Your Majesty and the Savior who is about to recompense you."

Louis raised his eyes to the sky. "You are right," he said. "Nothing less than his example should make me submit to such a degradation." He turned to the gendarmes. "Do what you will, I will drink of the cup even to the dregs."

Louis leaned on the abbé's arm as he walked toward the guillotine, which was mounted on a scaffold so the crowd could witness the former king's final moments. He was moving so slowly the priest feared he wouldn't make it, but he released his grip as they neared their destination. "I die innocent of all the crimes laid to my charge," he declared defiantly. "I pardon those who have occasioned my death, and I pray to God that the blood you are now going to shed may never be visited on France." He would have said more, but a soldier on horseback waved his sword and ordered the drummers to drown him out. The executioners seized the former king, secured him in the pillory, and released the blade.

It was over in an instant. A teenage soldier circled the scaffold with the severed head, displaying it to the masses. For a few moments there was stunned silence, followed by scattered shouts of *"Vive la republique!"* The cries multiplied as a few spectators scrambled to the base of the scaffold to dip their handkerchiefs in the victim's blood, while others carried off scraps of his clothing. One of the executioners sold strands of Louis's hair and the ribbon that tied it. "The late king of this country has been publicly executed. He died in a manner becoming his dignity," Morris reported to Jefferson. "Mounting the scaffold, he expressed anew his forgiveness of those who persecuted him and a prayer that his deluded people might be benefited by his death." The executioners were so eager to complete the job, Morris added, they "let fall the axe before his neck was properly placed, so that he was mangled."

★

Despite his diplomatic status, Morris's ties to the king and the old government made him a target. He was arrested twice during the first three months of 1793 for lacking the proper documents. He was quickly released on both occasions, but there was no telling what might happen next in blood-soaked Paris. Many other diplomats were fleeing the country, and some of Morris's friends and relatives urged him to do the same, even before the execution of Louis Capet. "The date of this letter will show you that I did not, as you hoped, abandon my post, which is not always a very proper conduct," Gouverneur wrote to his half brother Staats Long on January 14. "You are right in the idea that Paris is a dangerous residence. But it is better that my friends should wonder why I stay than my enemies inquire why I went away." Staats Long had advised his brother that he'd be far happier living a comfortable life at Morrisania, but Gouverneur disagreed. "The first of all enjoyments is that which results from doing our duty," he responded. Nevertheless, Morris concluded in the spring of 1793 that it would be safer to perform that duty from somewhere outside the capital. In May, he moved to a twenty-acre country estate at Seine-Port, twenty-seven miles from Paris. He described his new residence to Robert Morris as "a neat little house on the banks of the Seine" with pear, plum, peach, apricot, apple, and almond trees.

In the fall of 1793, the revolutionaries turned their attention to the hated Marie Antoinette. During the trial of the "Widow Capet," they produced letters proving she had treasonously corresponded with the Austrian court in the run-up to the war. With flimsier evidence, they said she had persuaded Louis to veto anticlerical legislation, masterminded the royal family's flight to Varennes, and aided the Swiss Guards in their defense of the Tuileries. Much of their case hung on Marie Antoinette's character, especially her supposed sexual deviancy. The prosecutors claimed, among other imaginary offenses, that the wilted, white-haired woman before them had taught her eight-year-old son to masturbate and had forced the dauphin to commit incest with his mother and aunt. Inevitably, she was convicted and sentenced to death.

France's rulers sent Louis to the guillotine in a closed carriage, to spare him the abuse of the crowds. For Marie Antoinette, they opted for an open cart. Griffith, the young traveler from Baltimore, reported that Parisians pelted her with "the most vulgar epithets" as she passed by. She wore a plain white robe and cap, and sat with "her back to the driver, like the vilest convict." *Le Père Duchesne*, a radical newspaper, was disappointed that the former queen was so composed. "The bitch was audacious and insolent right to the very end," it reported. "However, her legs failed her at the moment of being tipped over *jouer la main chaude* [to shake the hot hand]," the paper's nickname for the guillotine. Nevertheless, the account continued, it was "the greatest of all the joys of the *Père Duchesne*, having with his own eyes seen the head of the female veto separated from her fucking tart's neck." Such were the vicissitudes of the revolution that Jacques Hébert, the paper's editor, was guillotined less than six months later for allegedly betraying the cause. When it was Hébert's turn, he failed to match the self-possession of the doomed queen.

In a letter to Washington two days after Marie Antoinette's execution, Morris described the French government as "a despotism both in principle and practice." The most radical members of the National Convention were running the country, he told the president, and they were punishing their enemies. "It is an emphatical phrase in fashion among the patriots that *terror is the order of the day*," he wrote. As the Reign of Terror—during which an estimated seventeen thousand people were executed and at least three hundred thousand were arrested—spiraled, Morris's position became increasingly untenable. Not only had he been a friend to the monarchy, but radical legislators also feared he would turn America against revolutionary France. In November 1793, what must have been one of Morris's gravest concerns was realized: Local officials with a warrant barged into his Seine-Port home to arrest Countess Harriet de Damas, the wife of a French officer who had fought in the American Revolution and had fled to Italy. Morris vociferously protested, arguing that the arrest of the countess, who had been taking refuge in his home since the previous spring, was a violation of America's extraterritorial rights. The dispute further antagonized French officials, and they began asking Washington to recall Morris. At home, politicians who were more sympathetic to the revolutionaries also ramped up their criticism of America's envoy. Washington, once again, was loyal to his old friend, but eventually he bowed to the pressure: In the spring of 1794, he appointed James Monroe to replace Morris as minister to France. "The difficulty (under existing circumstances) of knowing what to write to you, had determined me to write nothing, but to let the matter rest altogether upon the public communications from the Secretary of State," a sheepish Washington wrote to Morris on June 19. The president reconsidered, he explained, "in order to assure you that my confidence in, and friendship & regard for you remains undiminished."

And so, with the Terror reaching its bloody climax and even old alliances cracking under the strain, Gouverneur Morris prepared at last to leave the country he had tried, in his way, to steady—still loyal to Washington and still convinced that the fate of nations should turn on principle, not passion.

TWENTY-ONE

A TOUR OF THE OLD WORLD

Morris departed France on October 20, 1794, two months after Monroe arrived. He was glum about leaving the country that had been his home for nearly six years, but relieved to be breaking free of the chaos and violence that had enveloped it. "I saw misery and affliction every day and all around me without power to mitigate or means to relieve, and I felt myself degraded by communications I was forced into with the worst of mankind for the injuries sustained by my fellow citizens," he told Washington. The day he left France, Morris resumed writing in his diary, an activity he had stopped in January 1793 for fear of endangering others.

Instead of immediately returning to America, Morris embarked on a tour of Europe. He was eager to explore unfamiliar countries, close a few land deals, and do what he could to free Lafayette, who was still being held by the Austrians and Prussians. He started in Switzerland and spent time in Lausanne and Basel before making his way to Germany. A curious and observant tourist, he recorded his impressions of rivers and forests, soil and livestock, palaces and salt works. On November 22, at the Bell Inn in Künzelsau, in south-central Germany, he sampled "the best bread I ever saw or tasted"—underlining the statement for emphasis. Two days later, he marveled at "a gallery of paintings, if they can be called by that name," in the palace of Franz Ludwig von Erthal, the prince-bishop of Würzburg. The artworks were "compositions of feathers, silk, flax, hair, wood, seeds, moss, etc., so put together as to represent to the life the various objects," he wrote, "and not only birds and beasts but perspective and even a sea storm, the falls of the Rhine at Schaffhausen and another fall in Switzerland." He pronounced the artworks "the greatest curiosity I believe in Europe." Sometimes what sparked his amazement was more mundane. "On the road this day I saw some mules at least sixteen hands high and extremely well made—they must be of prodigious force," he wrote on November 26.

Curiosities, artwork, and artisanal bread notwithstanding, the trip was not without its challenges. Morris was beset by broken-down carriages and mediocre food. He also suffered through flare-ups of gout and venereal disease. Sexually transmitted diseases were extremely common in the 1790s, particularly in large cities like Paris, London, and Hamburg. Indeed, syphilis was sometimes euphemistically called "the French disease." Morris also complained about being ripped off by crooked innkeepers but decided that "the best way is to pay with good humor and jog patiently on. The art of living consists I think in some considerable degree in knowing how to be cheated."

As 1794 ended, Morris found himself in frigid Hamburg, feeling uncharacteristically gloomy. "Another year is added to the many which have been lost in the abyss of eternal duration," he wrote on the last day of the year.

But his spirits rose as he waded into Hamburg society, and he decided to remain in the region for an extended period. At the end of February, he rented a house in the nearby Danish town of Altona, on the Elbe River. Two months later, he was joined there by an old friend.

★

Though Adèle had written Gouverneur in January 1793 vowing to return to France, she wasn't insensible to the perils of Paris—especially after the trial and execution of Citizen Louis Capet. Ultimately, she decided that returning home was too dangerous for an aristocrat like her. She remained in England, where she reconnected with Lord Wycombe, the British aristocrat who had been Morris's rival for her affections in Paris. He helped her publish a semiautobiographical novel, *Adèle de Sénange*, which sold briskly. Now she had the financial means to support herself and her son—and to help other émigrés as well.

By the time Gouverneur left Paris, Adèle was living in Bremgarten, near Zurich. At the end of January 1795, she wrote to him about her efforts to help twenty-one-year-old Louis-Philippe, the Duc d'Orléans. Louis-Philippe was the son of Morris's friend the Duchesse d'Orléans, and a possible heir to the French throne. Originally a supporter of the revolution, the young duke became a lieutenant-general in the French army, but he was dismayed by the execution of Louis XVI and the increasing radicalism of the government. After French forces were defeated at the Battle of Neerwinden in March 1793, he deserted and fled to Switzerland, where he lived under an assumed name and worked as a teacher. Louis-Philippe was desperate to get to Hamburg so he could sail to safety in America, but he was virtually penniless. Adèle asked Gouverneur to give him money, which he did. In a follow-up letter the next month, she told Morris she would accompany Louis-Philippe to Hamburg, and asked him to rent lodgings for them.

They arrived on April 1. Gouverneur suppressed the complicated emotions he must have been feeling when he finally saw Adèle again after nearly three years. "Madame de Flahaut arrives this morning," he wrote blandly in his diary. "In the afternoon, I place her companion Mr. Muller [the alias that Louis-Philippe was using] in the apartments I had taken for them." In the following weeks, Gouverneur often visited and dined with Adèle, but his diary doesn't include any sexual innuendo or hints that their love had been rekindled—save one. On

April 18, he picked some flowers for her on his way to her lodgings, presenting them to her with a poem:

Take the first fruits that I have just picked;
You know that they are all for you—
My work and my cares, my jests and my leisure,
The flowers of spring and the fruits of summer.

See winter come, with a giant's step,
When the day is so sad, and the night is so good;
Then let us celebrate, my dear child,
Because already I'm in the midst of fall.

It was a wistful gesture, from a man perhaps less interested in conquest than in remembrance.

However sweet his poems to her—"It surely must be love that inspires," he wrote in May—Adèle could no longer afford to be distracted by poetry. Adèle was thirty-three; Gouverneur, ten years older. He was a bachelor, she a widow (her husband had been arrested and executed in Paris) who now had to make her own living. Exiled from her homeland and separated from her son, she was no longer interested in a dalliance that would not bring her security, and Gouverneur had not proposed marriage. Furthermore, Morris was not welcome in Paris, and someday she hoped to return there. When they dined together that spring, her laughter was softer, the quick wit dimmed by fatigue. There were also signs of illness. One evening in April she was "taken with a bleeding from the breast"—an episode that moved him to quiet dread. He did not name it, but he sensed it might be the beginning of something grave. His verses to her grew tender, touched with concern, as though he feared time might be working against them.

When they dined together in early June, Adèle once again suffered bleeding from her breast. "We converse on her dreary situation in life, with which she is strongly affected," Gouverneur wrote in his diary. Three days later, he left for London.

★

Morris told Washington he was going to England to wrap up "some affairs," presumably business matters, but he also continued to serve in a quasi-diplomatic role and frequently sent letters to the president updating him on the situation in Europe. In London, he would be able to provide intelligence on whether Britain meant to widen its war with revolutionary France, tighten its naval blockade, or challenge America's fragile neutrality. He met with Lord William Wyndham Grenville, the British foreign secretary, and Prime Minister Pitt, still trying to steer the fragile republic he served toward respectability in the eyes of Europe. Morris also traveled outside of London, visiting a number of factories in the industrializing north. The hum of looms, the clang of forges, the traffic of new canals and engines—these were the sounds of a new age, an industrial one.

In Scotland he saw it perhaps most clearly, when he was shown an engineering marvel that ignited his imagination: a new canal that connected the Firth of Forth on the North Sea coast to the Firth of Clyde. "When I see this," he wrote, "my mind opens to a view of wealth for the interior of America which hitherto I had rather conjectured than seen." He saw, in those locks and waterways, the architecture of a nation's future—the possibility of binding distant regions into one economic body. The idea that would become the Erie Canal, that great artery of American commerce, took shape in a moment of clarity on a gray Scottish afternoon.

The next month, Grenville presented Morris at court to King George III, the monarch whose transgressions had spurred Morris and his countrymen to break free of British rule. At first, the king mistook Morris for an Englishman. Grenville gently corrected him, noting that Morris had been America's minister to France—and had been disliked by that country's revolutionary government.

"I suppose Mr. Morris is too much attached to regular government," the king joked.

"Yes, Sir, and if Your Majesty would send thither your discontented subjects, it would do them much good," Morris replied.

"Well, if you'll contrive it for me, I'll give my hearty consent."

"There are enough of them, sir," Grenville interjected.

"Oh, aye, quite enough," said the king, exhibiting a jaunty sense of humor despite his troubles.

★

Morris was still in London in May 1796 when he received disconcerting news from a French émigré: Adèle was engaged to José Maria de Souza-Botelho Mourao e Vasconcellos, the Portuguese minister to Denmark. Fascinated by one of Adèle's novels, the thirty-eight-year-old de Souza had traveled to Hamburg to meet the author. Gouverneur noted the news in his diary with a matter-of-fact restraint that thinly masked the blow—but he immediately made plans to return to Hamburg.

Morris returned in the middle of June. He saw Adèle at least four times before they broached the subject of her engagement. It was a steamy Monday, and on a carriage ride together she disclosed, finally, "whereabouts she is with her Portuguese lover." Whatever Adèle said, it must not have augured well for the future of their own romance; the lovers who hadn't been able to resist coupling in carriages and convents in Paris preserved their platonic relationship in Hamburg. In the middle of July, Gouverneur headed south on another road trip.

★

In the eight months that followed, Morris moved through Berlin, Dresden, and Vienna with the same mix of curiosity and purpose that had always defined him. In each city, he was both observer and participant—dining with ministers, meeting exiles, and studying how power, wealth, and culture survived amid the wreckage of revolution. As usual, he leavened his travels with sexual escapades.

In Berlin, where Prussian discipline met libertine indulgence, he found a capital that reflected Europe's contradictions: elegant, corrupt, and restless for change. In Dresden, he saw French refugees fleeing east to avoid their country's advancing soldiers; German officials did not let them remain in any one place for more than three days, but they made sure to see the sights before they moved on. "Unhappy people," he wrote, "yet serene, even gay." And in Vienna, he saw the grandeur of an empire and the fragility of those who ruled it. Between dinners with diplomats and audiences with Austrian officials, he quietly lobbied for Lafayette's release from prison and lent his own money to save the marquis's family from ruin.

Through it all, Morris chronicled what he saw not just as a sightseer but as a man measuring the Old World against the possibilities of America.

His sympathy for Europe's doomed aristocrats and his affairs with women like Adèle would later be used to paint him as an anachronism—a man too loyal to rank, too indulgent in pleasure. But Morris's faith was not in kings but in structure—in the belief that order could coexist with liberty, that beauty and reason could still govern human ambition.

He spent a month in Berlin, which had "an air of dissoluteness" that reminded him of the Palais-Royal in Paris. One morning, he recorded in his diary, a young woman came to his room selling fruit. He had declined on several previous occasions, but this time she would not take *nein* for an answer. The fruit seller marched into his room and shut the window next to Gouverneur's seat. Then, "*sans cérémonie*," she knelt before him and performed "an operation which boys are too apt to perform for themselves." Initially, the woman had tried to sell him a pineapple for eight reichsthalers, and he had offered to pay four. Now she demanded five.

On September 14, he reached Vienna. The Austrian capital was a tourist's delight: Gouverneur gawked at a polar bear at the Schönbrunn Palace zoo; toured the Medico-Surgical Joseph's Academy of Vienna, which featured nearly twelve hundred anatomical wax models;

and sampled local delicacies, including cockchafer beetles preserved in sugar.

Since the United States did not have diplomatic relations with Austria, the British ambassador presented Morris at court to Emperor Francis II. In mid-December, he obtained an audience with the Austrian foreign minister, using the opportunity to press for the release of Lafayette, who was being held along with his family at a fortress in Olmütz, Austria. Morris already had done much to help Lafayette and his wife. In June 1794, when the French authorities arrested Adrienne de Lafayette and imprisoned her in Paris, Morris and an agent successfully petitioned for her release on behalf of the US government, likely saving her from the guillotine. In January 1795, she went to Vienna and received permission to join her husband in prison at Olmütz, along with their daughters. Morris arranged for money to be sent to Lafayette to improve his living conditions and gave Adrienne a substantial loan—nearly a full year of his ministerial salary—so she could pay her husband's "debts of honor." Lafayette would finally be released in the fall of 1797 as part of the negotiations that led to the Treaty of Campo Formio, which ended the war between France and Austria.

Morris also had a brief romantic fling in Vienna, this time with Emilie de Litta, an Italian noblewoman from Milan. He met the marquise one December evening at the home of a friend and called on her the next morning. Their visit was interrupted by her husband, but Gouverneur perceived an unspoken invitation to return later, when she would be alone. "Her look tells me that we shall be tête à tête, and mine is full of tenderness, gratitude and desire." When Gouverneur came back that evening, he confirmed that his instincts had been correct.

After nearly four months, Morris departed Vienna on January 10, 1797. On his way back to Hamburg, he stopped for a few days in Leipzig, where he met Henriette von Crayen, the wife of Wilhelm von Crayen, a Prussian diplomat and banker. On February 10, the day after their first meeting, they happened to attend the same soiree; Gouverneur was enchanted by her. When the evening ended and his carriage didn't show up, Henriette offered him a ride in hers. Sensing a mutual attraction, he made a pass at her in the carriage, and she was receptive—to a point. "I am *un peu entreprenant* [a little enterprising], and if the distance had been greater, should I think have succeeded," he wrote. They consummated the relationship the following day. The lovers reluctantly parted on the twelfth, when Morris left Leipzig to attend to business in Berlin—but their affair wasn't over yet. The day after Gouverneur arrived in Berlin, he went to deliver a letter from Henriette to her sister, only to stumble upon Henriette herself. He pretended to be surprised, but he had urged Henriette to use her sister's illness as a pretext for meeting him in Berlin.

One night, Gouverneur cautioned Henriette that she was being too obvious in her affections. "Why conceal my passion?" she said. "I glory in it." He took her home in his carriage, and along the way they made love, with some difficulty. "This town is very badly paved," Gouverneur complained. Henriette was inconsolable at the end of February, as her return to Leipzig drew near. On March 2, Gouverneur went to say a final goodbye. "I dare not ask, I cannot expect that you will love me, but do not—I beseech you—quite forget me," Henriette said as they parted. She wrote to him at least six times over the next six months.

Morris arrived back in Hamburg at the end of March. Adèle's betrothal to de Souza was on hold, and Gouverneur visited her often. But they did not revive their affair. Adèle was still in touch with Talleyrand, and when he regained a position of power in Paris, she decided it was time to return home. On September 21, she told Gouverneur she was "quite content" with the latest French government, and confident that it wouldn't execute previous decrees against émigrés; she returned to France a short time later. A few years later, she and de Souza were married in Paris. There is no evidence that Gouverneur and Adèle saw each other, or exchanged letters, ever again. She died in Paris in 1836.

As Morris prepared to return to America, the revolution he had witnessed still smoldered behind him. France had traded one despotism for another, and across Europe the old courts had become anxious citadels—places where sovereigns feared their own subjects as much as their rivals.

The Grand Tour that his mentor, William Smith, had advised him to postpone was finally behind him. He had watched an old world dying and glimpsed a new one being born. What Europe had squandered through privilege, America might gain through enterprise.

In his next chapter, Gouverneur Morris would do all he could to make sure his country fulfilled its potential.

TWENTY-TWO

FEDERALISTS AGAINST REPUBLICANS

After more than a decade wandering the courts, salons, and ministries of Europe, Gouverneur was ready to go home. On October 4, 1798, he boarded the merchant vessel *Ocean* and set sail for New York. It was a challenge to cross the North Atlantic at that time of year—especially traveling from east to west—and the *Ocean* was lashed by storms and stalled by currents for much of its sixty-day voyage to America. In the middle of October, Morris was so seasick he didn't leave his bunk for two days. One of his horses suffered a much worse fate: a protruding bolt in his stall gored him every time the ship heaved in the heavy seas, killing him before the situation was discovered. The crew made multiple navigational errors, and the captain of the *Ocean* was "a most disagreeable and impertinent fellow" who rubbed Morris the wrong way almost immediately. Finally, on December 2, the *Ocean* spotted land and a lighthouse. The captain and crew assumed it was Montauk Light at the eastern end of Long Island; it was Beavertail Light in Narragansett Bay, Rhode Island. The ship had strayed off course, and Morris's long journey dragged on. The *Ocean* waited in Rhode Island for the weather to break so it could continue to New York.

Fed up with the ship and its crew, Morris left the *Ocean* and booked passage on a local coastal vessel—but his bad luck continued. Soon after leaving Newport, stormy seas forced his new ship to turn back. On its next attempt, it had to seek refuge in New London, Connecticut. Finally, eighty days after leaving Hamburg, Morris disembarked in New York, two days before Christmas.

Before heading to Morrisania, Gouverneur spent two weeks in New York City, where he caught up with old friends and colleagues. On Christmas Day, Alexander Hamilton updated him on the "state of our affairs" and urged him to "take a share in the administration" of President John Adams, who had succeeded Washington in March 1797. Morris wasn't interested; he wanted to focus on Morrisania and his private business interests. "Some of my friends have, as you may readily suppose, been talking to me of public life, but I turn a deaf ear to all that can be said of that sort," he wrote to his Hamburg friend and business partner John Parish. Morris was "not meaning to embark again on the stormy ocean of politics, now that I have got safe into the port of private life, unless something should happen which I do not foresee to make it my duty."

On January 5, 1799, a day that was "cold and like for snow," Morris ate dinner and set out for Morrisania, arriving at dusk to find a house that was "leaky and looked ruinous." He spent the first weeks dealing with carpenters and masons, even as he entertained guests. He also focused on organizing his books and papers. The surroundings might have seemed modest to a man who had spent the past decade frequenting the palaces and castles of Europe, but Gouverneur was gratified to return to "a pretty good house . . . on the foundation of that in which I was born, and in which my parents died." He particularly enjoyed his terrace roof, where he could take in the view and breathe "the most salubrious air in the world."

But Morris's long stint in Europe had reinforced his aristocratic tastes. Always a dandy, he was now even more out of step with the republican ethos of his native land. One traveler who crossed paths with him at an inn noted that he was accompanied by two French valets and had his "hair buckled up in about a hundred *papillotes* [paper curlers]." The innkeeper's dumbfounded reaction to the wooden-legged Morris and his companions "gave me some idea how the natives looked when poor [British explorer James] Cook made his entrée at the friendly isles," the traveler recalled.

At the same time, the forty-seven-year-old bachelor was thinking about leaving at least some of his European habits behind. "I do not know but you are right in the idea, that I should provide myself with a helpmate," he wrote to Parish that January. "It is not good, say the Scriptures, for a man to be alone, and when the winter of the year adds frosts to the winter of life, I suspect that the long evenings may grow somewhat dull, and force me to town." Morris was open to the idea of marriage, but instead of actively seeking a wife, he was happy to wait to see who fate would bring his way or "trust myself to the stream of time, and float as fate may order, fully convinced that the best pilots know little of the matter."

★

As Gouverneur reacquainted himself with the comforts of Morrisania, his old partner Robert Morris was in Philadelphia, residing in a two-story brownstone enclosed by a twenty-foot stone wall: the Prune Street Jail. Robert landed in the debtors' prison following the collapse of the North American Land Company, which he had formed with some associates (Gouverneur was not involved) without clear title to the land it held. Europeans balked at buying the land, and even after Robert forfeited his personal land holdings, he did not have enough money to pay his creditors. He had been imprisoned since February 16, 1798, when a sheriff arrested him in his rented Philadelphia home, in front of his wife and children. "I am told that his family exhibited a dreadful scene of distress, that Mrs. Morris was almost frantic, and flew upon the people who brought him to town and would have committed violence but was prevented," a young Massachusetts congressman told his wife.

The Prune Street Jail was part of a larger prison complex that included the New Gaol, a four-story facility for common criminals that opened just before the war. The New Gaol inmates were separated from the debtors by a wall that bisected the common exercise yard, but they frequently scaled it to rob the white-collar criminals on the other side—even though many of the debtors were similarly penniless. The Prune Street prisoners were charged for their room and board, and those who couldn't pay much were hungry, ill-clothed, and packed into cramped cells. For the first week of his imprisonment, Robert did not have a bed, much less a cell of his own. Gradually he settled into his new situation. With money that Mary obtained, he secured his own room—"the best in this house," he told a friend—and furnished it with three writing desks, a borrowed mahogany table, a worn Windsor settee and eight chairs, and six chests filled with letters and business papers. He woke up early and took long walks around the exercise yard, tracking his progress by dropping a pebble each time he completed a lap. The inmates were not confined to their cells, and they could receive visitors from daylight until nine at night. Mary came every afternoon, usually with their teenage daughter, Maria. Staring at the whitewashed walls, under a window with an iron grate, Robert had plenty of time to contemplate his dramatic fall. "A man that cannot hear and face misfortune should not run risks," he wrote to his son Thomas. "But I have been too adventurous and therefore it is my duty to meet my fate with fortitude, and I do it."

Many people had turned against Robert. Investors who had purchased his stock offerings and merchants who held his worthless notes cheered his punishment. Even among ordinary Philadelphians, there was schadenfreude at the financial titan's demise. But Gouverneur remained loyal. During a weeklong visit to Philadelphia in April 1799, he visited Robert five times. Their emotions got the better of them at their first meeting; Gouverneur noted in his diary that the two men were "strongly affected" by the hard facts of Robert's situation. After leaving Prune Street, Gouverneur went to visit Mary, who put on "an air of firmness which she cannot support and was wrong to assume." The next day, he dined in the prison with Robert, Mary, and some of their children, bending the jailhouse rules by lingering until after nine p.m. He did his best to lighten the mood with "a very lively strain of conversation," but noticed "with infinite concern that [Robert's] mind is more made up to his situation than I could have believed." Gouverneur also did what he could to improve the family's financial predicament, arranging an annuity of fifteen hundred dollars a year for Mary, who used the money to rent a small house.

★

When Gouverneur left for France in 1788, America had no political parties. But during Washington's second term as president, two distinct factions emerged.

The Federalists, led by Hamilton, favored an energetic central government. They believed America's future lay in commerce and industry, and they drew their strength from the merchant and manufacturing centers of the Northeast.

Opposing them were the Republicans, later known as the Democratic-Republicans, led by Jefferson and Madison. Fearing the rise of a new monarchy, they distrusted concentrated power and championed state sovereignty. They imagined an agrarian republic of independent farmers and looked to the south and the western frontier for most of their support.

The Federalists were skeptical of unchecked democracy, while the Republicans celebrated it. They clashed over everything from the need for a central bank—supported by Hamilton, opposed by Jefferson—to the proper American response to the French Revolution. When France declared war on Britain in February 1793, the Republicans' sympathy for the French cause clashed with the Federalists' instinctive tilt toward Britain.

Despite being a Virginian, Washington generally sided with the Federalists. But he tried to stay above the fray and worried about what the rise of factions might do to the fragile republic. In his Farewell Address, he warned that political parties gave narrow factions "an artificial and extraordinary force," allowing "cunning, ambitious and unprincipled men" to subvert the common good. He implored Americans to guard against "the baneful effects of the spirit of party."

Nevertheless, partisanship hardened during the presidency of Federalist John Adams, fueled by tensions with France. In a violation of US neutrality, French ships had begun seizing American merchant vessels trading with Britain. Hoping to ease the crisis, Adams sent three envoys to Paris in 1797. But Talleyrand—Morris's old adversary, now the French foreign minister—brushed them off after a perfunctory fifteen-minute meeting. His intermediaries, later known only as *X*, *Y*, and *Z*, demanded bribes and loans as the price of negotiation. The Americans refused.

The XYZ Affair, as it became known, inflamed anti-French sentiment and raised fears of war. Adams responded by building up the navy and expanding the army, measures that alarmed the Republicans, who saw the shadow of despotism. His administration then passed the Alien and Sedition Acts, empowering the government to deport foreigners deemed dangerous and prosecute citizens who criticized the president or Congress. Republican newspapers were shut down, their editors jailed. Adams's critics branded him a would-be monarch.

Morris, ever a believer in strong federal authority and chastened by what he had witnessed in revolutionary France, leaned Federalist—but he detested the hysteria consuming both camps. Federalists called their rivals "Jacobins," likening them to the blood-soaked radicals of Paris; Republicans, in turn, mocked the Federalists as closet monarchists. To Morris, both sides misunderstood the lessons of the Old World.

"Hamilton tells me I must take an active part in our public affairs, for that the anti-Federalists are determined to overthrow our Constitution," he noted in his diary on November 28, 1799. "This is a painful idea [in] every way."

Eleven days later, he appealed to the one man who still stood above the noise. Disparaging Adams as unfit, Morris urged Washington to return to office for a third term. "During a late visit to New York, I learned that the leading [Federalist] characters (even in Massachusetts) consider Mr. Adams as unfit for the office he now holds," Morris wrote on December 9, 1799. "You will easily conceive that his predecessor was wished for and regretted." If Washington declined, Morris warned, "no man will be chosen whom you would wish to see in that high office."

Washington never read the letter. Five days later, on December 14, 1799, he died of a sudden throat infection at Mount Vernon at age sixty-seven.

Morris received the news while hosting the Duc d'Orléans—the future King Louis-Philippe and the son of the duchess he had befriended in France—at Morrisania. The City of New York asked him to deliver a eulogy at St. Paul's Chapel. "In him were the courage of a soldier, the intrepidity of a chief, the fortitude of a hero," Morris said. "He loved glory, but still more he loved his country." Though he fretted afterward that he had botched the delivery, he sent copies of the address to friends in Europe—a gesture not of vanity but of reverence. Washington had been his moral compass; he wanted the Old World to know what America had lost.

In March 1800, Hamilton urged him to run for Congress. Morris declined—yet fate had other plans. At dinner with Hamilton less than a month later, he learned that the New York legislature had elected him to fill a vacant US Senate seat. "Informed that I am elected senator, which is unfortunate," he wrote in his diary. Despite his reluctance to reenter public life, Morris accepted the appointment.

On May 3, he presented his credentials at Congress Hall in Philadelphia. Eleven days later, the Senate adjourned—its next meeting to be held in the new federal city on the Potomac, named for the man whose absence was everywhere felt.

★

During the Senate recess, Morris set out on a northern adventure—part inspection tour, part pilgrimage into America's untapped future. He wanted to see for himself the land he owned in upstate New York, and the wilderness beyond it. Leaving Morrisania in mid-July, he sailed up the Hudson River to Albany, then pressed north through the crystalline waters of Lake George and Lake Champlain to Montreal.

He was half explorer, half poet. "The shores of Lake George are bold, chiefly mountainous, frequently steep, sometimes perpendicular," he wrote to John Parish, his Hamburg confidant. "Although these mountains are far from being so high as the Alps, the lake is on the whole a finer object than that of Geneva, because it combines better the sublime with the beautiful." He marveled at its clarity—"a liquid crystal"—and at the ease with which he forgot, for a time, national politics.

Even the journey's dangers exhilarated him. On the St. Lawrence River near Montreal, when his boatmen refused to shoot the Rapides du Sault Normand after dark, Morris, with his wooden leg braced against the boards, told them to go on. "To conclude, [one boatman] tells me that he never went through after sunset in his life," he recorded with dry amusement. "I reply very coolly that this then will be the first time."

From Montreal he followed the St. Lawrence to Lake Ontario, then westward to Niagara Falls and Lake Erie. There, amid the roar of the cataract and the immensity of the lake, his imagination surged into the new century. "Hundreds of large ships will, in no distant period, bound on the billows of these inland seas," he wrote to Parish. "One tenth of the expense borne by Britain in the last campaign would enable ships to sail from London through Hudson's River into Lake Erie." By "the last campaign," Morris meant Britain's wars in Europe. The point, as always with him, was practical and prophetic: what Europe wasted on destruction, America would invest in creation.

He saw in that wilderness a network of waterways that could link the Atlantic to the Great Lakes—a canal that would bind the young republic's Eastern Seaboard to its vast interior. "As yet, my friend," he wrote, "we only crawl along the outer edge of our country. The interior excels the part we inhabit in soil, in climate, in everything. The proudest empire in Europe is but a bauble, compared to what America *will* be, *must* be, in the course of two centuries; perhaps of one!"

The vision he sketched on that journey would, within a generation, become the Erie Canal, which joined the Hudson River to Lake Erie and transformed New York into the nation's commercial heart. Standing on those northern shores, Gouverneur Morris—veteran of one revolution and witness to another—looked at the continent and saw not what it was, but what it would be: a republic of motion and industry, drawing its strength not from kings or crowns but from the ceaseless flow of its own ambition.

★

Morris arrived in snowbound Washington on November 21. The new capital, carved from a swamp between Maryland and Virginia, was still more an idea than a city. Congress met in an unfinished Capitol; Adams delivered a welcome address in the unheated Senate chamber, where the breath of lawmakers fogged in the cold. "I congratulate the people of the United States on the assembling of Congress at the permanent seat of their government," the president began gamely. "Accommodations are not now so complete as might be wished," he conceded, "yet there is great reason to believe that this inconvenience will cease with the present session."

That was wishful thinking. Washington in 1800 was a muddy experiment in capital-building—a scattering of grand public buildings surrounded by tree stumps, shanties, and work yards. The air rang with the hammering of carpenters and the crack of gunfire from hunters stalking wild turkey and quail in the brush. Barely fourteen thousand people lived there: ten thousand whites, seven hundred free Black residents, and three thousand enslaved men and women. Most of the workers who built the Capitol and the White House, those monuments to liberty, were slaves. Abigail Adams, gazing from her window at enslaved laborers clothed in rags, felt the bitter irony. "Two of our hardy New England men would do as much work in a day as the whole twelve," she wrote to a friend. "It is true *Republicanism* that drives slaves half-fed and destitute of clothing . . . whilst an owner walks about idle, though one slave is all the property he can boast."

Morris's own reaction was barbed and urbane. Writing to his friend the Princess of Thurn and Taxis, a German aristocrat and salon hostess he had met during his European years, he painted a portrait both comic and caustic. "We want nothing here but houses, cellars and kitchens, well-informed men, amiable women and other trifles of the kind to make our city perfect," he quipped. Washington had "abundant fieldstone," he admitted, and boundless promise—but little else. "There is no want of sites for magnificent hotels," he teased, "and contemplated canals can bring a vast commerce to this place . . . it is the very best city in the world for a *future* residence."

By the time Gouverneur Morris arrived in the capital, the presidential election of 1800 had ground to a deadlock that threatened the Constitution he had helped draft. Electoral votes were allotted to each state according to its number of senators and representatives, just as they are today, but the mechanics of choosing electors were still unsettled. Only five states—Kentucky, Maryland, North Carolina, Rhode Island, and Virginia—allowed the people to vote directly. In the rest, state legislatures made the selection. Under the system that would stand until the Twelfth Amendment of 1804, each elector cast two votes for president but couldn't cast both for the same candidate. The candidate with the highest total became president; the runner-up became vice president.

That autumn, the new machinery of democracy jammed. For the first time, members of Congress had caucused along party lines to select candidates. The Federalists put forward President John Adams for the top job and Charles Cotesworth Pinckney of South Carolina for vice president. The Republicans, their opponents in the still-young party system, chose Thomas Jefferson for president and Aaron Burr of New York for vice president. When the votes were tallied, however, Jefferson and Burr each had seventy-three. Adams and Pinckney trailed behind. That meant the election would be decided in the House of Representatives, with each of the sixteen state delegations receiving a single vote. To win the presidency, Jefferson or Burr had to secure at least nine votes; the loser would be vice president.

The mood was electric. Partisan hostility had reached new heights, and Jefferson's supporters feared the Federalists might exploit the deadlock to cling to power. Morris confirmed that the fear was not unfounded. "It was proposed," he wrote to Hamilton, "to prevent any election, and thereby throw the government into the hands of a president of the Senate—it even went so far as to cast about for the person." He tried to dissuade the plotters, warning that such a maneuver would destroy the young republic's legitimacy. Though he disagreed with Jefferson on almost every principle, Morris believed the people's will was plain. "Since it was evidently the intention of our fellow citizens to make Mr. Jefferson the president," he wrote, "it seems proper to fulfill that intention."

Hamilton had played a pivotal role in the campaign. In a blistering fifty-four-page pamphlet he wrote that autumn, he had savaged Adams—his own party's leader—as unfit for office. Like Morris, Hamilton differed with Jefferson on just about everything. Yet the alternative alarmed him even more. Burr, he warned Morris, "has no principle public or private—could be bound by no agreement—will listen to no monitor but his ambition." Many Federalists, nevertheless, preferred Burr to Jefferson, whom they regarded as an atheist and a Jacobin eager to import the guillotine to America. Morris observed wryly that most of his fellow Federalists were "moved by passion only," adding that "it is dangerous to be impartial in politics. You who are temperate in *drinking*"—a teasing reference to Hamilton's public admission of his affair with Maria Reynolds after he had been blackmailed by her husband—"have never perhaps noticed the awkward situation of a man who continues to be sober after the company are drunk."

The House balloting began on February 11, 1801, in a chamber thick with distrust. During the first twenty-hour session, which didn't adjourn until nine the following morning, congressmen slept on the floor. One delegate, ill and bedridden, was carried through the snow and laid on a cot outside the chamber so his vote could be counted if needed. Nineteen ballots produced the same impasse: eight states for Jefferson, six for Burr, and two—Maryland and Vermont—divided, denying either candidate the ninth vote required to win. Rumors swirled. Some Federalists whispered of elevating Secretary of State John Marshall to an interim presidency and then calling a new election. "If that party wish to disorganize, *that* is the way to do it," James Monroe, now governor of Virginia, warned Jefferson from Richmond. "If the union could be broken, that would do it."

After seven tense days and thirty-six ballots, exhaustion accomplished what argument could not. The Federalist holdouts from Maryland and Vermont abstained, allowing the pro-Jefferson electors from those states to put them in Jefferson's column. Finally, the Virginian had secured ten state delegations and with them the presidency.

Morris, more serene than most of his peers, had seen the crisis as a natural convulsion in a still-forming republic. Months earlier he had written to Rufus King, "*nil desperandum de Republica* [Don't despair of the Republic] . . . Let the chair of office be filled by whomsoever it may, opposition will act as an outward conscience and prevent the abuse of power." Now, as others fumed or sulked, he observed dispassionately, "this farce of life contains nothing which should put us out of humor."

On March 4, 1801, Morris took his seat among the senators listening to Jefferson's inaugural address. The new president sought to calm a fractured nation: "Every difference of opinion is not a difference of principle. . . . We are all Republicans; we are all Federalists." Morris, who had spent a lifetime trying to balance liberty and order, could appreciate the sentiment. The next day the Senate adjourned, and he returned to Morrisania—to his books and his fishing, with the quiet satisfaction of a man who had helped design a government sturdy enough to survive its first true crisis.

★

Morris began his ten-day journey back to Washington on December 8. On the way, he stopped in Philadelphia to visit his old partner Robert Morris, newly released from debtors' prison after years of confinement. He also read Jefferson's First Annual Message, delivered to Congress on the day Morris departed from Morrisania. President Adams had addressed Congress in person, but Jefferson preferred to transmit the message in writing, a practice that endured until Woodrow Wilson revived the in-person speech—now called the State of the Union address—in 1913. Clerks copied Jefferson's message and circulated it immediately. Morris, reviewing the text as he rode south through frost-hardened towns, felt his temperature rise as he read Jefferson's words. The new president called for abolishing internal taxes, shrinking the army and navy, reducing the diplomatic corps, and eliminating "the great mass of public offices." To Morris, this sounded like the slow strangulation of federal authority. "The destruction of the general government," he called it—by which he meant not literal demolition, but a weakening drift back toward the laxity and fragmentation of the Articles of Confederation.

In January 1802, Jefferson's allies in Congress—the now-dominant Republicans—proposed abolishing the seven district and sixteen circuit court judgeships created by the outgoing Federalists during Adams's final weeks in office. The appointment of these "midnight judges" were, to Jefferson and the Republicans, a partisan entrenchment. To Morris, however, the judgeships were a structural safeguard, and the effort to repeal them was a direct threat to judicial independence.

On January 8, Morris rose in the Senate and spoke for nearly an hour. "Did the people of America vest all powers in the Legislature?" he demanded. They did not, because they wanted the judiciary to be "a check of the first necessity—to prevent an invasion of the Constitution by unconstitutional laws." The judiciary, Morris warned, must be a bulwark to "prevent any faction from intimidating or annihilating the tribunals themselves." It was a masterful defense of constitutional balance—precisely the equilibrium he had championed in Philadelphia fifteen years before.

Later that afternoon, Jefferson, perhaps hoping to cool tempers after the morning's clash, invited the senator to a tea he was hosting. The two men had, of course, known each other since Paris, sharing salons, carriage rides, and cautious confidences. They admired some of the same French thinkers and disagreed on the wisdom of others. But their friendship was now fraying under the strain of American democracy.

At the President's House, the gathering was modest: Jefferson, Secretary of State James Madison, and Madison's vivacious young wife, Dolley, who softened Jefferson's austere manner with her warmth. The president was "very civil," Morris noted, "but with evident marks of constraint." Dolley, meanwhile, was all sparkle and ease. Morris, in the private tone of a man who found her charm disarming, later confided to his diary that he thought she might even be interested in an amorous adventure, which didn't surprise him given the "shriveled condition" of her husband, seventeen years her senior.

Morris's arguments failed to sway the Republicans. On January 22, Congress voted to abolish the new judgeships. To Jefferson and his followers, the repeal reaffirmed popular sovereignty by undoing what they saw as the partisan overreach of the outgoing Federalists. To Morris, it was something else entirely: evidence that the revolution's democratic fervor had begun to tilt the balance too far, eroding the constitutional guardrails he believed essential to the Union's survival.

In the months that followed, Morris and his dear friend Hamilton exchanged anguished letters on the state of the country—and their places in it—as Jefferson's vision triumphed. Both New Yorkers, both graduates of King's College, they had long been intellectual kin, bound by their shared belief in order and energy in a strong central government. Hamilton was five years younger (or perhaps just three years—historians disagree on whether he was born in 1755 or 1757) and slighter than the imposing Morris, but he also cut a dazzling figure. His posture, one observer said, was "remarkably erect and dignified." He wore his reddish-brown hair brushed back, and his eyes, a deep blue verging on violet, glowed against a fair complexion and "the almost feminine rosiness of his cheeks." At dinner, Hamilton spoke in "a deliberate and serious" tone, his voice "engagingly pleasant." Yet when women entered the room, Hamilton adopted a "social and playful manner, as though in this he was alone ambitious to excel."

Both men had known hardship, but where Morris's wounds were physical, Hamilton's were psychic. Born to an unwed mother in the West Indies, abandoned by his father, orphaned at eleven, he had been forging himself ever since. Ambition was his armor. Unlike Morris, he lacked the balm of humor.

Hamilton's outlook grew darker after the death of his nineteen-year-old son, Philip, killed in a duel in 1801. "Never did I see a man so completely overwhelmed with grief," a friend wrote. Even after returning to work, "his countenance [was] strongly stamped with sorrow." The tragedy had stripped away the last of Hamilton's optimism. "Perhaps no man in the United States has sacrificed or done more for the present Constitution than myself," he wrote to Morris at the end of February 1802, "[and] yet I have the murmurs of its friends no less than the curses of its foes for my rewards. . . . Every day proves to me more and more that this American world was not made for me."

Hamilton added, half in jest, half in despair, that Morris, too, was out of step with the times. "You, friend Morris," he wrote, "are by *birth* a native of this country, but by *genius* an exotic. You mistake if you fancy you are more a favorite than myself." Morris replied with the same dry self-possession that had steadied him since Paris. "You say I am not more a favorite than you are—I believe that I am much less a favorite."

By spring, however, his own doubts had begun to bloom. Writing to Robert R. Livingston, now minister to France, Morris lamented what he saw as the dismantling of the federal framework he had helped build. "We have here as yet done nothing of importance," he wrote with acid irony, "except destroying the Constitution by repealing the judiciary law of last session." The government, he said, was "reducing the military establishment" and repealing taxes "because our wise ones think they have too much revenue."

When the session finally ended in May, he called on Jefferson out of courtesy. The old Parisian cordiality was gone; instead, the president was "as cold as a frog."

That summer, Gouverneur retreated to Morrisania, where he found more success tending to his gardens and friendships. Robert and Mary Morris came to stay, weary from scandal and debt. "[Robert] came to me lean, low-spirited, and as poor as a commission of bankruptcy can make a man," Gouverneur told John Parish. "I sent him home fat, sleek, in good spirits, and possessed of the means of living comfortably the rest of his days. So much for the air of Morrisania." The grand business ventures the two had once plotted in Europe—schemes of debt conversion and land speculation—had evaporated. What remained was friendship and loyalty.

On February 1, 1803, the New York legislature—now firmly Republican—voted against reelecting Morris to the Senate. "My political enemies have had the goodness to relieve me," he wrote to John Dickinson of Delaware, his old colleague from the Constitutional Convention. The Federalists were spent, the Jeffersonians triumphant. If "the voice of my country should call for my services," he added, "they shall certainly be rendered—but I hope that no such circumstances will arise."

After decades of war, diplomacy, and revolution, Gouverneur Morris was ready, or so he claimed, to happily "trifle life away."

★

Aaron Burr's dalliance with the Federalists during the deadlocked 1800 election had poisoned his relationship with Jefferson, and he knew the president planned to drop him from the Republican ticket in 1804. To salvage his political career, Burr turned his attention to the governorship of New York, which he hoped to win by cobbling together a coalition of Federalists and disaffected Republicans.

Some New York Federalists—resentful of Virginia's dominance in national politics and alarmed by the possibility that slavery might expand westward after the 1803 Louisiana Purchase—flirted with the idea of secession. They whispered of a Northern confederacy, with New York at its head. Burr, ever the opportunist, let them believe he might support it.

Hamilton stood apart from the would-be secessionists. "You know there cannot be any political confidence between Mr. Jefferson and his administration and myself," he reportedly said. "But I view the suggestion of such a project with *horror*." Federalist leaders, recognizing that no candidate of their own could prevail—Jefferson's popularity after the Louisiana Purchase was near its zenith—resolved to back the least objectionable Republican. When they met in Albany to make their choice, Hamilton argued passionately against Burr. He still distrusted him and feared that, as governor, Burr would act on the secessionist plot. Burr, in turn, seethed. "Hamilton is intriguing for any candidate who can have success against A[aron] B[urr]," he told his daughter.

The press joined the fray. On March 1, 1804, the *American Citizen*—a Republican newspaper in New York—printed a scathing attack that echoed Hamilton's long-standing assessment of his rival: "General Hamilton did not oppose Mr. Burr because he was a *democrat* . . . but because HE HAD NO PRINCIPLE, either in morals or in politics." Its editor, James Cheetham, claimed to possess a list of "*upwards of twenty women of ill fame* with whom [Burr] has been connected," along with another of "chaste and respectable ladies whom he had attempted to *seduce*." Anonymous broadsides plastered on New York's taverns and street corners made similar charges. Burr blamed Hamilton.

Burr tried to weather the storm, but the April vote was devastating:

He lost in a landslide to Gouverneur's old friend Morgan Lewis—30,829 to 22,139. Burr's political career lay in ruins, and he held Hamilton responsible.

It was a dinner party in March, however, that sealed their fate. Hamilton, in conversation, reportedly called Burr "a dangerous man, and one who ought not to be trusted." Weeks later, a physician named Charles Cooper, who had been present, alluded to Hamilton's remark in a private letter. Extracts from the letter appeared in the *New-York Evening Post.* Hamilton's father-in-law, Philip Schuyler, rushed to his defense, prompting Cooper to double down with a second letter—this time claiming that he had been "unusually cautious," since he could "detail . . . a still more despicable opinion which General Hamilton has expressed of Mr. Burr." In other words, Hamilton had said even worse things about Burr.

The *Albany Register* printed that letter on April 24. When Burr read it on June 18, his fury boiled over. Feverish and wrapped in scarves, he summoned a confidant, William P. Van Ness, to his estate at Richmond Hill and dictated a challenge. Van Ness carried the note to Hamilton's office. Burr demanded an explanation.

Hamilton's reply—cool, legalistic, and evasive—only enraged him further. "'Tis evident," Hamilton wrote, "that the phrase 'still more despicable' admits of infinite shades, from very light to very dark. How am I to judge of the degree intended?" The exchanges that followed devolved into insults. On June 27, Van Ness delivered a formal challenge to a duel to Hamilton's second, Judge Nathaniel Pendleton—Burr's way of demanding satisfaction according to the code of honor.

Neither man could back down. "Everything in Alexander Hamilton's life pointed to the fact that he would not dodge a duel or negotiate a compromise," historian Ron Chernow observed in his biography of Hamilton. He "was incapable of turning the other cheek." The duel was set for July 11, 1804, five days after Hamilton concluded his Supreme Court work, so that no client would be left unattended.

At dawn that Wednesday, two small boats slipped across the

Hudson toward the cliffs of Weehawken, New Jersey. One carried Burr and Van Ness, the other Hamilton and Pendleton. The Hudson River Palisades form a steep cliff at Weehawken, rising nearly two hundred feet above the river. At low tide, the receding water revealed a slender beach, with a narrow path leading to a rocky ledge, about twenty feet above the river. Edged by boulders and mostly hidden by the trees, the ledge provided the discreet ground so often chosen for "affairs of honor."

Burr and Van Ness arrived at half past six and scrabbled up the path. Reaching the ledge, they removed their jackets and cleared away some underbrush and debris while they waited for Hamilton and Pendleton. The second barge touched the beach a little before seven o'clock. In addition to Hamilton and Pendleton, it carried Dr. David Hosack, a surgeon who waited below the ledge—close enough to provide emergency aid, but far enough away to avoid being a witness to whatever transpired above.

When the duelists and their seconds were on the ledge, Pendleton and Van Ness marked out ten paces and drew lots to determine which man would stand on which side. Then the seconds loaded the pistols, ornate weapons with lacquered walnut handles and gold mountings along their brass barrels. Hamilton and Burr stood sideways, to narrow their silhouettes. Hamilton asked for a moment to put on his spectacles. After retrieving them from his pocket and putting them on, he aimed his pistol in several directions before indicating he was ready to proceed.

"*Present*," Pendleton said, signaling Hamilton and Burr to raise their pistols.

The sharp crack of pistols split the air.

TWENTY-THREE

THE DEATH OF HAMILTON

That afternoon, Gouverneur's nephew brought the horrifying news to Morrisania: Alexander Hamilton was dead, shot by Vice President Aaron Burr in a duel. When Morris ventured into town the next day, however, he learned that Hamilton was still alive—barely.

After the duel, Pendleton and Hosack had carried Hamilton down the path, laid him in the bottom of the boat, and set out for Manhattan. "Let Mrs. Hamilton be immediately sent for," the wounded man gasped as they neared the dock belonging to his friend William Bayard, the director of the Bank of New York. "Let the event be gradually broken to her, but give her hopes." Hamilton, Pendleton, and Hosack had departed that morning from Bayard's dock; Bayard was waiting there when they returned. Spying his friend sprawled in the bottom of the boat, the bank director began to weep. Servants placed Hamilton on a cot and carried him to a second-floor bedroom in Bayard's mansion, located at what is now 80-82 Jane Street in lower Manhattan.

Morris rushed to Hamilton's side as soon as he heard that his friend was still alive. There were more than twenty family members and friends packed into the darkened chamber, most of them kneeling in prayer. Morris was so overcome by the scene that he fled to Bayard's garden, where he walked until he could regain his composure. The previous day, Hamilton had tried to comfort his wife by urging her to take solace in her spirituality—"Remember my Eliza, you are a Christian," he repeated—but now Hamilton could hardly speak. As the end drew near, Eliza held up their two-year-old son Philip—named for his slain older brother—so his father could kiss him goodbye. Then she lined up all seven of their children at the foot of his bed. "He opened his eyes, gave them one look, and closed them again till they were taken away," Hosack recalled. When Hamilton died at two in the afternoon on Thursday, July 12, 1804, Morris was sitting next to him.

Eliza read the letter her husband had left for her, then called Morris into another room. Weeping, she told him he had been her husband's best friend (notwithstanding Hamilton's subversion of Morris's diplomatic mission to London more than a decade before). She begged him to join her in praying for her own death, and to act as her children's father when she was gone. "The big tears that flowed down Morris's cheek bespoke the anguish of his soul," one witness recalled. That evening, Morris was asked to deliver a funeral oration, but he wasn't sure he could manage it. "I promise to do so if I can possibly command myself enough, but express my belief that it will be utterly impossible," he wrote. "I am wholly unmanned by this day's spectacle."

Morris wasn't just worried about holding himself together; he agonized over what he should say. His "indiscreet and opinionated" friend had lived a complicated life and had espoused some beliefs that Morris found troubling. This "stranger of illegitimate birth" had publicly admitted to cheating on his wife—that was messy enough. Even worse, in Morris's view, was that Hamilton "was on principle opposed to republican and attached to monarchical government." This was an overstatement—and a curious one coming from a man who, like Hamilton, believed in a strong executive and had been unfairly accused of being a monarchist. And then there was the manner of Hamilton's death: He had been killed in a duel, despite being firmly opposed to the practice. Morris was wary of fueling partisan strife by casting too much blame on Burr. "I cannot thoroughly excuse him without criminating Colonel Burr, which would be wrong and might lead to events which every good citizen must deprecate," he wrote in his diary. Morris didn't have much time to figure it all out. "In addition to all the difficulties of this subject is the impossibility of writing and committing anything to memory in the short time allowed," he fretted. "The corpse is already putrid and the funeral procession must take place tomorrow morning."

On Saturday morning, mourners gathered in front of the Robinson Street (now Park Place) home of John Church and his wife Angelica, Hamilton's beloved sister-in-law. Every shop in the city was shuttered. Church bells chimed, guns fired from the Battery, and ships in the harbor flew their flags at half-mast. The funeral procession began around noon, led by New York militia units marching to the doleful beat of muffled drums. The soldiers, the muzzles of their weapons flipped toward the cobblestones, were followed by clergymen and members of the Society of the Cincinnati, founded in 1783 by officers of the Continental Army. Then came Bayard and seven other pallbearers carrying the mahogany casket, with Hamilton's hat and sword on top. Two young Black servants wearing white turbans led Hamilton's riderless gray horse, clopping behind the casket with the fallen general's empty boots reversed in the stirrups. Hamilton's four eldest sons walked behind the horse, followed by other relatives, foreign diplomats, and a wide assortment of New Yorkers: politicians, lawyers, doctors, merchants, ship captains, artisans, and Columbia College (the new name of King's College) students and professors. People lined the streets, filled every door and window, and perched on roofs to watch the procession pass by. Many women were weeping.

Morris rode in a carriage. Even as the procession threaded through Beekman, Pearl, and Whitehall Streets and crawled up Broadway to Trinity Church, he was grappling with how to eulogize his friend. How could he mention the duel, without inciting the crowd against Burr? He was reluctant to dwell on Hamilton's domestic life, given his well-publicized affair with Maria Reynolds. But how else could he arouse pity for a family left in desperate financial straits? It was nearly two o'clock when Morris rose to speak, standing on a stage hastily constructed in the portico of the church. He was flanked by Hamilton's sons, who were six, eleven, sixteen, and eighteen. "Far from attempting to excite your emotions, I must try to repress my own," he began, "and yet I fear that instead of the language of a public speaker, you will hear only the lamentations of a bewailing friend." Morris took a deep breath—he was "so much affected," the *New-York Evening Post* reported, it "almost deprived him of the power of utterance." Gouverneur soldiered on, running through some of the highlights of Hamilton's legendary life: brilliant scholar at King's College; military aide to Washington; victorious officer at Yorktown; delegate to the Constitutional Convention. Seizing on this last accomplishment, he deftly defended Hamilton's—and his own—controversial stances during the summer of 1787. Hamilton had argued that the new republic required a strong central government and had even suggested a president and senators serving for life—ideas that to many smacked of monarchy. "In signing that compact [the Constitution] he expressed his apprehension that it did not contain sufficient means of strength for its own preservation, and that in consequence we should share the fate of many other republics and pass through anarchy to despotism," Morris said. "We hoped better things. We confided in the good sense of the American people, and above all we trusted in the protecting Providence of the Almighty."

Morris said Americans had benefited from Hamilton's fidelity to his unpopular beliefs, "saving your dearest interests, as it were, in spite of yourselves." He concluded by urging his listeners to control their anger at Burr. "You all know how [Hamilton] perished. On this last scene, I cannot, I must not dwell. It might excite emotions too strong for your better judgment," he said. "Suffer not your indignation to lead to any act which might again offend the insulted majesty of the law." Morris was not used to speaking outside, and many of his words dissolved in the open air. He suspected he had disappointed even the small fraction of the audience that could hear him. "I find that what I have said does not meet the general expectation," he reflected later. "This I knew would be the case—it must even happen to him whose duty it is to allay the sentiment which he is expected to rouse. How easy would it have been to make them for a moment absolutely mad!"

Posterity judged the eulogy much as Morris had feared: less a stirring oration than an act of moral composure. Yet in its restraint lay its power. Where others demanded retribution, Morris offered dignity; where grief might have flamed into civil chaos, he preached order and mercy. History came to see it not as a failure of passion, but as the last service one founder could render another—a farewell that steadied a mourning nation rather than inflaming it.

★

As 1804 ended, Morris was increasingly disappointed by the policies—and popularity—of Jefferson's administration. To Morris, Jefferson's program pointed toward the erosion of national strength: a retreat from federal power, a shrinking army and navy, and a naive faith that a republic could survive without the firm scaffolding of central authority. Yet true to his temperament, he retained hope that his countrymen would eventually come to their senses—a faith not unlike that of his late friend Hamilton, who had also believed that experience, not argument, would teach Americans the value of order. "Nations, like individuals, are not to be reasoned out of vice, much less out of folly, but learn wisdom and virtue in the school of application," Morris wrote on December 28 to Aaron Ogden, a New Jersey lawyer and entrepreneur with whom he had served in the Senate.

The quiet of Morrisania now seemed the proper antidote to the noise of Washington. For the next several years, Morris largely stayed at his estate, where he lived "literally like a nobleman," according to Jonathan Mason of Massachusetts, who had served with him in the Senate and visited in the fall of 1804. One is "continually attracted by a profusion of plate, gold and mirror," Mason wrote in his diary. "He has all this world can give him but a good wife and amiable children. . . . He also laments that he did not, twenty years since, unite his talents with some corresponding female mind to make each other happy."

Though public life no longer claimed Morris, the habits of activity remained. His remit now measured not in debate or diplomacy, but in business and the care of property. He made quick trips to the city to conduct transactions and occasional jaunts upstate to look at land he owned. In the summer of 1806, for example, he made two trips upstate, where he bathed in mineral waters and reveled in his physical prowess, proud that neither his wooden leg nor his advancing age impeded his ability to paddle, hike, or ride. "I row about nine miles on our return, the boatmen being much jaded and besides not excellent at the oar," he wrote after a late-August excursion on Lake George, and "am the least fatigued of our party." Even so, he was periodically plagued by flare-ups of gout, and the amputation of his leg could still cause him discomfort. In August 1805, he complained of "a good deal of pain from an ugly little ulcer which has tormented the stump of my amputated leg for near two months."

Financially, things could have been better. He had a hard time finding buyers for his upstate properties, and the Lafayettes still had not repaid the large loan he had given them. He kept busy organizing Hamilton's papers and overseeing the workers who were still repairing and refurbishing Morrisania after his long absence. For recreation, he read, wrote, socialized, and fished.

On July 22, 1808, he wrote a muted entry in his diary that offered no hint of the day's towering significance. "A little rain this morning which clears away at nine. Go to Mr. Varick's to see Mr. DeWitt who is in town—call at Alderman Lennox's and on Martin Wilkins and Mr. Popham," he recorded. "Then visit Miss Randolph at Mrs. Pollock's to answer letter from Rhode Island."

TWENTY-FOUR

MR. MORRIS TAKES A BRIDE

Morris first encountered Ann Cary Randolph, known as Nancy, in the 1780s. She was the daughter of Colonel Thomas Mann Randolph, a member of one of Virginia's most prominent families and a close friend of Jefferson's. The Randolphs owned Tuckahoe, a plantation on the James River west of Richmond. Twice during that decade, Morris visited Tuckahoe while managing Robert Morris's tobacco contracts. If he noticed Nancy, who was only thirteen when he last visited in 1788, he made no mention of her in his letters.

A year later, Nancy's older sister Judith married her first cousin Richard Randolph, and later Nancy went to live with the couple at Bizarre, their plantation on the Appomattox River. Before long, misfortune and rumor would conspire to make her name infamous.

Richard's younger brothers, Theodorick and John, were both infatuated with Nancy and proposed to her in turn. She accepted Theodorick's suit, but he died of tuberculosis in February 1792, before they could marry or even announce their engagement. That September, Richard, Judith, Nancy, and John traveled to Glentivar, a cousin's estate thirty miles away. What happened that night became one of the most notorious scandals of early America.

Nancy arrived feeling unwell, dressed oddly for the warm weather in a heavy buttoned coat. She retired early to a small upstairs bedroom adjoining the one Richard and Judith shared. In the middle of the night, screams pierced the quiet house. When their hostess, Mary Harrison, rushed upstairs with laudanum to help, Richard barred her from entering Nancy's room. Later, footsteps were heard descending the stairs, but by dawn, the household fell into uneasy silence. The next morning, Nancy stayed in bed while the others went out. Two days later, the Randolphs departed.

Soon, whispers spread across Virginia. Servants at Glentivar, it was said, had found the body of a white infant on a pile of shingles outside. The story grew darker with every retelling: Nancy had given birth, Richard was the father, and he had murdered the child to hide their affair, which under Virginia law was incestuous because Richard was Nancy's brother-in-law.

To clear his name, Richard published a letter in the *Virginia Gazette and General Advertiser* in April 1793 proclaiming his innocence and inviting his accusers to confront him. He announced that he would appear at the next session of the county court to meet them face-to-face. But when he arrived at court to defend himself, the sheriff was waiting with a warrant. Richard was arrested for "feloniously murdering a child said to be borne of Nancy Randolph."

Richard turned to two of Virginia's most celebrated lawyers for his defense—Patrick Henry, the Revolutionary War orator who had declared "Give me liberty or give me death!," and John Marshall, who would become the nation's longest-serving Supreme Court chief justice. They refused to concede that Nancy had been pregnant, let alone that a child had been born. Under Virginia law, their case was helped by the fact that the Black witnesses who had discovered the dead baby on the shingles were barred from testifying against white defendants. Judith, meanwhile, stood firmly beside her husband and sister. The jury quickly acquitted Richard of all charges.

The verdict meant that legally, Nancy was innocent too, but her reputation was destroyed. In defending Richard, Henry and Marshall implied that if she had given birth, the father must have been her late fiancé, Theodorick. Virginia's moral codes were harsh: premarital relations, even with a betrothed, were viewed as shameful and was illegal in most of eighteenth-century America. (It would not become legal in Virginia until 2020.) Though the courts had cleared her, the stain of scandal made Nancy a poor prospect for marriage. She remained with Judith and Richard, who continued to support her.

When Richard died suddenly of fever in 1796, the household at Bizarre fell into decline. John, distraught over his brother's death, took over the plantation, but tobacco prices were declining and Richard had left the family deeply in debt. To make matters worse, the family had recently concluded that the eldest of Judith and Richard's two sons, five-year-old St. George, was deaf and mute. In that somber house, Nancy's vitality only deepened the resentments of others. Her laughter and love of life clashed with John Randolph's bitterness; in the spring of 1805, he asked her to leave—banishing her from Bizarre, the only home she had left.

Homeless and disgraced, Nancy made her way north. She stayed briefly in Rhode Island, perhaps teaching to survive, and later in Fairfield, Connecticut, where she befriended a widow, Mrs. Pollock, who owned a boardinghouse at 54 Greenwich Street in New York City.

From there, she wrote to Gouverneur Morris, hoping he might remember the girl he had once met at Tuckahoe and offer kindness to a woman now nearly penniless. After they met again at Mrs. Pollock's in October 1808, she wrote to thank him for his generosity in visiting her and for the simple courtesy that few others had shown her. "Talk not of gratitude, my dear Madam," Morris replied in March 1809, "but communicate so much of your situation as may enable me to be useful." He brushed away the gossip that had haunted her for years, telling her that virtue lay in "a pure heart, a chastened spirit, fortitude, benevolence, charity."

Morris was fifty-seven, a lifelong bachelor famed for his wit and gallantry; Nancy, thirty-four, was still beautiful, if weary from scandal. Their correspondence grew frequent and tender. Morris proposed that she come to Morrisania as his housekeeper—a respectable position, though he hinted that affection might grow between them. "Time, in taking away the ardor, has not wholly quelled the rashness of youth," he wrote. "I can only answer that I will love you as little as I can." Nancy accepted.

On April 28, 1809, he drove to Mrs. Pollock's boardinghouse and brought Nancy home. By December, affection had deepened into attachment, and Morris—mindful of his public stature—sought reassurance from his old acquaintance John Marshall, now chief justice. He asked what reputation Miss Randolph had left in Virginia. Marshall replied that the affair had been "ambiguous," the rumors "invented by the malignant," and that Judith Randolph herself, who had the best reason to believe Nancy guilty, had kept her under her roof for years afterward.

That was enough for Morris. On Christmas Day 1809, before a gathering of unsuspecting nieces, nephews, and cousins at Morrisania, he married Nancy Randolph. He gave her a string of pearls; she wore a patched gown, one of only two she owned. "I glory that I was married in a gown patched at the elbows," she wrote to a friend.

His family was scandalized. His relatives, who had expected to inherit his estate, called the marriage folly. One niece, Gertrude Meredith of Philadelphia, even wrote to scold him for marrying beneath him. Morris replied with characteristic wit and finality: "If the world were to live with my wife, I should certainly have consulted its taste; but as that happens not to be the case, I thought I might, without offending others, endeavor to suit myself, and look rather into the head and heart than into the pocket."

Gouverneur Morris had at last done what he had spent a lifetime avoiding: he had chosen permanence over pleasure, affection over ambition. And in doing so, he found in Nancy Randolph—the woman the world had cast aside—the partner he had long claimed not to need.

TWENTY-FIVE

A GRAND CANAL

DeWitt Clinton hadn't come to western New York for sport. He was reconnoitering a route that, if it could be cut through this mud and timber, would bind the interior of America to the Atlantic coast. The vision wasn't his alone. For decades, Morris had insisted that a man-made river could marry the Great Lakes to the Hudson—and make New York master of the continent.

The inn where Clinton was staying on July 15, 1810, was cramped, filthy, and filled with noisy drunks—and that included the innkeeper, his wife, and their son. Even so, he hoped for a restful night's sleep after a grueling day on the water. Though just forty-one, Clinton had just finished his second stint as New York mayor; now he was traveling across the state on an official mission that would shape his city's future.

The inn was at a place called Three-River Point, named for the confluence of the Oneida, Seneca, and Oswego Rivers, about one hundred and fifty miles northwest of Albany. When Clinton arrived shortly before sundown, a respectable-looking girl showed him a room crowded with cupboards and a weaver's loom, but it had two beds and was, she assured him, *not* infested with bedbugs. It certainly seemed preferable to the rooms in the attic, which *were* populated with bedbugs, the girl admitted—and by several "villainous-looking fellows" who were unappealing roommates. Clinton left the attic rooms to three of his companions, while he bunked with a fourth in the room downstairs.

Soon after he tumbled into bed, Clinton wondered if he had made a mistake. He was assaulted by the stench of boiled pork, and the raucous drunks in the next room couldn't drown out the crickets chirping in the hearth and the rats scrabbling in the walls. Mosquitoes and bats whizzed around his head. Women trudged in and out of the room to fetch plates, knives, and spoons from the cupboards, and when they did, dogs scampered under his bed. Clinton also heard his restless colleagues rolling around in their beds upstairs—tortured, no doubt, by the bedbugs. He congratulated himself on escaping that torment, until he lit a candle and examined his own sheets. The girl had lied: his room was infested with bedbugs, too.

Clinton got dressed, lit a cigar, and went outside, where another companion was sleeping in a tent. The moon was full, and he sat down on a hill overlooking the spot where the Oneida and Seneca Rivers combined into a single majestic torrent. A number of boats were moored on the banks, and flocks of white geese frolicked on the water. Frogs croaked, bloodhounds barked. Outside a hut on the opposite shore, an Indian man and his family prepared for the coming day. Settling into a tranquil state of mind, Clinton stumbled into the tent and found a spare mattress, where he collapsed into a couple hours of sleep.

★

Over the years, Morris had often expounded on his dream of a man-made waterway, hundreds of miles long, connecting New York City to the interior of the continent. This grand canal, he proclaimed, would unleash the nation's economic potential, bind the original states on the Atlantic Seaboard to the nascent states beyond the Appalachian Mountains, and make New York City the hemisphere's dominant metropolis. As it was, people and trade were largely confined to coastal areas, cut off from the valuable farmland, timber, and minerals of the Northwest Territory—the future states of Illinois, Indiana, Michigan, Ohio, Wisconsin, and part of Minnesota. It took weeks to cross the mountains on the rutted turnpike roads, mostly old Indian trails that were oppressively dusty in dry weather, a muddy slop the rest of the time. In the swampiest areas, the roads were made up of logs laid across the path with earth between them, to keep the route from sinking into the marsh. Travelers had to ford many of the streams that crossed the route, since there were few bridges. Without a strong connection to the coast, he and many others feared, the lands west of the mountains might be seized by a European power or even become their own country, leaving the original thirteen states pinched between the mountains and the sea.

Morris was consumed by the idea of a canal even during the bleakest days of the Revolutionary War, when it didn't seem likely the United States would win its independence, let alone develop the continent. In the summer of 1777, after the British forced General Philip Schuyler (Alexander Hamilton's future father-in-law) and his troops to abandon Fort Ticonderoga, Washington sent Morris and several other men to meet with Schuyler at Fort Edward, about fifty miles north of Albany. Washington wanted his emissaries to suss out the strategic situation; Morris regaled the group with descriptions of his canal, declaring that "at no very distant day, the waters of the great western inland seas, would, by the aid of man, break through their barriers and mingle with those of the Hudson," according to his boyhood friend Morgan Lewis, who was also at Schuyler's headquarters. Many streams already ran along the desired path, Morris pointed out, so all that needed to be done was to dig deeper and wider waterways along the same route.

Morris's belief in the project was reinforced by the canal he saw in Scotland and by his trek to Niagara Falls and Lake Erie in 1800. Three years after that trip, he happened to be staying at the same Schenectady inn as the surveyor-general of New York State, Simeon De Witt. The two men passed the evening together, and Morris promoted his plan of "tapping Lake Erie," as De Witt recalled, and "leading its waters, in an artificial river, directly across the country to Hudson's river." A geographer who would retain his job as surveyor-general for fifty years, De Witt knew something about the region's topography, and he was skeptical: The hills and valleys between the lake and the river were "insuperable obstacles," he told Morris. The older man waved away De Witt's objections, insisting that "the object would justify the labor and expense, whatever that might be."

The surveyor considered the idea "a romantic thing, and characteristic of the man." Nevertheless, he mentioned it to other leading New Yorkers, including at least one state legislator. He also discussed it with a struggling flour merchant from Geneva, New York, named Jesse Hawley. Hawley was frustrated by the time and money it took to ship flour to New York City—and it took longer and cost more in the summer months, when the water level in the Mohawk River dropped. In 1806, Hawley went bankrupt and was sentenced to twenty months in debtors' prison. During his confinement in 1807 and 1808, he wrote a series of fourteen essays for the *Genessee Messenger* explaining the need for a canal and laying out—in great detail—how it might be constructed. Many settlers in central New York, who were producing more crops but struggling to get them to market, welcomed Hawley's public-relations gambit. Joshua Forman, a member of the state assembly from the region, was well aware of his constituents' concerns. In 1808, he introduced a resolution calling for a survey of a possible canal route. The legislature approved the survey—but allocated just six hundred dollars to get it done. Forman was undaunted; he didn't expect his colleagues to pony up any *state* money for the canal. Instead, the resolution hopefully stated that *Congress* would surely spend whatever it took to realize "that great national project."

After all, the federal government had money to spare. In his second inaugural address in 1805, President Jefferson had touted the nation's growing budget surplus, boasting that the government would retire the national debt ahead of schedule. He suggested "the revenue thus liberated" might be used to build and improve "rivers, canals, roads, arts, manufactures, education, and other great objects within each state." Two years later the surplus was larger still, and Jefferson again recommended federal spending on internal improvements. Forman took him at his word. At the beginning of 1809, he went to Washington to lobby Jefferson. Forman began his meeting with the president by ticking off the many benefits of the canal: it would promote settlement of western lands and enhance their value; open a channel of commerce between those territories and Atlantic ports; speed the movement of troops and supplies in case of war; and cement the union among the states. Jefferson, an inventor and innovator with a passion for technology, listened intently before rendering a verdict: The New Yorkers were nuts. The project "might be executed a century hence," Jefferson allowed, but it couldn't possibly be built anytime soon. The president noted that a much smaller Potomac River canal project, pushed by none other than George Washington, had stalled because nobody would fork over the two hundred thousand dollars necessary to complete it. "And you talk of making a canal of three hundred and fifty miles through the wilderness!" Jefferson exclaimed. "It is little short of madness to think of it at this day." Forman was unbowed. With federal help or without, he told the president, New York would "never rest until it was accomplished."

In March 1810, New York state legislators appointed a seven-member, bipartisan commission to determine the feasibility and cost of building the canal. They tapped Morris, a prominent Federalist, to chair the panel, and DeWitt Clinton, the former New York mayor, as its leading Republican member. Morris was eager to serve and as bullish as ever about what a canal would do for New York and America—he just doubted state and federal leaders were wise enough to pay for it. The project was "the most extensive theater for the display of skill and industry which can be found on this globe," he wrote to the Washington, D.C., architect Benjamin Henry Latrobe, who had designed and built the Capitol's south wing, "but I fear that our minds are not yet enlarged to the size of so great an object."

★

When Clinton stayed at the Three-River Point inn in July 1810, he was eleven days into a summer-long trip to explore the likely canal route. He and several of his fellow canal commissioners traveled together on a bateau, a flat-bottomed boat equipped with sails, but which also could be propelled by long poles and oars. They embarked from Schenectady on July 4, planning to travel up the Mohawk River as far west as they could go, roughly one hundred miles to Rome, New York. The commissioners jokingly called their bateau the *Eddy*, in honor of their colleague Thomas Eddy, a Quaker merchant and social reformer. The vessel had an awning and curtains, to protect the passengers from the sun and rain, and was manned by a captain and crew. A second bateau carrying about a ton and a half of baggage and provisions trailed behind them. They named that boat the *Morris*—but their chairman was not with them.

Having toured Europe and made several expeditions upstate, fifty-eight-year-old Gouverneur knew better than to brave an adventure on the river. Instead, he and Nancy explored the proposed canal route in a luxurious carriage, trailed by a second coach carrying their French cook. They also brought along an English painter named James Sharples, who had been a houseguest at Morrisania while he painted the couple's portraits. The Morrises had entertained Sharples and his wife Ellen in high style, serving them three-course dinners each day on "a magnificent service of silver" and dessert on "the most beautiful French china," according to Ellen. Her husband was eager to see Niagara Falls, so Gouverneur invited him to come along. In addition to the French cook, the Morrises' second coach carried servants and "every luxury that could be thought of, that no inconvenience might be experienced in passing through the uncultivated part of the country," Ellen wrote.

On July 24, Morris and his party viewed Niagara's Horseshoe Falls from Table Rock, on the Canadian side of the border. Gouverneur was overwhelmed—despite having seen the falls before. Wondering why, he decided that his mind just couldn't absorb the enormity of what he was seeing, no matter how many times he saw it. Clinton and the other river travelers didn't arrive until a week later. The former mayor had never seen the falls before, and he was transfixed. "The spray of the waters enveloped us with a mist as penetrating as rain," he gushed after taking in the same view from Table Rock. Clinton was fascinated to hear that some animals that plunged over the falls somehow survived. "There is a dog at Chippewa which escaped with a broken rib, and two sheep were once found below the cataract, one of which was alive," he wrote in his journal. "On the other hand, the chance is greatly against life. Wild geese, fish, deer, and other creatures are to be seen dashed to pieces." The commissioners dined together several times over the next couple of days and held one official meeting. Apparently, there were disagreements over how to proceed, though neither Clinton nor Morris detailed what they were. "I suspect that when we come to make up our report, there will be a variety of opinions and I fear that the most correct will not be the most prevalent," Morris wrote on August 3.

The next day, the commissioners began the long journey home. On the way, the Morrises visited a community of Shakers, a religious sect known for their frenetic style of worship. An offshoot of the Quakers, they espoused celibacy, communal living, and trance dancing. Morris listened to a sermon denigrating "worldly pursuits, pleasures and enjoyments, and, more especially, the conjugal pleasures." He thought it was ridiculous; rejecting recreational sex was "an unnatural (and therefore impious) doctrine."

Gouverneur and Nancy returned to Morrisania on September 7. Six months later, the canal commission issued a report calling for a single, continuous waterway from Albany to Lake Erie. The commissioners estimated the cost at five million dollars (about $127 million in 2026 dollars), and recommended that state leaders seek federal funding rather than private or state loans. By this time, James Madison had succeeded the skeptical Jefferson as president, and the commissioners hoped Madison and Congress would see that "too great a national interest" was at stake to deny New York the money. In December 1811, Morris and Clinton traveled to Washington to make the case. They met with Madison, Vice President George Clinton, and various members of Madison's cabinet, and testified before the House of Representatives. More than a dozen years later, a congressman vividly recalled Morris's "grand and luminous" testimony, which demolished the "ignorance and prejudice" of his skeptical listeners. The initial response from Madison and other administration officials was somewhat positive, even though some of them snickered that Clinton was using the canal project as a launching pad for his presidential ambitions. Morris and Clinton delayed their departure from Washington for several weeks, hoping that Congress would move forward.

★

Even as he awaited Congress's decision on the canal, Morris was deeply engaged in another project vital to New York's future: the creation of the Manhattan street grid.

The population of New York City (which was just Manhattan until 1874) doubled between 1790 and 1800. By 1810, New York was America's largest city, with nearly a hundred thousand residents, and its undisputed commercial capital. The burgeoning metropolis had steadily marched north from the southern tip of Manhattan Island, outstripping its warren of short streets, country lanes, and Native American and animal trails. It was an increasingly chaotic place, where dogs and hogs roamed freely, excrement overflowed from privies, and stagnant water bred mosquitoes. Refuse and offal clogged the streets, sidewalks were uneven, and there were frequent fires. Residents lived in fear of yellow fever, cholera, consumption, typhus, and smallpox, scourges which killed thousands when they swept through the city. City leaders agreed that New York needed a rational street plan to guide its growth.

In 1807, the city's governing council appointed Morris, the surveyor Simeon De Witt, and John Rutherfurd, a businessman and former New Jersey senator who happened to be married to Morris's niece, to draw up that plan. The three men rode all over Manhattan to explore its farthest reaches, then hired a young surveyor named John Randel Jr., who was only in his early twenties, to map it. Every morning, Randel hiked from his home in lower Manhattan to the panel's headquarters at the corner of Christopher and Herring (now Bleecker) Streets, which was then in the country. One landmark along the way was Thomas Paine's house, where in fair weather Randel always saw the political philosopher in his window, absorbed in a book with his chin resting on his left hand and a decanter of rum or brandy on the table in front of him. Randel and his assistants spent their days rambling over every inch of the island, sometimes tromping through thickly wooded areas that were "impassable without the aid of an ax." They also had to contend with angry property owners and squatters who didn't relish thc idea of the city running new streets through their land. When they saw Randel and his men approaching with their maps and measuring tools, they sicced their dogs on them or, on one occasion, pelted them with cabbages and artichokes. Late in the evenings, Randel trudged home through narrow streets sparsely lit by whale-oil lamps.

Randel later said that he tried to avoid "rocks, precipices, steep grades and other obstacles" in plotting the streets and avenues, but the map that Morris and his colleagues finally issued in the spring of 1811 essentially ignored the island's natural features. Their uncompromising grid plowed through hills and forests, swamps and streams. Morris was often accused of being an aristocrat or even a monarchist, but his plan (and it was largely drafted by Morris and De Witt, since Rutherfurd rarely attended the meetings) was positively democratic compared with the broad avenues and triumphant circles of royalist Europe. New York's avenues and streets would be numbered, not named for prominent personages. And its roughly two thousand city blocks (up to 155th Street), all the same size, would split up the country estates of the upper classes.

The plan laid out twelve avenues, each a hundred feet wide, running north from Houston Street (roughly the edge of town). Every two hundred feet, fifty- or sixty-foot-wide streets crossed the avenues at right angles. Every half mile or so, an east-west street widened to one hundred feet. The panel had no use for the circles, ovals, and stars that Pierre L'Enfant had used in designing Washington, D.C. Instead, its pragmatic grid system emphasized equality and uniformity. "Straight-sided and right-angled houses," the commissioners stated flatly in remarks drafted by Morris, "are the most cheap to build, and the most convenient to live in." Morris acknowledged that "it may be a subject of merriment that the commissioners have provided space for a greater population than is collected at any spot this side of China." But he projected that New York's population might quadruple by 1860, and preferred creating too much room for growth as opposed to too little. As it turned out, he and De Witt weren't optimistic enough: by 1850, there were more than half a million people living in Manhattan.

★

Frustrated by the inaction on Capitol Hill, in January 1812 Morris and Clinton went ahead and drew up a canal funding bill for Congress to consider. Morris was optimistic after they presented it to a House panel. "The most difficult point is accomplished," he wrote in his diary on January 11. "They might have met occasionally for a month without getting so far advanced. What remains is [to] get them into a humor to report the bill, instead of wasting weeks in amendments to make it worse." In a meeting with Madison two days later, however, the president cast doubt on the constitutionality of the measure, darkening its prospects. Meanwhile, a whispering campaign against Morris and Clinton erected unseen barriers. On January 12, Senator James Asheton Bayard wrote to a fellow Delaware Federalist that even though the New Yorkers' "ostensible object" was the canal, "the real one is supposed to be a political intrigue." Bayard told another correspondent that "the characters of the two men are pretty well-known and it is rather supposed that they mean to open a road to the presidency than a canal from the lakes."

There was a light dusting of snow on the ground when Morris went back to the House on January 16. He heard "favorable sentiment" from some members, but the committee chairman told him he was inclined to table the bill; New York would not be getting any help from Washington, at least not anytime soon. Morris left the capital for Morrisania at the end of the month.

Morris and Clinton chalked up Congress's reluctance to jealousy; New York State was growing in population and political power, and representatives of the states it had surpassed were loath to give it another boost. Whatever the reason, they weren't going to let it stop their canal. Several days after arriving home, Morris set out for Albany to tell state legislators what had happened and to propose next steps. Above all, Morris wrote in a March report, New York should ignore "the sneers and sarcasms of men, who, with too much pride to study, and too much wit to think, undervalue what they do not understand, and condemn what they cannot comprehend." If Washington would not provide the money, the report said, then New York could borrow it from European bankers. Morris was confident the state could obtain a five-million-dollar loan at an annual interest rate of about six percent.

Three months later, however, a second war with Great Britain would upend not only the prospects for the canal but also the fortunes of the nation—and Morris's place in it.

TWENTY-SIX

MR. MADISON'S WAR

The Greek temple loomed ghostly white in the dark. In another half-century, a soaring dome would join its twin sandstone wings, but on August 24, 1814, the US Capitol consisted of two unfinished blocks connected only by a wooden passageway. British troops advanced across the eastern grounds, formed a firing line, and sent a volley through the windows—testing for American sharpshooters who never answered back. A lieutenant kicked in the doors, and the soldiers surged inside.

What they found astonished them. Corinthian columns soared twenty-six feet into the air. A giant carved eagle presided over the rostrum. The craftsmanship, one officer sniffed, revealed that Americans were "somewhat infected with an unseemly bias for monarchical splendor." They fanned out into the empty chambers, helping themselves to souvenirs. A rear admiral pocketed a slim gilt-stamped volume marked *The President of the United States*—a ledger of federal revenues. In a room next to the Senate chamber, another soldier sliced the portraits of Louis XVI and Marie Antoinette from their frames.

At nearly ten that night, the admiral—forty-two-year-old Sir

George Cockburn—stood on the House rostrum beneath a marble sculpture of Liberty holding the Constitution in her hand. "Shall this harbor of Yankee democracy be burned?" he bellowed. His men shouted their assent.

In the House chamber, they chopped apart doors and paneling, tore down the visitors' gallery, and hurled furniture into a great heap in the center of the room. Rockets failed to ignite the metal-sheathed roof, but once all the mahogany chairs, desks, and tables were piled in the middle of the floor and doused in powder, a second barrage fired into the heap turned the chamber into a furnace so hot it cracked stone, melted glass, and burned marble to lime. The Senate wing went up quickly, its older timbers eager for flame. The Library of Congress vanished. The House's secret journals curled into ash. Red morocco chairs and silk curtains, paperwork and portraits, all fed the conflagration. Flames whooshed through the doors and windows, shot through the roof, and streaked toward the streets to the north and east, painting the night sky a blazing red. Across the city, the Navy Yard burned too—set ablaze by Americans desperate to deny its stores to the enemy. British reinforcements marching toward Washington found their way illuminated by the capital's funeral pyre.

★

President James Madison had galloped away from the White House that morning, dressed in his customary black and armed with two borrowed dueling pistols. Five days earlier, forty-five hundred British troops had disembarked at the Chesapeake Bay town of Benedict, Maryland, about forty-five miles southeast of Washington. Madison meant to ride eight miles east to the heights above Bladensburg to see how far the invaders had advanced, before returning for a dinner Dolley was preparing. She recalled his anxious question: Did she have "courage or firmness" to remain until his return? She assured him she feared only for him—and for their army.

Events would prove she had more courage than most of the men assigned to defend the capital.

At half past noon, American cannons and sharpshooters fired on British troops crossing the bridge into Bladensburg, but the redcoats—scarred veterans of Napoleon's wars—pressed forward. The British drove the American riflemen into the woods, an American surge chased the British troops back to the river's edge. The balance tipped when men under the command of a blue-eyed Irishman named Major General Robert Ross deployed Congreve rockets. The shrieking missiles—terrifying and unfamiliar—sent two American regiments reeling in panic. A third regiment held briefly, then crumpled when its flanks evaporated. Officers begged men to stand their ground. Few listened. The road to Washington was soon clogged with fleeing militiamen, giving the humiliating rout its enduring nickname: the "Bladensburg Races."

Madison and his cabinet secretaries, who had watched from the heights, had long since fled westward toward Virginia. Dolley received frantic penciled notes from her husband urging her to be ready "at a moment's warning" to flee. She loaded trunks with public and private papers, scanned the horizon through a spyglass, and saw only chaos: soldiers wandering aimlessly, citizens pouring across the bridge into Virginia, and horses and wagons jamming every road.

The two artillery crews assigned to protect the White House abandoned their posts. When dusty messengers arrived at three o'clock with word that Madison wanted her to flee, Dolley reluctantly agreed—but only after she and her servant used a carving knife and an ax to cut Gilbert Stuart's majestic portrait of George Washington from its frame. She entrusted the canvas to two New Yorkers who swore to keep it safe.

"I confess that I was so unfeminine as to be free from fear, and willing to remain in the Castle," she later wrote. "If I could have had a cannon through every window—but alas! Those who should have placed them there fled before me."

★

That night, as the Capitol smoldered, Cockburn and Ross led a hundred and fifty redcoats up Pennsylvania Avenue. They marched in eerie silence past scattered wooden houses until the avenue widened into a tree-lined promenade. At a boardinghouse, Ross politely requested supper from its panicked proprietor, Barbara Suter. Suter and her servant warmed up some bread and went out to kill a few chickens in the yard. At around eleven p.m., Ross, Cockburn, and their staff officers led a small detachment to the residence across the road, a fourteen-year-old whitewashed mansion that locals had begun calling "the White House."

Inside, the British found a dinner frozen in time: roasting joints, warming pots, a table set for forty with fine silver and crystal. The aroma of cooking meat lingered in the air. On the sideboard, they found ale, cider, and several kinds of wine, including the president's favorite Madeira, cooling in cut glass decanters. Most of the British soldiers were famished—they hadn't eaten since breakfast at five or six that morning—and they heartily dug in. They drank to the health of the prince regent, and to the triumph of British arms on sea and land. The British troops had scooped up a Washington bookseller on the way to the mansion and pressed him into service as a guide; Cockburn forced the humiliated man to drink to the health of "Jemmy" Madison. Satiated, they scavenged freely—seizing a medicine chest, the president's shirts, shoe buckles, a ceremonial sword—and stacked furniture for kindling.

"Our sailors," one navy captain boasted, "were artists at the work."

Fifty men ringed the mansion, thrust burning poles through its windows, and stepped back. The blaze leapt instantly—mahogany, velvet, damask, the pianoforte, draperies, even brass dissolved into molten drops. The French ambassador watched the inferno in awe: "I never saw a scene at once more terrible or more magnificent."

When a violent storm finally doused the flames, someone chalked a bitter epitaph on the Capitol's scorched stone: "George Washington founded this city after a seven years' war with England," the message read. "James Madison lost it after a two years' war."

★

Morris could not have foreseen the nightmare of August 24, 1814, but for nearly a decade he had warned that Jefferson's and Madison's policies were steering the nation toward disaster. The war that would squelch his Erie Canal dream—at least for the time being—had long been in the making.

The roots of the War of 1812 lay in the Napoleonic Wars. By 1803, Napoleon dominated much of continental Europe and was preparing to invade Britain. In trying to strangle each other's commerce, both France and Britain seized neutral American ships. British captains also impressed American sailors into the Royal Navy—disputing their citizenship, claiming them as British subjects, and dragging thousands into service. Perhaps as many as three-quarters of the men impressed from US ships were genuine Americans, but there were thousands of Royal Navy deserters on American vessels, and when the British boarded them, they often struggled to sort out their countrymen from Americans who looked and spoke English the same way. Phony American birth certificates circulated widely. Furthermore, the British refused to recognize the naturalization clause in the Constitution, which gave Congress the power to determine who could become a citizen; to them, many so-called Americans were actually British subjects.

Morris understood Britain had to take a tough line to discourage desertions, and that the Royal Navy was desperate to replenish its ranks to repel the threatened French invasion. Impressment was an affront to national honor, but to Morris it was a diplomatic challenge, not a justification for war.

Jefferson, determined to avoid conflict, responded with the Embargo Act of 1807, cutting off all American exports. He and the Republicans predicted the embargo would force the British and French to change their behavior and, as an additional benefit, encourage domestic manufacturing. Not incidentally, Republicans also knew that New York and New England merchants—mostly Federalists—would suffer the most. The Federalists protested that the embargo would be economically ruinous for Northeastern states and the country as a whole. They also insisted that France, not England, had been the greatest offender, and that by denying US exports to both countries, Jefferson was doing Napoleon's bidding.

To Morris, the embargo was "so hostile to freedom" that even King George III would not have imposed it on his own subjects. How could a democratic government deprive its own people of their livelihoods, their property, and their mobility—crippling commerce not to defend liberty but to make a political point?

The economic results were catastrophic. Exports collapsed by 80 percent; imports fell nearly 60 percent; shipbuilding plummeted; farmers went bankrupt; unemployment soared. Smugglers flourished—some brazen enough to float a fortified half-mile-long barge down Lake Champlain from Canada. Congress eventually abandoned the embargo a few days before Jefferson left office in March 1809, but its replacement laws were equally ineffective.

In addition to their anger over impressment, many Americans resented Britain's continuing influence with frontier Indian tribes in the Northwest Territory, which threatened western expansion. However, there was another factor that was driving America toward war with Britain, one that had less to do with honor than with glory.

A new generation of young legislators—the "War Hawks," mostly young Southerners and Westerners such as Henry Clay and John C. Calhoun—dreamed of conquering Canada. Clay boasted that Kentucky militiamen alone could seize Montreal, the hinge of British power in North America, as well as the modern-day province of Ontario. Montreal was Britain's commercial and military hub, commanding the St. Lawrence River, the vital passage connecting the Atlantic to the Great Lakes. Whoever held Montreal controlled the flow of troops, supplies, and trade through the entire region. Conquering it could have severed Britain's grip on Canada and effectively toppled British rule on the continent. Demographics seemed to support Clay's bold prediction: the United States had nearly six million free inhabitants to Canada's five hundred thousand, and many Canadians were of French descent or American birth.

Jefferson, ever the optimist, claimed the campaign would be "a mere matter of marching."

War fever outran reality. On June 18, 1812, Congress declared war on Britain by narrow margins, exposing a deep regional divide. New England and New York largely opposed war; the South and West overwhelmingly favored it.

Morris and the Federalists were aghast. The United States had almost no army and a negligible navy. Worse, Britain was fighting Napoleon—a tyrant Morris viewed as the inevitable product of the excesses of the French Revolution. Napoleon's ambitions threatened not only Europe but the American continent. To attack Britain while she resisted such a conqueror, Morris argued, was to place the United States on the wrong side of the struggle for freedom. "Can we hope for, shall we dare ask for mercy, if we shed the blood of man in an unrighteous quarrel?" Morris warned in a public letter to his fellow New Yorkers.

To Morris, the origins of the war lay not in London but in Washington. He believed the conflict revealed how the slaveholding South, aided by the political bonus granted by the Three-Fifths Clause, had come to steer the nation's destiny. Because enslaved people counted toward congressional representation—even though they had no rights—the South held more seats in the House and more electoral votes than its free population warranted, and thus controlled the country's politics. Morris saw a pattern: Southern-led coalitions had pushed through the Eleventh Amendment, shielding states from certain lawsuits and strengthening state sovereignty; they had repealed Adams's new judgeships, weakening the federal judiciary that Federalists viewed as a vital check on legislative overreach; and they had backed Jefferson's embargo, which devastated Northern merchants. Now, with the South championing war against Britain—an adventure the North overwhelmingly opposed—Morris feared that a minority interest, fortified by slavery, was dragging the entire Union into catastrophe.

The invention of the cotton gin in 1793 had transformed slavery from an institution many assumed would fade into oblivion into one that was expanding aggressively. Enslavers were making so much money from growing cotton that they became hungry for more slaves and more land to cultivate. The number of enslaved people in America had nearly doubled, and Southerners were eager to expand their "peculiar institution" to new states.

The North and South, Morris believed, were becoming like different nations. Commerce and slavery, he wrote, were "mortal foes"—one would eventually destroy the other. "I cannot blame Southern gentlemen for striving to put down commerce, because commerce, if it survives, will, I think, put them down," he wrote.

By early 1813, some New England Federalists were even proposing secession. Morris, who had spent his life fighting for union, began to wonder privately whether the country could—or should—hold together.

★

Reality soon humbled the War Hawks; the opening campaigns in Canada were disasters.

In the middle of July, an American force under the command of Brigadier General William Hull rowed across the Detroit River and landed on the Canadian shore without encountering any resistance. Basking in his apparent victory, Hull issued a giddy proclamation promising that Canadians would be "emancipated from tyranny and oppression"—and then lost his nerve.

When Hull learned the American garrison at Fort Mackinac, Michigan, had surrendered to a combined British and Indian force without firing a shot, he unaccountably ordered the evacuation of Fort Dearborn, on Lake Michigan in what is now Chicago. The sixty-six soldiers, nine women, and eighteen children who abandoned Fort Dearborn were supposed to be escorted to Fort Wayne by a trader named William Wells and thirty Miami warriors. Instead, five hundred Potawatomi and Winnebago warriors set upon the group as they crossed the sand dunes about a mile outside Fort Dearborn, slaughtering most of them. Wells was singled out for special treatment: the warriors reportedly beheaded him and ate his heart.

Then Hull received word that British Major General Isaac Brock was approaching with an unknown number of reinforcements. Thoroughly unnerved, Hull skulked back to Fort Detroit. The British seized the advantage, pounding the fort with cannon and mortar fire from the Canadian side. After a day, Hull sent his son across the river under a flag of truce and gave up the fort, and his entire army, to the British. He was later court-martialed, convicted of cowardice and neglect of duty, and sentenced to death, though the court spared his life in light of his advanced age and Revolutionary War service.

Two other American invasions at the beginning of the war fared no better. New York militiamen refused to cross into Canada at Queenston Heights, leading to a bloody defeat. Another offensive failed to even reach the border. One observer called that fiasco "a miscarriage, without even [the] heroism of disaster."

Morris's fellow canal commissioner DeWitt Clinton was a member of Madison's party—now commonly known as the Democratic-Republicans—but he ran against the incumbent in 1812 on an antiwar platform, hoping to attract some Federalist support. Madison won comfortably and, in his second inaugural address, declared the war "just . . . necessary and noble"—a statement so detached from reality that Morris wondered whether the president was "out of his senses." In a letter to a friend, Morris said he had been told that Madison "never goes sober to bed. Whether intoxicated by opium or wine was not said, but I learned last winter that pains in his teeth had driven him to use the former too freely."

Antiwar sentiment was spreading, even in the formerly enthusiastic South and West. America's first war as an independent nation produced its first peace movement, as many citizens exercised their constitutional right to dissent by signing petitions and holding rallies. Many state militiamen ignored callups; Clay's Kentucky supplied only four hundred recruits in 1812.

Yet in 1813, Americans scored some successes—most notably a naval triumph on Lake Erie that allowed them to retake Detroit, regain control of the Northwest Territory, and make another push into Canada. They also won the Battle of the Thames, where Tecumseh, a Shawnee chief who had united several tribes to fight American expansion, fell and his confederacy collapsed. But the tide soon turned again. In October 1813, Napoleon suffered a decisive defeat at the Battle of Leipzig and six months later, he abdicated his throne. Britain shifted thousands of seasoned troops to America. With the French threat removed, by late 1813 the Royal Navy had blockaded much of the East Coast, throttling commerce. In New York, ships lay idle, shops closed, and citizens pleaded for relief.

A war meant to defend trade, protect sailors, and perhaps conquer Canada had instead brought economic ruin—and, by August 1814, the burning of the nation's capital.

The British were not yet finished.

★

Baltimore was a thriving port, a Republican stronghold, and a spawning ground for privateers who tormented British shipping. Unlike Washington, it was both a strategic and symbolic target. But here the Americans stood their ground.

The morning after torching Congress and the White House, the British completed their desecration of the American capital by burning the State and War departments. Then, after a spectacular afternoon storm—a hurricane, most likely—that toppled some buildings, tore the roofs off others, and launched cannons into the air, the redcoats marched back to the fleet waiting at Benedict.

At three in the morning on September 12, 1814, they landed at North Point, at the mouth of the Patapsco River, and began marching toward Baltimore. They encountered little resistance at the beginning of their fourteen-mile march to the city, but unlike at Bladensburg, the Americans didn't panic—they held firm.

Fort McHenry, located on the peninsula dividing two branches of the river, was the key to Baltimore's defenses. The fort was a five-pointed star constructed of masonry and dirt fill, and above it flew a giant American flag, thirty feet tall and forty-two feet wide. The river was shallow near Fort McHenry—too shallow for large ships. So, at dawn the next day, the British sent smaller bomb ketches to approach the fort and bombard it with two-hundred-pound mortar shells, hoping to degrade it enough to outflank the Americans on the peninsula and clear the way for the infantry to advance into Baltimore. The ketches were beyond the reach of American guns, and for twenty-five hours, rockets and mortars rained down on the fort in a relentless barrage, continuing all through the day and night of September 13.

One of the people who witnessed the assault was a thirty-five-year-old Georgetown lawyer named Francis Scott Key. Key had been temporarily detained by the British while he was seeking the release of Dr. William Beanes, a Maryland doctor the British arrested after he helped detain six of their stragglers as prisoners of war. As night fell, Key and the doctor paced the deck of a British ship under the "red glare" of Congreve rockets, watching the mortars, which had fuses timed to explode over the fort, bursting like bombs in the air.

Again and again the doctor asked: "Can you see the flag? Is the flag still there?"

At dawn—through smoke, mist, and first light—they saw it: the enormous American flag still waving above Fort McHenry.

Baltimore had held.

Key scribbled the first lines of a poem on the back of an envelope. Published soon after in a Maryland newspaper, it bore a title that would become sacred: "The Star-Spangled Banner."

TWENTY-SEVEN

"LET US FORGET PARTY"

Six weeks after US forces repulsed the redcoats at Baltimore's Fort McHenry, Morris had to repel an attack on his wife's reputation—from her own relatives.

In April 1814, Nancy had received a letter from her sister Judith's son, Tudor. Now a Harvard student, Tudor asked his "dear, good Aunt" if he could borrow thirty dollars—a strange request, since Nancy hadn't seen her sister since leaving Virginia under a cloud of scandal in 1805. In fact, the only contact she had had with her relatives was in December 1811, when she accompanied Gouverneur on his trip to Washington to lobby for the Erie Canal. While there, the couple had visited with John Randolph, the cousin who had exiled her from Bizarre some six years earlier and was then serving in Congress. Nevertheless, Nancy sent the money and even gave her nephew a bit more after he made a second request a few weeks later. In July, Tudor wrote again to say that he'd like to visit Morrisania, setting the stage for a family reunion that quickly went awry.

When Tudor arrived at Morrisania by boat at the beginning of August, he was seriously ill. Nancy put him right to bed, and Morris soon felt compelled to write John that the boy was "deeply, perhaps mortally diseased" and that he and Judith should come immediately. He assured John that if Judith could make the journey, she would be treated to "good air, milk, vegetables and fruit" and would find "a comfortable house, an affectionate sister, and a good friend. You will both find a hearty welcome." John replied that he and Judith would wait to see how Tudor's illness progressed before embarking on the trip. But in late September, after Morris reported to them that Tudor had begun to suffer "violent bleeding from the lungs," John and Judith decided they shouldn't wait any longer.

When the two arrived on October 22, John took Nancy in his arms and kissed her on the lips; apparently, the family feud was over. The next day, Morris's physician announced that Tudor was improving and might soon be able to travel. After dinner, John handed Gouverneur a note granting his formal consent for Judith and Tudor to remain at Morrisania for the fall and winter, if they liked. Before leaving for New York City, John hugged Nancy and whispered to her, "Remember the past."

Later that day, John's coach toppled over after crashing into a pile of stones on Cortlandt Street. John was ailing even before the accident, having fallen down a staircase at an inn on his way to Morrisania, and this latest mishap aggravated his injuries. Gouverneur, Nancy, Judith, and the recovering Tudor hurried to New York to see him. While they were there, John and Tudor had an opportunity to talk in private, and they compared notes on Nancy and the situation at Morrisania. John was in a bitter mood—he had lost his seat in Congress, though he would soon regain it—and likely was taking opium to dull the pain from his injuries.

In contrast, Gouverneur and Nancy's family life couldn't have been happier. In February 1813, Nancy had given birth to a baby boy, making Gouverneur a first-time father at age sixty-one. Blessed with a wealthy, loving husband and a young son, Nancy was blissfully content; John, rejected by her years before, was miserable. Behind Morris's back, John had also spoken to Gouverneur's nephews, learning that they were in debt to their rich uncle. Eager to bolster their inheritances, the nephews shared John's desire to break up Gouverneur and Nancy's marriage. One of the nephews, David Ogden, claimed the Morrises' marriage was a fraud, and that little "Gouverno" was not Gouverneur's son but "the offspring of an illicit amour" with a servant at Morrisania. Ogden also accused Nancy of scheming to kill anyone who knew the truth. On a recent visit to Morrisania, he told John, Nancy had tried to kill *him* with a "noxious and offensive-smelling vapor" she released into his bedroom.

John sat down on All Hallows' Eve and penned an extraordinary letter to Nancy, addressed to Gouverneur as head of the household. In it, he accused her of murdering not only the baby found on the shingle pile at Glentivar in 1792, but the man rumored to have been the father, Richard Randolph. "My brother died *suddenly* in June 1797, only three [*sic*] years after his trial," John wrote. "Tudor, because he believes you capable of anything, imparted to me the morning I left Morrisania his misgivings that you had been the perpetrator of that act, and, when I found your mind running upon poisonings and murders, I too had my former suspicions strengthened . . . a dose of medicine was the avowed cause of his death." There is no evidence Nancy had been morbidly "running upon poisonings and murders" in her conversations; that line appears to be John's embellishment, twisting ordinary talk about illness and accusation into fuel for his suspicions. John went on to accuse Nancy of taking an enslaved man as a lover at Bizarre and working as a prostitute after leaving Virginia. "Chance has again thrown you under my eye. What do I see? A vampire that, after sucking the best blood of my race, has flitted off to the North, and struck her harpy fangs into an infirm old man." He concluded with a warning for Gouverneur. "If he be not both blind and deaf, he must sooner or later unmask you unless *he too die of cramps* in his *stomach*. You understand me . . . Repent before it is too late."

After writing the letter, John spread his accusations far and wide.

Nancy, horrified, fell ill "under the wounds inflicted by relations, whom she believed to be friends," according to Gouverneur. When she rallied, she was itching to respond. Some of the couple's friends urged them to sue John, but Gouverneur could "see no use in keeping up, much less spreading his filthy tales." The accusations did not weaken his faith in his wife; she had been forthcoming about her travails in Virginia and "her candor had blunted [John's] arrow." From early in their courtship, she had told him, in painful detail, about the night at Glentivar. There were no revelations in John's letter that Morris had not already heard from Nancy herself. He didn't see the point in seeking revenge. As far as he was concerned, "those who cried aloud against this houseless child of want that I took to my bosom and hate her because she is happy" would have to answer to God.

Nevertheless, in January 1815, Nancy wrote a long letter to John defending herself against his accusations. Then she mailed copies to twenty of his political opponents. "When you entered this house, and when you left it, you impressed upon my lips a kiss which I received as a token of friendship from a near relation. Did you then believe that you held in your arms, that you pressed to your bosom, that you kissed the lips of a common prostitute, the murderess of her own child and of your brother?" Yes, Nancy acknowledged, she had given birth at Glentivar on that night in 1792. But she didn't murder the baby—it was stillborn. And the father was Theodorick, the man she planned to marry, and not his brother Richard.

Nancy reminded John that she had rejected his romantic advances so many years ago because of his "stormy passions," "mean selfishness," and "wretched appearance." Now, with Gouverneur, she had found true love. "I loved my husband before he made me his wife. I love him still more now that he has made me the mother of one of the finest boys I ever saw; now that his kindness soothes the anguish which I cannot but feel from your unmanly attack."

★

As the Morrises fought to preserve Nancy's reputation, America was fighting to preserve its independence.

British troops had occupied eastern Maine and were making plans to absorb it into Canada. The redcoats were threatening to invade upstate New York, raiding the Atlantic coast with impunity, and advancing toward New Orleans. The US Army, hampered by desertions and a lack of recruits, had largely left it to militiamen to defend the states. And the American economy, especially in New York and New England, was in ruins. "We are in a deplorable situation," Massachusetts state legislator Daniel Sargent told his colleagues, "our commerce dead; our revenue gone; our ships rotting at the wharves. . . . Our treasury drained—we are bankrupts."

In the face of the crisis, some formerly antiwar Federalists rallied around the flag. Morris's old friend Rufus King, in his second stint as a senator from New York, had once disparaged the conflict as "a war of party and not of the country." Now, as ordinary New Yorkers pitched in to build forts, breastworks, and blockhouses to defend their city against an expected British invasion, King urged citizens to set aside their reservations about the war. "The enemy is at our doors, and it is now useless to inquire how he came here," he proclaimed at a public meeting shortly after the sacking of Washington. "He must be driven away—and every man join heart and hand, and place shoulder to shoulder to meet him."

Morris was appalled. He told King that Congress should cut off all funding for the war. "I feel myself bound in duty and honor to declare that anything like a pledge by Federalists to carry on this wicked war strikes a dagger to my heart," he wrote. "How often—in the name of God, how often!—will you agree to be cheated? What are you to gain by giving Mr. Madison men and money?"

Many New Englanders also wondered why they were sending their tax dollars to Washington. With its long seacoast, New England was the region most exposed to British marauders, yet the federal government had been unable—or unwilling—to defend it. The Madison administration had destroyed New England commerce, led the country into an unjust war, and then left New England to its fate. Something had to change. In October 1814, the Massachusetts legislature invited the other New England states to a regional convention to hammer out a plan for their common defense. They also hoped to lay the groundwork for a second Constitutional Convention by drafting proposed amendments. This second convention, to include all the states, would revise the nation's charter "on the basis of fair representation"—in other words, it would eliminate the Three-Fifths Clause. Connecticut accepted immediately and invited the delegates to convene in Hartford. Rhode Island also agreed to participate, and though New Hampshire and Vermont declined to send official state delegates, each was represented by county officials.

The Federalist leaders of the Hartford Convention insisted their aim was to save the Union. Democratic-Republicans didn't believe it, and the secrecy of the proceedings—kept private for the same reasons the Constitutional Convention shut its doors to the public—stoked their blackest fears. They suspected New England planned to make a separate peace with Britain and accused the delegates of plotting to secede. They denounced the Hartford Convention as a conspiracy of traitors, and for years afterward beat the fading Federalists over the head with it until their rivals ceased to be a viable political party.

Undoubtedly, secession *was* on the minds of many New Englanders in the fall of 1814. In November, *The Boston Gazette* predicted that if Madison were still president on the next Fourth of July, "a new form of government will be in operation in the eastern section of the Union." The *Columbian Centinel* ran a series of editorials by a writer who chose the pseudonym Epaminondas, the Theban general who pushed for the independence of several states from the Athenian confederacy. The author urged the delegates in Hartford "not to be entangled by the cobwebs of a compact which has long ceased to exist," arguing that the Union had once been a blessing but was now, under Madison, a curse. When Connecticut and Rhode Island agreed to participate, the

Centinel heralded them as the second and third pillars of "a new federal edifice." At the end of November, the newspaper laid out a plan of action for the Hartford delegates: refuse to pay federal taxes until New England's claims were heard; conclude a separate peace with Britain; and convene the Northern states to write a new federal constitution. Even the Democratic-Republican *Boston Patriot* acknowledged a week before the convention that about half the people in Massachusetts favored disunion.

Yet according to the leading historian of the period, the late Samuel Eliot Morison, the participating states sent moderates to Hartford "who wished to avoid secession at all costs," thereby ensuring the convention would reject the most radical path. "We are going to keep you young hotheads from getting into mischief," is how white-haired, sixty-two-year-old George Cabot of Massachusetts, the presiding officer, described his role. Broad-shouldered and over six feet tall, Cabot reminded some of Washington. Courtly forty-nine-year-old Harrison Gray Otis of Massachusetts—the man Democratic-Republicans accused of being the arch instigator—insisted the convention was supposed to be "a safety valve by which the steam arising from the fermentation of the times might escape, not as a boiler in which it should be generated."

Morris was thrilled by the idea of a regional alliance, and hopeful that New York would eventually join it. His eyes were "fixed on a star in the east," he told Timothy Pickering, a Massachusetts congressman, a week after the delegates convened in mid-December. He thought the convention might be "the day-spring of freedom and glory," and that "the madmen and traitors assembled at Hartford will, I believe, if not too tame and timid, be hailed thereafter as patriots and sages of their day and generation."

In fact, Morris had been calling for such a meeting for several years. Six weeks before war was declared, he told DeWitt Clinton the only way to "rescue the country from her present miserable and ridiculous condition" was to call a convention of the Northern states "to take the ground no longer to allow a representation of slaves," forcing the South to "either submit to what is just or break up the Union." About a year later, he wrote Otis in a similar vein, suggesting a public debate on whether it was "conducive to the happiness or consistent with the freedom of the Northern and Eastern states to continue in union with the owners of slaves."

In his lowest moments, Morris wondered whether *any* constitution could restrain the worst inclinations of human beings. "What does it signify that men should have a written constitution, containing unequivocal provisions and limitations?" he wrote to Pickering. "The idea of binding legislators by oaths is puerile. Having sworn to exercise the powers granted according to their true intent and meaning, they will, when they feel a desire to go further, avoid the shame, if not the guilt, of perjury by swearing the true intent and meaning to be according to their comprehension that which suits their purpose."

In 1787, Morris had done all he could to abolish slavery, or at least curb it; he had failed. Slave-owning Virginians had held the presidency since John Adams left office, and Democratic-Republicans—hostile to a strong central government and to economic development—dominated national politics. New states were clamoring to join the Union, and the West appeared to be aligned with the South. How could the Northeastern states flourish under such a regime?

Morris did not organize the Hartford Convention, nor did he attend it. His home state didn't even participate. Nevertheless, his apparent enthusiasm for secession would sully his legacy. For decades, historians skated over the hypocrisy of the Founders who espoused universal ideals of freedom and liberty while enslaving other human beings. They had a harder time excusing an architect of the Union who—troubled by that hypocrisy—considered breaking it up. Morris had reached the same conclusion Lincoln would nearly a half-century later: The Union could not endure half-slave and half-free. The difference, of course, was that Lincoln held fast to his vision of an imperishable Union that was wholly free. Morris, to his historical detriment, no longer believed that was possible. By 1814, he doubted that the Union could survive so long as slavery remained entrenched; in his bleakest letters he seems to accept that either the Constitution would have to be remade on free principles or different sections of the country would eventually go their separate ways.

As the twenty-six delegates met in the Old State House in Hartford, a small detachment of US troops under the command of an old Irishman wearing "fantastic military dress" marched around the building playing "The Rogue's March." In the end, however, the Hartford Convention did not come close to calling for secession. Its final report complained that the ill-conceived invasion of Canada had left New England vulnerable to British attacks—"the enemy scours the sea coast, blockades our ports, ascends our bays and rivers, makes actual descents in various and distant places, holds some by force, and threatens all that are assailable with fire and sword"—and proposed that states be permitted to redirect some of their federal taxes into their own treasuries to pay for their defense. It also assailed the Three-Fifths Clause as "unjust and unequal" and took a swipe at Virginia, arguing that the repeated election of the president from a single state encouraged "intrigue," "undue local influence," and "the domination of particular states." It proposed to amend the Constitution to scrap the Three-Fifths Clause; require a two-thirds vote of the House and Senate to admit new states, interdict trade with foreign nations, or declare war; limit any future embargoes to sixty days; exclude naturalized citizens from holding public office; and bar both the reelection of presidents and the consecutive election of presidents from any one state. These amendments, the delegates said, would *strengthen* the Union by ensuring fair and equal representation and placing new limits on executive powers that had been abused, thereby "removing the grounds of existing jealousies."

Morris believed the delegates had been too timid. From his perspective, the Republicans had killed the Constitution when they repealed Adams's judgeships, turning the judiciary from an independent check into just another prize of party warfare, and had dissolved the

Union by trying to conquer Canada instead of defending the states. "A government without force, without money, without talent, and generally despised cannot stand," he wrote to Rufus King in January 1815. "If not overthrown, it must tumble down and the convention have, out of pure malice perhaps, left it to the latter as being the more humiliating alternative." He sounded more optimistic in a letter he wrote a few days later to Moss Kent, a Federalist congressman from New York. The Hartford delegates had been "prudent," he told Kent, but he thought their humble language and modest proposals masked a determination to pursue a more radical course if they were rebuffed, as Morris fully expected them to be.

A few weeks after the convention adjourned, Massachusetts and Connecticut dispatched representatives to Washington to push their proposals for bolstering the states' defenses. By the time they arrived, however, their mission had become irrelevant.

★

On Saturday, February 11, 1815, a crowd was enjoying an evening concert at the City Hotel, on the west side of Broadway in lower Manhattan. At about eight o'clock, a man burst through the doors to the assembly room, breathless with excitement. He climbed onto a table and began to twirl a white handkerchief in the air. "Peace! Peace! Peace!" he cried. The audience gasped, the musicians set down their instruments, and everybody streamed outside to join a joyous mass that multiplied into the tens of thousands. People lit candles, lamps, and torches and paraded through the streets, echoing the shouts of the man with the handkerchief: "Peace! Peace! Peace!" The celebration continued all night long. "We were all Democrats, all Federalists!" recalled one participant, a visitor from Connecticut. "Old enemies rushed into each other's arms. Every house was in a revel. Every heart seemed melted by a joy which banished all evil thought and feeling." The man, swept along by the tide, didn't realize he was shouting, too, until he woke up hoarse the next morning.

British and American representatives had signed the Treaty of Ghent on December 24, 1814, but because news could travel only as fast as a winter ship could cross the Atlantic, America didn't learn the war was over until forty-nine days later. In the intervening time, Brevet Major General Andrew Jackson defeated the British at the Battle of New Orleans. He had read the terrain with ruthless clarity, throwing up earthworks in front of the city, stacking cotton bales as improvised ramparts, mixing regular soldiers with frontiersmen and free Black militiamen, and forcing the redcoats to march straight into carefully sighted American fire. In less than half an hour, his line shredded an elite British assault and turned a vulnerable city into an unlikely fortress. The victory cemented Jackson's status as an American hero and launched him on a trajectory that would end in the White House. Even though the Treaty of Ghent essentially restored the status quo before the war, most Americans viewed it as a victory. They had not conquered Canada, nor even gotten the British to end impressment. They had, however, withstood the might of the British Empire and maintained their independence.

The end of the war erased New England's fears of invasion and ended any talk of secession. The laying aside of old enmities the Connecticut visitor witnessed on Broadway rippled across the country, spreading from city to city in similar celebrations and softening, at least for a time, the hard edges of partisan suspicion, as peace ushered in what became known as the Era of Good Feelings. For about a decade, the partisan warfare between Federalists and Democratic-Republicans died down as Americans, united with a new sense of purpose, concentrated on building up their young nation. The political peacemaking and the gradual extinction of the Federalists even led to a short-lived belief that America had moved beyond competing political parties. Morris still loathed the Madison administration and Democratic-Republican policies, but he accepted the fact that peace had snuffed out any possibility of secession. He urged his fellow Federalists to move on, and he followed his own advice.

★

At home, Gouverneur's querulous nephews continued to make financial demands, but the furor over John Randolph's attack on Nancy had died down. For the most part, domestic tranquility reigned in the manor house at Morrisania. One day in June 1815, Gouverneur, Nancy, and two-year-old Gouverno walked a mile and a half through the woods and meadows of the estate to the cherry orchards. High in the branches, wild pigeons pecked at the sun-dappled fruit ripening in the trees. All seemed right with the world: Napoleon had just met his final defeat at Waterloo, trade with Britain had resumed, and workers in Washington were busy removing and replacing the sooty stone of the burned-out Capitol. When the content family returned to the house, Gouverno drank some wine and milk (wine and cider were everyday table drinks for children, so long as they were diluted), and frolicked around the house for the next two hours, energized rather than fatigued by the long walk. Less than a month later, Morris reflected on all that had transpired since he had left Europe. "How large a portion of human life! How eventful a period in the history of mankind!" he wrote to John Parish, his old friend from Hamburg. "I lead a quiet and, more than most of my fellow mortals, a happy life." Morris told Parish he was married to a woman with "much genius" and an "affectionate temper," and that he spent most of his time with his son. "Behold your friend as he descends with tottering steps the bottom of life's hill," Morris wrote, "supported by a kind companion, a tender female friend, and cheered by a little prattler who bids fair . . . to fill in due time the space his father leaves."

Morris knew just how damaging the Hartford Convention and the outcome of the War of 1812 had been to the Federalists' political prospects. As the presidential election of 1816 approached, he advised his party colleagues to temporarily cede the field to the Democratic-Republicans, who would "split and abuse each other" if they didn't have the Federalists to kick around. "If you come forward, Democrats will stifle their feelings to support their party, not so much because they love it, as because they hate you," he wrote to a meeting of Federalists in Philadelphia several months before the election. "Charges, which in their mouth will produce distrust of their leaders, would in yours increase their confidence."

Morris even seemed to have set aside some of his personal animus toward the Democratic-Republicans; around the same time, either he or Nancy wrote to Jefferson proposing that they visit Monticello sometime that fall. "I shall be very happy indeed to receive you here and to give you personally assurances of my continued esteem," Jefferson replied on October 20. "You will find me enjoying general good health, but much enfeebled by age, as at that of seventy-three ought to be expected." Jefferson said he was about to depart for one of his properties elsewhere in Virginia and would be "really mortified" if he missed them. He assured them, however, that his daughter would happily host them in his absence.

The Morrises never made that trip to Monticello.

At sixty-four, Morris's long life of indulging in fine food and wine had caught up with him. His gout—inflammatory arthritis caused by a buildup of uric acid in the body—was only getting worse, and he was in almost constant pain. He tried a wide variety of treatments—from bleeding to enemas, laudanum to laxatives—to alleviate his symptoms, but none provided much relief. On October 10, Morris wrote in his diary that he took advantage of the mild weather by taking a short walk. Based on the nine diary entries that followed—the last ones he wrote—it might have been the last time he walked outside. At some point in late October or early November, he experienced a blockage in his urinary tract that plunged him into agony and made him fear for his life. In desperation, he removed a piece of whalebone from one of Nancy's corsets and tried to clear the blockage himself. His clumsy attempt to operate on himself caused severe lacerations from which he never recovered. At five in the morning on Wednesday, November 6, 1816, Gouverneur Morris died.

At the time of Morris's death, the Constitution he had played such an instrumental role in creating still contained the contradictions that had haunted him; in forty-five years, those contradictions would explode into a fratricidal war that killed as many as 850,000 Americans. Nevertheless, in his final years Morris seemed to have moved beyond the idea that his political enemies were the enemies of his country. "But, gentlemen, let us forget party, and think of our country," he wrote to his fellow Federalists in August 1816. "The people will look out for men of sense, experience and integrity. Such men may, I trust, be found in both parties; and, if our country be delivered, what does it signify whether those who operate her salvation wear a Federal or Democratic cloak?

"Perhaps the expression of these sentiments may be imprudent, but when it appears proper to speak truth, I know not concealment," he concluded. "It has been the unvarying principle of my life, that the interest of our country must be preferred to every other interest."

AFTERWORD

When Gouverneur Morris stood on a stage in front of Trinity Church on a sweltering July afternoon in 1804, choking back tears to eulogize his friend Alexander Hamilton, he looked out at an audience of thousands. Twelve years later, when Morris himself died, there was no massed crowd. Newspapers hardly mentioned Morris's passing. "We are not sufficiently possessed of facts to attempt even a sketch of the life of the illustrious deceased," a two-paragraph item in the *New-York Evening Post* noted apologetically. Morris was buried the next morning in a cherry orchard at Morrisania, overlooking Mill Brook. The only mourners were his relatives and a handful of friends.

In the succeeding decades, some efforts were made to consecrate his burial ground. In 1841, Gouverneur Morris Jr. built St. Ann's Episcopal Church, named in memory of his mother (she died in 1837), on the site. He moved his mother's remains to a burial vault beneath the church, while leaving his father's remains in a tomb outside. Nearly a century later, in 1932, several thousand people, many clustered on rooftops and in the windows of flag-draped apartment houses, watched local politicians dedicate a modest marble tablet to Morris in the churchyard at St. Ann's, now located in the South Bronx. The engraving at the top of the tablet hailed Morris as "THE MAN WHOSE HAND WROTE THE CONSTITUTION OF THE UNITED STATES," and below that it listed many of his notable positions and accomplishments. At the bottom were these words: "AN AMERICAN THROUGH AND THROUGH." Today, protected from bustling St. Ann's Avenue by a black wrought iron fence, that tablet stands forlornly next to the church's garbage and recycling bins.

To be sure, there are sites named for Morris and his family all over the Bronx, from Gouverneur Morris Square to Morris Heights, Morris Educational Campus to the Gouverneur Morris Playground. But there are no soaring monuments or memorials to him, in New York or anywhere else. Few Americans, in the Bronx or beyond, have any idea who he was. Despite his friendship with Alexander Hamilton, the musical *Hamilton*, which reintroduced millions of Americans to their country's Founders, doesn't mention him at all.

Why have we forgotten Gouverneur Morris? One straightforward reason is that there isn't a fitting place to remember him: Unlike Mount Vernon and Monticello, Morrisania no longer exists. Early in the twentieth century, some local preservationists tried to turn Morris's manor house, where the floor still bore the marks from his wooden leg, into a museum, and the grounds into a public park. But around 1905, the New York, New Haven and Hartford Railroad bought the property and demolished the mansion to expand one of its railyards. Today, cement support columns and an entry ramp for the Robert F. Kennedy Bridge (formerly the Triborough Bridge) stand on the site.

Morris's name is another impediment; nobody is quite sure how to pronounce it. Based on its spelling, it should be "Goover*niere*." But many sources claim it should be pronounced "Governor," like a state's top elected official. Of course, that was one of the few roles Morris *didn't* play as a public servant, adding to the confusion. Abigail Adams, who sometimes spelled names phonetically, wrote Morris's first name as "Gove*neer*." Far better to be named "George," "John," or "Ben," if you'd like future generations to have your name on the tips of their tongues.

But the reasons for Morris's disappearance from the American story go much deeper than the destruction of his homestead or his challenging name. They are firmly rooted in the character and personality of the man himself.

As the author of this book, I toggled for months between calling it *The Forgotten Founder* and *The Forsaken Founder*. Both adjectives gesture toward the same puzzle: why a man so central to the making of the United States could become so marginal in its memory. But in the end, "forsaken" felt closer to the truth. *Forgotten* suggests accident; *forsaken* suggests a choice.

Morris possessed one of the keenest political intellects in the early republic—but also one of its sharpest pens and tongues. He punctured pretension, exposed hypocrisy, and said aloud what others whispered, especially about slavery. Southerners never forgave his speeches at the Constitutional Convention, where he unspooled blistering denunciations of human bondage and the spectacle of men who preached liberty while buying and selling Black people. He called slavery a "nefarious institution" that defied "the most sacred laws of humanity," and he meant every syllable.

Many critics, especially Democratic-Republicans, distrusted Morris's aristocratic tastes and his skepticism of unbridled democracy—that is, his belief that pure majority rule, unrestrained by law or institutions, could be as dangerous as any king. Throughout his life, from the eve of the Revolutionary War to the Constitutional Convention, from the French Revolution to the War of 1812, Morris maintained a mortal dread of mob rule and saw government as a bulwark against popular passions. To firebrands and ideologues, consumed by their desire for freedom and liberty at any cost, this made him suspect. Even after the Reign of Terror validated his fears in the bloodiest way imaginable, they denigrated Morris as a closet monarchist. Their criticisms tarnished his legacy.

During the War of 1812, when Morris warned that the South's dominance—amplified by the Three-Fifths Clause—threatened the Union itself, he terrified even some of his allies. That he dared to ask, in private letters, whether a Union built on human bondage *could* or *should* endure was politically ruinous, even if the question sprang from anguished patriotism.

His long and eventful bachelorhood also complicated his legacy. Morris never disguised his appetites. His diaries are unusually frank for the era, full of wit, sensuality, and sexuality—a window into a private world most statesmen concealed. The man who wrote the Constitution's final language did not fit the Victorian mold that nineteenth-century historians preferred to cast around the Founders.

Morris's facility with language and women, and his willingness to flaunt his brilliance and sexual successes, rankled many of his contemporaries and turned some of them into enemies. And despite his realistic assessments of humanity, he was naive when it came to individuals who surreptitiously sought to undermine him. William Short, Lafayette, even his good friend Hamilton—all of them denigrated him behind his back, even as he did his level best to help them when they were in trouble. Many historians took their unfounded accusations at face value.

Then there was his marriage. Nancy Randolph arrived in the North with a scandalous Southern past, which Morris understood, accepted, and actively defended. Their courtship and marriage were acts of compassion and conviction, but also of love and intellectual companionship. Even so, their union scandalized his nieces and nephews, discomfited elite society, and made later historians wary. It was easier, for some, to dismiss him than to explain him.

★

And yet, the case for his remembrance is overwhelming.

Morris left fingerprints on nearly every major institution of the early republic. During the Revolutionary War, he—alongside Robert Morris—salvaged the Continental Army's finances and kept Washington's troops from collapse. At the Constitutional Convention, he spoke more often than any other delegate—and more forcefully. And his denunciations of slavery marked him as a man unwilling to compromise on a moral issue others preferred to muffle or postpone.

He did not merely edit the Constitution; he shaped its voice. In effect, he wrote much of its final text. The Preamble, with its immortal opening words—"We the People"—flowed from his pen. So did the document's structural clarity: a strong executive, an independent judiciary, and a Congress capable of governing a continental nation.

His years abroad shaped American diplomacy at a moment when the nation was fragile, untested, and easily underestimated. In London he defended American commerce and American honor; in Paris he navigated the turbulence of the French Revolution, tried to aid the royal family and the Lafayettes at great personal risk, and kept US interests intact amid chaos. His Paris diaries remain among the most vivid eyewitness accounts of the French Revolution written by a foreign observer. What he saw there hardened his conviction that democracy without structure—without law, institutions, and habits of restraint—could devour itself, and those memories colored his later warnings during the War of 1812, when he feared that war fever, sectional passion, and populist anger might trample constitutional limits just as revolutionary zeal had done in France.

He also saw farther west and further ahead than most of his contemporaries. The Erie Canal was his vision before it was DeWitt Clinton's achievement. He sketched the idea during the Revolutionary War, refined it after touring European canals, and spent decades insisting that a waterway linking the Hudson River to the Great Lakes would transform the young nation. It would, he argued correctly, pull western commerce toward New York, knit the interior to the coast, and turn the state into the hinge of a continental economy. When the canal finally opened in 1825, it vindicated everything he had predicted. He did not live to see it, but the great waterway bore his imprint. So does the Manhattan streetscape; the rational, democratic pattern he created helped transform New York City into the nation's leading metropolis and continues to shape it today.

★

So why is Gouverneur Morris the forsaken Founder?

Not because he failed, but because he refused to fashion himself into the Founder the public expected. He did not sugarcoat his opinions. He did not flatter voters. He did not write a grand treatise to secure a place in posterity's syllabus. He did not mythologize himself; offered the chance to be one of the authors of *The Federalist Papers*, he politely declined.

In an age when the Founders are sculpted into marble saints or flattened into one-dimensional villains, Morris reminds us that members of the founding generation were as quarrelsome, brilliant, self-contradicting, flawed, and visionary as any that came after. He reminds us that the Constitution was crafted not by demigods but by human beings wrestling with their origin story and the nation's deepest sins. He reminds us that slavery was not incidental to the republic's creation—and that even in 1787 there were men, like Morris, who denounced it with prophetic clarity.

He reminds us to be wary of demagogues—from the left or from the right—who claim it's time to blow it all up. And he reminds us that the fight for American democracy has always involved people who loved their country even when they despaired of its direction.

He leaves us with a final admonition, written near the end of his life: "Let us forget party, and think of our country."

It is hard to imagine a more fitting epitaph for a man who spent his life helping to create America. In the twenty-first century, few pieces of advice from the eighteenth century feel so urgently needed.

Perhaps that is why he was forsaken.

Perhaps that is why he should now be remembered.

ACKNOWLEDGMENTS

It's often said that researching and writing a book is a solitary undertaking, but I wouldn't have been able to publish this one without a lot of help and support.

My agent, Victoria Skurnick, is unfailingly upbeat and encouraging, and she brings her positive predictions to fruition by being well-connected and resourceful. This is the second time she's helped me sell a biography of an American hero that most Americans have never heard of, and I'm so grateful to have her in my corner.

I also want to thank Dawn Davis, my incredible editor at Simon & Schuster. Dawn expertly identified the weaknesses in my initial draft and made suggestions that improved it immeasurably. She is a master at pacing and flow, and her edits helped me give the story of Gouverneur Morris the drama, color, and flair it deserves. It's a cliché to say that an editor made every page better, but Dawn really did. It was an honor to work with her.

Other members of the Simon & Schuster team also deserve my gratitude: Maria Mendez kept the project organized and on schedule and answered even my dumbest questions with patience and kindness. And I want to thank Rachael DeShano and Dominick Montalto for their meticulous copyediting and fact-checking work.

Though I didn't work with her directly, I want to tip my hat to

Melanie Randolph Miller, the editor of *The Diaries of Gouverneur Morris*, two volumes published in 2011 and 2018 by the University of Virginia Press. Miller's painstaking work in organizing and annotating Morris's wonderful diaries made them much more accessible to me and to other readers; this would be a much different, and lesser, book without her labors.

Closer to home, I want to thank my mother, Phyllis Greenberger, for a lifetime of love and support. My late father, Robert Greenberger, loved American history and had an abiding faith in our country. His sunny outlook on life rivaled Gouverneur Morris's own, and I miss him every day.

My daughter, Sydney, and my son, Eli, leavened the late nights and early mornings with their good humor and kept me grounded in the here and now, even as I wandered the highways and byways of the eighteenth and early nineteenth centuries. I'm grateful that I didn't have to wait as long as Morris did to experience the joys of fatherhood. And I want to thank Teddy, who can't read this but who stood—or more accurately, lay—by my side as I researched, wrote, and revised the book, at all hours of the day and night.

Most important, I want to thank my wife, Michele. She is the love of my life and marrying her was the best decision I ever made. I spent many weeks and months with my head buried in my research and writing, while she picked up the slack to keep our non-book lives running smoothly. I am deeply grateful for her love, patience, and support.

NOTES

PROLOGUE

1 *On July 6, 1816*: Gouverneur Morris to John Parish, July 6, 1816, in Anne Cary Morris, ed., *The Diary and Letters of Gouverneur Morris*, 2 vols. (Kegan Paul, Trench & Co., 1889), 2:600–601.

2 *The president was often drunk on wine or high on opium*: Morris, *The Diary and Letters of Gouverneur Morris*, 2:548.

2 *his wife had signaled her openness to an affair*: Diary entry for January 8, 1802, in Melanie Randolph Miller, ed., *The Diaries of Gouverneur Morris: New York, 1799–1816* (University of Virginia Press, 2018), 207.

2 *Unlike Jefferson, who elevated mankind*: Melanie Randolph Miller, *Envoy to the Terror: Gouverneur Morris and the French Revolution* (Potomac Books, 2005), 19.

2 *"Looking back, I can with some little self-complacency"*: Gouverneur Morris to John Parish, July 6, 1816, in Morris, *The Diary and Letters of Gouverneur Morris*, 2:601.

3 *"most noted antislavery men of those times"*: "Address at Cooper Institute," February 27, 1860, in Roy B. Basler, ed., *The Collected Works of Abraham Lincoln*, vol. 3, *August 21, 1858–March 4, 1860* (Rutgers University Press, 1953), 531.

3 *"There has never been an American statesman"*: Theodore Roosevelt, *Gouverneur Morris* (Houghton, Mifflin and Company, 1888), 364.

3 *"extreme, aggressive frankness"*: Roosevelt, *Gouverneur Morris*, 363.

ONE: CHOOSING SIDES

5 *At ten o'clock on the night of April 18, 1775*: Rick Atkinson, *The British Are Coming: The War for America, Lexington to Princeton, 1775–1777* (Henry Holt

and Company, 2019), 55–57; Elizabeth Ellery Dana, ed., *The British in Boston: Being the Diary of Lieutenant John Barker of the King's Own Regiment from November 15, 1774, to May 31, 1776* (Harvard University Press, 1924), 31–32; Hugh Boscawen, "The Origins of the Flat-Bottomed Landing Craft 1757–1758," *Journal of the National Army Museum* (1985), 24.

5 *The British knew local militiamen had been training*: Atkinson, *The British Are Coming*, 43, 53.

5 *"with proper preparation and secrecy"*: Quoted in ibid., 51.

6 *Gage even had a hand-drawn map*: Ibid, 53.

6 *who met regularly at Boston's Green Dragon Tavern*: Ibid.

6 *After receiving his instructions from Warren*: Letter from Paul Revere to Jeremy Belknap, circa 1798, Massachusetts Historical Society; Atkinson, *The British Are Coming*, 57–58.

7 *Hancock growled that he would stay and fight*: Atkinson, *The British Are Coming*, 59–60.

7 *"Keep your ranks"*: Quoted in ibid., 62.

8 *"Now the war has begun"*: Quoted in ibid., 68–69.

8 *"I had my hat shot off my head three times"*: Quoted in ibid., 71.

8 *"Whoever looks upon them as an irregular mob"*: Richard Wheeler, "Voices of Lexington and Concord," *American Heritage* 22, no. 3 (April 1971), 8–13.

9 *Morris's own family was split*: Max Mintz, *Gouverneur Morris and the American Revolution* (University of Oklahoma Press, 1970), 46–47; Richard Brookhiser, *Gentleman Revolutionary: Gouverneur Morris—The Rake Who Wrote the Constitution* (Free Press, 2003), 22.

TWO: A SLOOP IN THE FOREST

10 *The bewigged men wore waistcoats*: Edwin G. Burrows and Mike Wallace, *Gotham: A History of New York City to 1898* (Oxford University Press, 1999), 172–74.

11 *The first Morrises to gain a foothold*: Mintz, *Gouverneur Morris and the American Revolution*, 3–4.

11 *Once, he constructed a sloop*: Edward Floyd De Lancey, ed., *History of New York During the Revolutionary War, by Thomas Jones, Justice of the Supreme Court of the Province*, vol. 1 (New York Historical Society, 1879), 140n.

12 *Another oft-told tale*: Ibid.

12 *people referred to suspect stories*: Ibid.

12 *Judge Morris relished political combat*: Mintz, *Gouverneur Morris and the American Revolution*, 4–5.

12 *Instead of a hat*: Ibid., 7.

12 *Unlike the slave-owning planters*: Louis B. Wright, *The Cultural Life of the American Colonies* (Dover Publications, 2002), 21.

13 *A tally of Lewis Jr.'s property*: Mintz, *Gouverneur Morris and the American Revolution*, 7.

13 *about a fifth of New Yorkers were Black*: Burrows and Wallace, *Gotham*, 127, 184.

13 *the colonial authorities executed thirty slaves*: Andy Doolen, "Reading and Writing Terror: The New York Conspiracy Trials of 1741," *American Literary History* 16, no. 3 (Autumn 2004), 377; Thomas J. Davis, "The Great Negro Plot of 1741," *History Now* 60 (Summer 2021).

13 *many in the English-speaking world*: Burrows and Wallace, *Gotham*, 184.

13 *At one thirty in the morning*: Mintz, *Gouverneur Morris and the American Revolution*, 5; William Howard Adams, *Gouverneur Morris: An Independent Life* (Yale University Press, 2003), 13; Morris, *The Diary and Letters of Gouverneur Morris*, 1:1.

14 *He held an unspecified grudge*: Mintz, *Gouverneur Morris and the American Revolution*, 15.

14 *"more knowledge (though still a youth)"*: De Lancey, *History of New York During the Revolutionary War*, 1:140n.

14 *"use their best endeavors to cultivate a good understanding"*: Quoted in Mintz, *Gouverneur Morris and the American Revolution*, 14.

15 *"My desire is that nothing be mentioned about me"*: Quoted in ibid., 13.

15 *"a Negro boy called George"*: Quoted in ibid., 15.

15 *"It is my desire"*: Quoted in ibid.

15 *"the arts of reasoning exactly"*: *A History of Columbia University, 1754–1904* (Columbia University Press, 1904), 444.

15 *Gouverneur was particularly skilled at math*: Jared Sparks, *The Life of Gouverneur Morris, with Selections from His Correspondence and Miscellaneous Papers*, 3 vols. (Gray & Bowen, 1832), 1:5–6.

16 *"One circumstance I think is a little unlucky"*: Bayrd Still, *Mirror for Gotham: New York as Seen by Contemporaries from Dutch Days to the Present* (New York University Press, 1956), 34.

16 *"children planted by our care"*: Quoted in Edmund S. Morgan and Helen M. Morgan, *The Stamp Act Crisis: Prologue to Revolution* (The University of North Carolina Press, 1953), 67.

17 *Three days later, frigates in New York Harbor*: This account of the Stamp Act protests in New York comes from Burrows and Wallace, *Gotham*, 198–200; and F. L. Engelman, "Cadwallader Colden and the New York Stamp Act Riots," *The William and Mary Quarterly* 10, no. 4 (October 1953): 560–78.

18 *"cram the stamps down their throats"*: Burrows and Wallace, *Gotham*, 199.

THREE: WIT AND BEAUTY

19 *Surely, he had been warned to stay out of the kitchen*: This account of Morris's accident comes from Julia Delafield, *Biographies of Francis Lewis and Morgan Lewis* (Anson D. F. Randolph & Company, 1877), 74–75; and Mintz, *Gouverneur Morris and the American Revolution*, 23.

19 *Caregivers likely turned to the few remedies available*: Amer Hussain and Fouzia Choukairi, "To Cool or Not to Cool: Evolution of the Treatment of Burns in the 18th Century," *International Journal of Surgery* 11, no. 7 (August 2013): 503–6.

20 *"the passions of barbarians"*: Mintz, *Gouverneur Morris and the American Revolution*, 23–24.

20 *Morris chose to pursue a career in the law*: Ibid., 25–26.

20 *"How many hours have I hunted"*: Ibid., 26–27.

21 *"rub off in the gay circle"*: Gouverneur Morris to William Smith, February 20, 1772, in Sparks, *The Life of Gouverneur Morris*, 1:16–18.

21 *Smith urged caution*: William Smith to Gouverneur Morris, February 25, 1772, in ibid., 1:18–19.

21 *the second-largest city in British America:* Carl Bridenbaugh, *Cities in Revolt: Urban Life in America, 1743–1776* (Capricorn Books, 1964), 216.

21 *Broadway was paved and lined with poplars and elms*: Mintz, *Gouverneur Morris and the American Revolution*, 32–33.

21 *The city's diversity set it apart*: Edward L. Glaeser, "Urban Colossus: Why Is New York America's Largest City?," *Federal Reserve Bank of New York Economic Policy Review* (December 2005), 9.

22 *"With all the opulence and splendor of this city"*: Adams, *Gouverneur Morris: An Independent Life*, 18; Diary entry for August 23, 1774, in L. H. Butterfield, ed., *The Adams Papers, Diary and Autobiography of John Adams, Diary, 1771–1781*, vol. 2 (The Belknap Press of Harvard University Press, 1961), 109.

22 *Tall—about six foot four—broad-shouldered, with light-brown hair*: Mintz, *Gouverneur Morris and the American Revolution*, 36; Howard Swiggett, *The Extraordinary Mr. Morris* (Doubleday, 1952), 4.

22 *Morris became captivated by her sister Catherine*: This description of Morris's infatuation with Kitty Livingston comes from Swiggett, *The Extraordinary Mr. Morris*, 15–18; Mintz, *Gouverneur Morris and the American Revolution*, 40–41; and Brookhiser, *Gentleman Revolutionary*, 19.

23 *It was nearly sundown*: Benjamin Woods Labaree, *The Boston Tea Party* (Oxford University Press, 1964; repr. Northeastern University Press, 1979), 141.

23 *another rainy, raw New England day*: William M. Fowler Jr., *The Baron of Beacon Hill: A Biography of John Hancock* (Houghton Mifflin, 1980), 160.

23 *"Who knows . . . how tea will mingle with salt water?"*: Quoted in ibid., 161.

24 *Now the firebrand Samuel Adams rose*: Ibid.

24 *his head and hands trembling*: Elan D. Louis, "Samuel Adams' Tremor," *Neurology* 56, no. 9 (June 2001), 1201–5.

24 *"This meeting can do nothing more"*: Quoted in Fowler, *The Baron of Beacon Hill*, 161.

24 *That was the signal*: This account of the Boston Tea Party comes from Labaree, *The Boston Tea Party*, 141–45; account by Samuel Cooper, Boston Tea Party Historical Society; account by John Andrews, Boston Tea Party Historical Society; *Massachusetts Gazette and the Boston Weekly News-Letter*, December 23, 1773, https://www2.umbc.edu/che/tahlessons/pdf/historylabs/Road_to_Revolut_student:_RS14.pdf.

24 *"This destruction of the tea is so bold"*: Diary entry of December 17, 1773, in Butterfield, *The Adams Papers*, 2:86.

24 *"They highly extolled the Bostonians"*: *Boston-Gazette and Country Journal*, January 3, 1774.

24 *"Politics I dislike"*: Sparks, *The Life of Gouverneur Morris*, 1:20–21.

25 *he was "much hurt"*: Quoted in Atkinson, *The British Are Coming*, 13.

25 *"a great wrath"*: Quoted in Labaree, *The Boston Tea Party*, 179.

25 *"revert to her primitive insignificancy"*: Quoted in Atkinson, *The British Are Coming*, 14.

25 *"The die is now cast"*: Quoted in ibid., 15.

26 *"Yesterday I was present at a grand division of the city"*: Sparks, *The Life of Gouverneur Morris*, 1:24–25.

27 *"a most daring spirit of resistance"*: Quoted in Atkinson, *The British Are Coming*, 15.

27 *"You may depend on my taking the most speedy and effectual measures"*: Quoted in ibid., 22.

27 *Soon after, an American artist visiting London*: Ibid., 23–25.

27 *"The people here are very much divided"*: Quoted in Still, *Mirror for Gotham*, 39.

27 *"who can boast the glorious title of free-born Americans"*: Quoted in Mintz, *Gouverneur Morris and the American Revolution*, 46.

27 *"was the germ of American freedom"*: Quoted in ibid.

27 *"Could the American contest have been decided without blood"*: Gouverneur Morris to Peter Van Schaack, September 8, 1778, in Henry C. Van Schaack, *The Life of Peter Van Schaack* (D. Appleton & Co., 1842), 131.

FOUR: THE COMMANDER IN CHIEF

29 *"I heard the bullets whistle"*: George Washington to John Augustine Washington, May 31, 1754, in W. W. Abbot, ed., *The Papers of George Washington, Colonial Series*, vol. 1, *1748–August 1755* (Charlottesville: University Press of Virginia), 118.

30 *"so much martial dignity in his deportment"*: Benjamin Rush to Thomas Rushton, October 29, 1775, in Lyman Henry Butterfield, ed., *Letters of Benjamin Rush*, vol. 1 (Princeton University Press, 1951), 92.

30 *"Though I am truly sensible of the high honor done me in this appointment"*: Worthington Chauncey Ford, ed., *Journals of the Continental Congress, 1774–1789*, vol. 2, *1775 May 10–September 20* (US Government Printing Office, 1905), 92.

30 *the reluctant general left Philadelphia to take command of the troops*: This account of Washington's stops in New Jersey and New York comes from De Lancey, *History of New York During the Revolutionary War*, 556; Burrows and Wallace, *Gotham*, 225–26; Isaac Newton Phelps Stokes, *The Iconography of Manhattan Island*, 6 vols. (New York: 1915–1928), 4:894.

31 *"With the spring of a deer"*: John C. Dann, ed., *The Revolution Remembered: Eyewitness Accounts of the War for Independence* (University of Chicago Press, 1980), 409.

31 *"the best horseman of his age"*: Quoted in David McCullough, *1776* (Simon & Schuster, 2005), 47–48.

31 *He was said to have hurled a stone*: Ibid., 48.

31 *He rode in an elegant green coach*: Ibid., 46.

32 *an "unaccountable kind of stupidity"*: George Washington to Richard Henry Lee, August 29, 1775, in Worthington Chauncey Ford, ed., *The Writings of George Washington*, vol. 3, *1775–1776* (G. P. Putnam's Sons, 1889), 97.

32 *"Gentlemen in the other colonies have large plantations of slaves"*: John Adams to Joseph Hawley, November 25, 1775, in Robert J. Taylor, ed., *Papers of John Adams*, vol. 3 (The Belknap Press of Harvard University Press, 1979), 316.

32 *grouping them with children and old men*: General Orders, November 12, 1775, in Philander D. Chase, ed., *The Papers of George Washington, Revolutionary War Series*, vol. 2, *16 September 1775–31 December 1775* (University Press of Virginia, 1987), 353–55; Brad Meltzer and Josh Mensch, *The First Conspiracy: The Secret Plot to Kill George Washington* (Flatiron Books, 2019), 83.

33 *"appeared to have comprehended it throughout"*: Quoted in Mintz, *Gouverneur Morris and the American Revolution*, 48–49; Sparks, *The Life of Gouverneur Morris*, 1:39n–40n.

33 *"most arrant nonsense"*: Gouverneur Morris to John Jay, June 30, 1775, in Elizabeth M. Nuxoll, ed., *The Selected Papers of John Jay*, vol. 1, *1760–1779* (University of Virginia Press, 2010), 126–28.

33 *"the torrent of violence has been strong enough"*: From "His Majesty's most gracious speech to both Houses of Parliament, on Thursday the 26th of October 1775," accessed at https://quod.lib.umich.edu/e/eccodemo/K124613.0001.001.

34 *the redcoats were running short of food, fuel, and tents*: Phillip Papas, *Renegade*

Revolutionary: The Life of General Charles Lee (New York University Press, 2014), 130.

34 *"The cold is so intense"*: Quoted in Atkinson, *The British Are Coming*, 219.

FIVE: WAR COMES TO NEW YORK

35 *Moody, coarse, and unkempt*: Atkinson, *The British Are Coming*, 330; Burrows and Wallace, *Gotham*, 227–28.

36 *"To see the vast number of houses shut up"*: Quoted in Still, *Mirror for Gotham*, 40.

36 *He ordered the construction of thirteen forts*: Burrows and Wallace, *Gotham*, 228–29.

36 *Only twenty-four, Morris was prime military age*: Mintz, *Gouverneur Morris and the American Revolution*, 56; Sparks, *The Life of Gouverneur Morris*, 1:89n.

37 *Washington immediately moved eight thousand troops south*: Washington's preparations to defend New York are described in Burrows and Wallace, *Gotham*, 229; and McCullough, *1776*, 117.

37 *The farmers and artisans who made up the bulk of the Continental Army*: McCullough, *1776*, 33–34; Alexander Graydon, *Memoirs of His Own Time*, ed. John Stockton Littell (Lindsay & Blackiston, 1846), 147–48.

38 *"a common story of a certain juggler"*: Morris's speech may be found in Sparks, *The Life of Gouverneur Morris*, 1:95–107.

38 *Responding to a summons to appear before the committee*: Mintz, *Gouverneur Morris and the American Revolution*, 63–64; "Letter in answer to summons of 27 June from Committee of the Congress of New York," in William Smith Jr. Papers, New York Public Library, Manuscripts and Archives Division.

38 *"The future consequence of every gentleman in the country"*: Quoted in Mintz, *Gouverneur Morris and the American Revolution*, 65.

39 *The ringleaders were royal officials*: This account of the conspiracy to capture George Washington comes from Meltzer and Mensch, *The First Conspiracy*, 217; Mintz, *Gouverneur Morris and the American Revolution*, 62; Washington Irving, *The Life of George Washington*, vol. 2 (G. P. Putnam's Sons, 1889), 519–20; Douglas Southall Freeman, *George Washington: A Biography*, vol. 4 (Charles Scribner's Sons, 1951), 115–20; Benson J. Lossing, "Washington's Life Guard," *The Historical Magazine* 2, no. 5 (May 1858), 130–31; Carl Van Doren, *Secret History of the American Revolution* (The Viking Press, 1941), 13–15; Atkinson, *The British Are Coming*, 315–16.

40 *At about nine the next morning*: This account of the arrival of the British armada comes from Atkinson, *The British Are Coming*, 316–17; McCullough, *1776*, 134; Thomas Balch, ed., *Papers Relating Chiefly to the Maryland Line During the Revolutionary War* (T. K. and P. G. Collins, Printers, 1857), 40.

SIX: A NARROW ESCAPE

41 *Instead, the armada lingered*: McCullough, *1776*, 148.

41 *On July 9, Washington ordered his anxious men to assemble*: Atkinson, *The British Are Coming*, 348; Ron Chernow, *Washington: A Life* (Penguin, 2010), 237.

42 *Washington duly recited the twenty-seven separate grievances Congress had enumerated*: Atkinson, *The British Are Coming*, 348–49.

42 *Some soldiers, energized by the declaration*: Ibid., 349–50.

42 *Three days later, five British warships fired a barrage*: Ibid., 351; Still, *Mirror for Gotham*, 49; Edward Bangs, ed., *Journal of Lieutenant Isaac Bangs, April 1 to July 29, 1776* (John Wilson and Son, 1890), 59–60.

42 *More British ships arrived throughout July and August*: McCullough, *1776*, 148.

42 *On August 22, the British finally made their move*: Ibid., 157.

43 *That night, aided by fog and a favorable wind*: Ibid., 187–91.

43 *"The merry tones on drums and fifes had ceased"*: Diary of Ewald Shewkirk, August 30, 1776, in Henry P. Johnston, *The Campaign of 1776 Around New York and Brooklyn*, part 2 (Long Island Historical Society, 1878), 115.

43 *Washington met with his war council and made the painful decision*: McCullough, *1776*, 208.

44 *"Gouverneur, through what cause God alone knows"*: Quoted in Mintz, *Gouverneur Morris and the American Revolution*, 69.

44 *"I am amazed at Gouverneur!"*: Quoted in ibid., 69–70.

44 *"a series of accidents too trifling for recital"*: Quoted in ibid., 70; *Journals of the Provincial Congress, Provincial Convention, Committee of Safety and Council of Safety of the State of New-York, 1775–1776–1777*, 2 vols. (Thurlow Weed, Printer to the State, 1842), 2:323.

45 *"a gang of villains"*: Quoted in Mintz, *Gouverneur Morris and the American Revolution*, 70–71; *Journals of the Provincial Congress, Committee of Safety and Council of Safety*, 1:764, 772.

45 *Morris wrote a series of short essays*: Mintz, *Gouverneur Morris and the American Revolution*, 73; J. Jackson Barlow, ed., *To Secure the Blessings of Liberty: Selected Writings of Gouverneur Morris* (Liberty Fund, 2012), 5.

45 *"We need not inquire whether mortal beings are capable"*: Barlow, *To Secure the Blessings of Liberty*, 6–7.

45 *Natural liberty, Morris observed*: Mintz, *Gouverneur Morris and the American Revolution*, 72–73; Barlow, *To Secure the Blessings of Liberty*, 7–11.

46 *Morris proposed that "for the preservation of their health"*: *Journals of the Provincial Congress, Committee of Safety and Council of Safety*, 1:842.

46 *"erect a wall of brass around the country for the exclusion of Catholics"*: This account of the debate comes from Mintz, *Gouverneur Morris and the American Revolution*, 75; Sparks, *The Life of Gouverneur Morris*, 1:124–25; and *Journals*

of the Provincial Congress, Committee of Safety and Council of Safety, 1:845–46, 860–61.

46 *Morris's proposal for a strong state executive*: Mintz, *Gouverneur Morris and the American Revolution*, 74; *Journals of the Provincial Congress, Committee of Safety and Council of Safety*, 1:834, 836, 860.

47 *"A regard to the rights of human nature"*: *Journals of the Provincial Congress, Committee of Safety and Council of Safety*, 1:887.

48 *Jay agreed with Morris on slavery*: Mintz, *Gouverneur Morris and the American Revolution*, 76.

48 *The convention at first tabled Morris's measure*: These details from the slavery debate come from *Journals of the Provincial Congress, Committee of Safety and Council of Safety*, 1:887; and Charles Z. Lincoln, *The Constitutional History of New York*, vol. 1, *1609–1822* (The Lawyers' Cooperative Publishing Company, 1906), 553–54.

48 *"the want of vigor in the executive"*: Gouverneur Morris to Alexander Hamilton, May 16, 1777, in Harold C. Syrett, ed., *The Papers of Alexander Hamilton*, vol. 1, *1768–1778* (Columbia University Press, 1961), 253–54; Mintz, *Gouverneur Morris and the American Revolution*, 77.

48 *William Smith heard that his old protégé protested*: William H. W. Sabine, ed., *Historical Memoirs of William Smith*, vol. 1 (Colburn & Tegg, 1956), 143.

SEVEN: "THE SKELETON OF AN ARMY"

49 *"If Congress have not yet left Philadelphia"*: Alexander Hamilton to John Hancock, September 18, 1777, in Syrett, *The Papers of Alexander Hamilton*, 1:326–27.

50 *"Believe me"*: Cornelius Hartnett to Thomas Burke, November 2, 1777, in Edmund C. Burnett, ed., *Letters of Members of the Continental Congress*, vol. 2, *July 5, 1776–December 31, 1777* (The Carnegie Institution of Washington, D.C., 1923), 562n; Mintz, *Gouverneur Morris and the American Revolution*, 88.

50 *There were fewer than three hundred houses*: Lynn Montross, *The Reluctant Rebels: The Story of the Continental Congress, 1774–1789* (Harper & Brothers, 1950), 210.

50 *"about twenty-one members"*: Quoted in ibid., 222.

50 *"Devil a foot will I go tonight!"*: Quoted in ibid.

50 *"first-rate abilities"*: Quoted in Clarence L. Ver Steeg, *Robert Morris: Revolutionary Financier, with an Analysis of His Earlier Career* (Octagon Books, 1976), 82; Mintz, *Gouverneur Morris and the American Revolution*, 89.

51 *In the courtroom where Congress met*: Montross, *The Reluctant Rebels*, 210.

51 *"I am now convinced beyond a doubt"*: George Washington to Henry Laurens, December 23, 1777, in Frank E. Grizzard Jr. and David R. Hoth, eds.,

The Papers of George Washington, Revolutionary War Series, vol. 12, *26 October 1777–25 December 1777* (University Press of Virginia, 2002), 683–87.

52 *Morris arrived at Valley Forge at the end of January*: This description of the conditions at Valley Forge comes from Chernow, *Washington*, 323–25.

52 *"I was there when the army first began to build huts"*: Moncure Daniel Conway, ed., *The Writings of Thomas Paine*, vol. 1, *1774–1779* (G. P. Putnam's Sons, 1894), 392.

52 *Instead of supplying the patriots*: Chernow, *Washington*, 328.

52 *with canvas strips they tore from tents*: Ibid., 325.

52 *"There comes a bowl of beef soup"*: Albigence Waldo, "Valley Forge, 1777–1778: Diary of Surgeon Albigence Waldo, of the Connecticut Line," *The Pennsylvania Magazine of History and Biography* 21, no. 3 (1897), 307.

53 *"One of them that attends my person and table"*: Quoted in Chernow, *Washington*, 325–26.

53 *"Our quartermaster and commissary departments"*: Gouverneur Morris to John Jay, February 1, 1778, in Henry P. Johnston, ed., *The Correspondence and Public Papers of John Jay*, vol. 1, *1763–1781* (G. P. Putnam's Sons, 1890), 173–74.

53 *"This is the seed time of glory as of freedom"*: Quoted in Mintz, *Gouverneur Morris and the American Revolution*, 94.

54 *"as a friend to offer my services to this most interesting republic"*: The Marquis de Lafayette to Adrienne de Noailles de Lafayette, June 7, 1777, in Stanley J. Idzerda, ed., *Lafayette in the Age of the American Revolution: Selected Letters and Papers, 1776–1790*, vol. 1, *December 7, 1776–March 30, 1778* (Cornell University Press, 1977), 58–59.

54 *Washington was impressed by Lafayette's performance*: Mike Duncan, *Hero of Two Worlds: The Marquis de Lafayette in the Age of Revolution* (PublicAffairs, 2021), 58–59; Chernow, *Washington*, 296.

54 *"I am deeply surprised at the mature judgment and solid understanding"*: Gouverneur Morris to Henry Laurens, January 26, 1778, in Edmund C. Burnett, ed., *Letters of Members of the Continental Congress*, vol. 3, *January 1, 1778–December 31, 1778* (The Carnegie Institution of Washington, D.C., 1923), 50.

54 *Morris likely met with Washington at the Isaac Potts House*: This description of Washington's headquarters at Valley Forge comes from Chernow, *Washington*, 324; and the National Park Service, "Washington's Headquarters," at Valley Forge National Historical Park, accessed at https://www.nps.gov/places/washingtons-headquarters.htm.

55 *their working relationship blossomed*: Mintz, *Gouverneur Morris and the American Revolution*, 97.

55 *Together they mapped out a plan*: Ibid., 95–97.

55 *The commander in chief made another move*: Chernow, *Washington*, 333–34.

56 *After a month of debate, Congress approved a compromise*: Mintz, *Gouverneur Morris and the American Revolution*, 99–100.

56 *"It is not what you wished but it may do"*: Gouverneur Morris to George Washington, May 15, 1778, in Edward G. Lengel, ed., *The Papers of George Washington, Revolutionary War Series*, vol. 15, *May–June 1778* (University of Virginia Press, 2006), 127–28.

56 *"singular pleasure"*: George Washington to Gouverneur Morris, May 18, 1778, in ibid., 156–57.

56 *"We are going on with the regimental arrangements as fast as possible"*: Gouverneur Morris to George Washington, May 21, 1778, in ibid., 184–85.

56 *He sent the final documents to Washington*: Gouverneur Morris to George Washington, June 9, 1778, in ibid., 368–69.

EIGHT: FRANCE COMES TO THE RESCUE

57 *the redcoats in Philadelphia waltzed through candlelit rooms*: This description of British amusements in Philadelphia comes from John W. Jackson, *With the British Army in Philadelphia, 1777–1778* (Presidio Press, 1979), 211–17.

57 *The redcoats drilled and paraded in almost every open space*: Ibid., 103.

57 *"You can have no idea"*: Rebecca Franks, "A Letter of Miss Rebecca Franks, 1778," *The Pennsylvania Magazine of History and Biography* 16, no. 2 (1892), 216.

58 *The climax was the* Meschianza: This description of the *Meschianza* comes from Jackson, *With the British Army in Philadelphia*, 240–47.

58 *with a wagon train trailing a dozen miles behind them*: Chernow, *Washington*, 339.

59 *some delegates walked a mile to a nearby farmhouse*: Montross, *The Reluctant Rebels*, 239–40.

59 *what the redcoats had wrought in America's proud metropolis*: Jackson, *With the British Army in Philadelphia*, 266–67.

59 *"which are here in the greatest possible numbers"*: Quoted in ibid., 267.

59 *"as fast as our cups were filled"*: Ibid.

59 *The homes of prominent patriots were singled out*: Ibid., 268; Montross, *The Reluctant Rebels*, 240.

59 *the occupiers had befouled the redbrick State House*: Jackson, *With the British Army in Philadelphia*, 268; Montross, *The Reluctant Rebels*, 240–41.

59 *"the offensiveness of the air in and around the State House"*: Henry Laurens to Rawlins Lowndes, July 15, 1778, in Burnett, *Letters of Members of the Continental Congress*, 3:332–33.

60 *The agreement between "the most Christian King and the United States of North America"*: *Treaty of Alliance with France; 2/6/1778* in *Perfected Treaties,*

1778–1945, Record Group 11, General Records of the United States Government, National Archives Building, Washington, D.C.

60 *a "matter for heartfelt joy"*: George Washington to Richard Henry Lee, May 25, 1778, in Worthington Chauncey Ford, ed., *The Writings of George Washington*, vol. 7, *1778–1779* (G. P. Putnam's Sons, 1890), 23.

60 *Washington viewed the British proposal as "diabolical"*: Quoted in Montross, *The Reluctant Rebels*, 233.

60 *"implies a criminality in our justifiable resistance"*: Ibid., 234; Worthington Chauncey Ford, ed., *Journals of the Continental Congress, 1774–1789*, vol. 10, *1778 January 1–May 1* (US Government Printing Office, 1908), 378.

61 *"Would you think that one so little of the man of the world as I am"*: Samuel Adams to James Warren, July 15, 1778, in Burnett, *Letters of Members of the Continental Congress*, 3:332.

61 *"Who would have thought"*: Quoted in Montross, *The Reluctant Rebels*, 241.

61 *On the morning of August 6, 1778*: This description of how Congress received Gérard comes from Mintz, *Gouverneur Morris and the American Revolution*, 109–10; Montross, *The Reluctant Rebels*, 242; and Elias Boudinot to Hannah Boudinot, August 8, 1778, in Burnett, *Letters of Members of the Continental Congress*, 3:363.

62 *"the just cause of all mankind"*: Gouverneur Morris to Peter Van Schaack, September 8, 1778, in Van Schaack, *The Life of Peter Van Schaack*, 131.

62 *"The towns on [Britain's] coast are at least as defenseless as ours"*: Quoted in Mintz, *Gouverneur Morris and the American Revolution*, 113.

63 *"Let me paint my situation"*: Gouverneur Morris to Robert R. Livingston, August 17, 1778, in Burnett, *Letters of Members of the Continental Congress*, 3:376–77; and Mintz, *Gouverneur Morris and the American Revolution*, 113–14.

64 *"but a higher duty has bound me to the service of my fellow creatures"*: Quoted in Mintz, *Gouverneur Morris and the American Revolution*, 127.

64 *A Loyalist regiment erected seventy huts on the estate*: Ibid., 128, 162.

64 *"I am now going into the wide world"*: Quoted in Van Schaack, *The Life of Peter Van Schaack*, 130.

65 *"daily employed in making oblations to Venus"*: Quoted in Brookhiser, *Gentleman Revolutionary*, 60.

65 *"a thing which I probably shall not get"*: Quoted in Mintz, *Gouverneur Morris and the American Revolution*, 138–39.

NINE: THE SCANDAL OF GENIUS

66 *"Gentlemen, I see around me the eminent men of your profession"*: Quoted in *The Historical Magazine and Notes and Queries Concerning the Antiquities, History and Biography of America*, vol. 3, second series (Henry B. Dawson, 1868), 194.

67 *On the day of the operation*: This description of what Morris's amputation must have been like, given the surgical practices of the time, comes from Sharon Z. Cotner, "Boning Up on Amputation," *Colonial Williamsburg Foundation Library*, Research Report Series, no. 323 (1989).

67 *Morris "bore the operation with amazing firmness"*: Quoted in Melanie Randolph Miller, *An Incautious Man: The Life of Gouverneur Morris* (ISI Books, 2008), 44.

68 *If he had been available*: Mintz, *Gouverneur Morris and the American Revolution*, 140.

68 *"with becoming fortitude"*: Quoted in ibid.

68 *"Let it pass"*: Quoted in ibid., 141.

68 *Drunk on champagne at an event in nearby Chester*: Eugene Parker Chase, ed., *Our Revolutionary Forefathers: The Letters of François, Marquis de Barbé-Marbois, During His Residence in the United States as Secretary of the French Legation, 1779–1785* (Books for Libraries Press, 1969), 167–68.

68 *"man of wit"*: Diary entry for June 22, 1779, in Charles Francis Adams, ed., *The Works of John Adams, Second President of the United States*, vol. 3 (Charles C. Little and James Brown, 1851), 219.

68 *"an eternal speaker"*: Josiah Bartlett to William Whipple, June 20, 1778, in Burnett, *Letters of Members of the Continental Congress*, 3:310.

68 *"often guardless and incautious"*: Henry Laurens to the Marquis de Lafayette, January 28, 1778, in Burnett, *Letters of Members of the Continental Congress*, 3:59–60.

TEN: THE POWER OF THE PURSE

70 *In the smoky half-light of their log huts*: This description of the conditions at Mount Kemble comes from Carl Van Doren, *Mutiny in January* (The Viking Press, 1943), 32–34, 38–43.

70 *"I know that I have the hearts of the soldiery"*: Quoted in ibid., 41.

70 *By December, the Continental currency*: Ibid., 34.

71 *"They have now served their country for near five years"*: Quoted in ibid., 33.

71 *officers tried to buy a little peace with celebration*: Ibid., 44–46.

71 *"If you mean to kill me"*: Quoted in ibid., 46.

72 *It took a week of pleading and negotiation to end the crisis*: Ibid., 46–52; Charles Rappleye, *Robert Morris: Financier of the American Revolution* (Simon & Schuster, 2010), 226.

73 *Born in Liverpool to a modest tobacco broker*: Rappleye, *Robert Morris*, 7–9.

73 *It didn't take long for the tall, sandy-haired teenager*: Ibid., 10–14.

73 *Robert amassed a fortune*: Ibid., 23–26.

73 *Robert hesitated for weeks*: Ibid., 231–32.

73 *"You are called on by the public"*: Quoted in ibid, 232.

74 *"Aided by your talents and abilities"*: Quoted in Mintz, *Gouverneur Morris and the American Revolution*, 144.

74 *When cash ran out, he invented his own currency*: Ibid., 150–51; Rappleye, *Robert Morris*, 258–59.

75 *the air smelled of fish entrails*: This description of Front Street in the late eighteenth century comes from John Harvey Powell, *Bring Out Your Dead: The Great Plague of Yellow Fever in Philadelphia in 1793* (University of Pennsylvania Press, 1949; repr. Time Life Books, 1970), 1; and Jim Murphy, *An American Plague: The True and Terrifying Story of the Yellow Fever Epidemic of 1793* (Scholastic, 2003), 2–3.

75 *the Morrises were bombarded*: John Dos Passos, "Robert Morris and the 'Art Magick,'" *American Heritage* 7, no. 6 (October 1956): 113.

75 *he could "do nothing" without Gouverneur*: Quoted in Mintz, *Gouverneur Morris and the American Revolution*, 145.

75 *"has more virtue than he shows"*: Quoted in ibid.

75 *"He has talents and much knowledge"*: Quoted in ibid.

75 *"appeared to me to possess the most spirit and nerve"*: Quoted in ibid., 146.

76 *"The first bank in the country"*: Quoted in ibid., 149.

76 *"the commonest things become intricate"*: Quoted in Rappleye, *Robert Morris*, 290.

76 *On August 14, 1781, Washington received word*: Chernow, *Washington*, 407.

77 *Troops under Lord Charles Cornwallis*: Ibid., 403.

77 *After casting anchor in the Potomac River*: Ibid., 399.

77 *Cornwallis ordered his men to dig trenches and construct earthworks*: Ibid., 407.

78 *Admiral Sir Thomas Graves and his nineteen warships*: Rappleye, *Robert Morris*, 275; Harold A. Larrabee, *Decision at the Chesapeake* (Clarkson N. Potter, Inc., 1964), 211–23.

78 *the Americans were dressed in rags*: Chernow, *Washington*, 413.

78 *At ten the following morning*: Ibid., 417.

78 *"In passing between the two armies, they showed the greatest scorn"*: Evelyn M. Acomb, ed., *The Revolutionary Journal of Baron Ludwig Von Closen, 1780–1783* (The University of North Carolina Press, 1958), 153.

79 *British fifes and drums played an English ballad*: Chernow, *Washington*, 418.

ELEVEN: "ALL THAT MEN CAN BEAR"

80 *"We have borne all that men can bear"*: Quoted in Richard H. Kohn, "The Inside History of the Newburgh Conspiracy: America and the Coup d'Etat," *The William and Mary Quarterly* 27, no. 2 (1970), 189.

81 *"permanent provision for the public debts"*: Quoted in Mintz, *Gouverneur Morris and the American Revolution*, 159.

81 *"During the war they find you useful"*: Quoted in Louis C. Hatch, *The Administration of the American Revolutionary Army* (Longmans, Green, and Co., 1904), 164.

81 *"When soldiers advance without authority"*: Nathanael Greene to Gouverneur Morris, April 3, 1783, in Sparks, *The Life of Gouverneur Morris*, 1:251–52.

81 *"As the present constitution is so defective"*: Henry Knox to Gouverneur Morris, February 21, 1783, in ibid., 1:256.

81 *he ordered his officers to convene in a wooden building*: Chernow, *Washington*, 435–36.

82 *"How inconsistent with the rules of propriety!"*: The text of Washington's Newburgh Address, delivered on March 15, 1783, may be found in John C. Fitzpatrick, ed., *The Writings of George Washington from the Original Manuscript Sources, 1745–1799*, vol. 26, *January 1, 1783–June 10, 1783* (US Government Printing Office, 1938), 222–27.

82 *Washington did something no one had ever seen him do*: Chernow, *Washington*, 435–36.

83 *One evening at a dinner table with Washington*: There are many versions of this possibly apocryphal story. They differ in some details, including when the episode occurred. This version comes from John Cochran, "Reminiscences and Anecdotes," *The American Historical Register and Monthly Gazette of the Patriotic-Hereditary Societies of the United States of America*, vol. 1 (January 1895), 432–39.

83 *"No treason has operated"*: Quoted in Rappleye, *Robert Morris*, 381.

84 *the two Morrises turned to private pursuits*: Mintz, *Gouverneur Morris and the American Revolution*, 163–65.

84 *"to which many gentlemen followed"*: Peggy Chew [to a girlfriend], June 23, 1784, in Elizabeth Read, "The Chews of Pennsylvania," *The Magazine of American History*, vol. 4 (March 1880), 202.

TWELVE: "AN ASSEMBLY OF DEMIGODS"

86 *An economic boom that followed the end of the revolution*: This summary of the causes of Shays's rebellion comes from David O. Stewart, *The Summer of 1787: The Men Who Invented the Constitution* (Simon & Schuster, 2007), 11–12; Leonard L. Richards, *Shays's Rebellion: The American Revolution's Final Battle* (University of Pennsylvania Press, 2002), 1; David P. Szatmary, *Shays' Rebellion: The Making of an Agrarian Insurrection* (University of Massachusetts Press, 1980), 69.

86 *"ostensible cause of the commotions"*: Henry Knox to George Washington, October 23, 1786, in W. W. Abbot, ed., *The Papers of George Washington, Retirement Series*, vol. 4, *20 April 1799–13 December 1799* (University Press of Virginia, 1999), 299–302.

87 *"nest of devils"*: Szatmary, *Shays' Rebellion*, 100.

87 *After firing warning shots*: Ibid., 102.

87 *"No morn ever dawned more favorable"*: George Washington to James Madison, November 5, 1786, in Robert A. Rutland and William M. E. Rachal, eds., *The Papers of James Madison*, vol. 9, *9 April 1786–24 May 1787 and supplement 1781–1784* (The University of Chicago Press, 1975), 161–62.

87 *Individual states issued their own currencies*: Stewart, *The Summer of 1787*, 18–22.

88 *"Never, in the flow of time"*: Gouverneur Morris in the United States Senate, January 8, 1802, in Max Farrand, ed., *The Records of the Federal Convention of 1787*, revised edition in 4 vols. (Yale University Press, 1937), 391.

88 *"an assembly of demigods"*: Thomas Jefferson to John Adams, August 30, 1787, in Julian P. Boyd, ed., *The Papers of Thomas Jefferson*, vol. 12, *7 August 1787–31 March 1788* (Princeton University Press, 1955), 69.

89 *Among the fifty-five representatives*: Mintz, *Gouverneur Morris and the American Revolution*, 178; Stewart, *The Summer of 1787*, 18–22.

89 *he took the floor one hundred and seventy-three times*: Mintz, *Gouverneur Morris and the American Revolution*, 181.

89 *"Gouverneur Morris was probably the most brilliant member"*: Max Farrand, *The Framing of the Constitution of the United States* (Yale University Press, 1913), 21–22.

89 *"winds through all the mazes of rhetoric"*: Charles C. Tansill, ed., *Documents Illustrative of the Formation of the Union of the American States* (US Government Printing Office, 1927), 101–2.

89 *"the political depravity of men"*: Quoted in Mintz, *Gouverneur Morris and the American Revolution*, 182.

89 *James Wilson, another Pennsylvania delegate*: Ibid.

90 *"to the brilliancy of his genius"*: James Madison to Jared Sparks, April 8, 1831, in Sparks, *The Life of Gouverneur Morris*, 1:286.

90 *"fickle and inconstant"*: Tansill, *Documents Illustrative of the Formation of the Union of the American States*, 102.

90 *"was admired more than he was trusted"*: Farrand, *The Framing of the Constitution of the United States*, 21.

90 *He was short and weighed barely a hundred pounds*: Stewart, *The Summer of 1787*, 8.

90 *hair he brushed forward to conceal his receding hairline*: Ibid., 48.

90 *reluctant to do or say anything that might call attention to himself*: Ibid., 28.

90 *He had already compiled a memorandum*: Gaillard Hunt, ed., *The Writings of James Madison*, vol. 2, *1783–1787* (G. P. Putnam's Sons, 1901), 361–67.

91 *Washington arrived in Chester*: Chernow, *Washington*, 526; Stewart, *The Summer of 1787*, 29–30.

91 *the general walked four blocks down Market Street*: Stewart, *The Summer of 1787*, 30.

91 *in his dining room with a cask of dark beer*: Walter Isaacson, *Benjamin Franklin: An American Life* (Simon & Schuster, 2003), 445.

91 *"in a very large circle of ladies"*: Diary entry for May 23, 1787, in Donald Jackson and Dorothy Twohig, eds., *The Diaries of George Washington*, vol. 5, *1 July 1786–31 December 1789* (University Press of Virginia, 1979), 160.

92 *accompanied by three of the men he enslaved*: Chernow, *Washington*, 526.

92 *Washington purchased soap powder*: Ibid., 531–32.

92 *the general rose early to ride*: Ibid., 531.

92 *"I hope it will not be conceived"*: George Washington to Robert Morris, April 12, 1786, in W. W. Abbot, ed., *The Papers of George Washington, Confederation Series*, vol. 4, *2 April 1786–31 January 1787* (University Press of Virginia, 1995), 15–17.

92 *At least a third of the delegates were slave owners*: Stewart, *The Summer of 1787*, 68–71.

92 *More than two thousand free Black people*: Ibid., 72–73.

93 *Only one, George Wythe*: Joyce Blackburn, *George Wythe of Williamsburg* (Harper & Row, 1975), 123.

93 *"I am persuaded his mind is too thoroughly tainted"*: James Madison to James Madison Sr., September 8, 1783, in William T. Hutchinson and William M. E. Rachal, eds., *The Papers of James Madison*, vol. 7, *3 May 1783–20 February 1784* (The University of Chicago Press, 1971), 304–5.

93 *"Where slavery exists, the republican theory becomes still more fallacious"*: Hunt, *The Writings of James Madison*, 2:361–63.

93 *"that slow poison"*: Robert A. Rutland, ed., *The Papers of George Mason, 1725–1792*, vol. 1, *1749–1778* (The University of North Carolina Press, 1970), 173.

93 *"a petty tyrant"*: Ibid.

93 *"In that case a new revolution will take place"*: Quoted in John J. Reardon, *Edmund Randolph: A Biography* (Macmillan, 1975), 173.

94 *long powdered hair and dark, piercing eyes*: James Haw, "John Rutledge: Distinction and Declension," in Scott Douglas Gerber, ed., *Seriatim: The Supreme Court Before John Marshall* (NYU Press, 1998), 70.

94 *"the most eloquent man in the United States"*: Farrand, *The Records of the Federal Convention of 1787*, 3:238.

94 *"an air of reserve, design and cunning"*: Diary entry for September 3, 1774, in Butterfield, *The Adams Papers*, 2:121.

94 *Rutledge was joined by a pair of cousins*: Stewart, *The Summer of 1787*, 40.

94 *"Dr. Franklin is well known to be the greatest philosopher"*: Tansill, *Documents Illustrative of the Formation of the Union of the American States*, 100.

94 *the library occupied the entire second floor*: This description of Franklin's library comes from William Parker Cutler and Julia Perkins Cutler, *Life, Journals, and Correspondence of Rev. Manasseh Cutler, LL.D.*, vol. 1 (Robert Clarke & Co, 1888), 269.

95 *"When I entered his house"*: Ibid., 267–68.

95 *Franklin's garden was just a few hundred yards from the State House*: Isaacson, *Benjamin Franklin*, 445.

95 *carried to the State House in a glass-windowed sedan chair*: Catherine Drinker Bowen, *Miracle at Philadelphia: The Story of the Constitutional Convention, May to September 1787* (Little, Brown, 1966), 34.

95 *he relied on fellow Pennsylvania delegate James Wilson*: Stewart, *The Summer of 1787*, 33–34.

96 *Franklin had recently accepted the presidency*: Ibid., 70–71.

96 *A steady rain was falling*: Ibid., 47.

96 *the city had scattered dirt and gravel*: Bowen, *Miracle at Philadelphia*, 23.

96 *Delegates approaching from the rear*: Cutler and Cutler, *Life, Journals, and Correspondence of Rev. Manasseh Cutler, LL.D.*, 1:263.

96 *covered in green baize*: Bowen, *Miracle at Philadelphia*, 23.

96 *The first order of business was to elect a presiding officer*: Chernow, *Washington*, 529.

96 *Robert and Rutledge escorted the general*: Ibid.

96 *Madison followed the trio to the front*: Stewart, *The Summer of 1787*, 48.

97 *A handful, including Franklin*: Ibid., 49.

97 *On the following Monday, the delegates adopted rules*: Ibid., 50–51.

97 *"a necessary precaution to prevent misrepresentations or mistakes"*: George Mason to George Mason Jr., June 1, 1787, in Farrand, *The Records of the Federal Convention of 1787*, 3:32–33.

97 *To protect their privacy*: Cutler and Cutler, *Life, Journals, and Correspondence of Rev. Manasseh Cutler, LL.D.*, 1:262; Stewart, *The Summer of 1787*, 51.

97 *"Gentlemen, I am sorry to find"*: Chernow, *Washington*, 530–31.

98 *In the predawn darkness of May 30*: Cutler and Cutler, *Life, Journals, and Correspondence of Rev. Manasseh Cutler, LL.D.*, 1:271–72; Stewart, *The Summer of 1787*, 42.

99 *Morris suggested that Randolph replace his fifteen points*: Farrand, *The Records of the Federal Convention of 1787*, 1:33; Dennis C. Rasmussen, *The Constitution's Penman: Gouverneur Morris and the Creation of America's Basic Charter* (University Press of Kansas, 2023), 66.

99 *Then South Carolinian Charles Cotesworth Pinckney rose to speak*: Tansill, *Documents Illustrative of the Formation of the Union of the American States*, 749.

99 *"We are not now under a federal government"*: Farrand, *The Records of the Federal Convention of 1787*, 1:43.

100 *"In vain will be their pretentions to a love of liberty"*: "Address by the Pennsylvania Society for the Abolition of Slavery," in James H. Hutson, ed., *Supplement to Max Farrand's The Records of the Federal Convention of 1787* (Yale University Press, 1987), 44–45.

100 *"had thought it advisable to let them lie over"*: Quoted in Hutson, *Supplement to Max Farrand's The Records of the Federal Convention of 1787*, 44.

THIRTEEN: NEITHER PEOPLE NOR PROPERTY

101 *On May 31, Morris left the convention and returned to New York*: Mintz, *Gouverneur Morris and the American Revolution*, 185.

101 *His mother had died eighteen months earlier*: Ibid., 172–74.

102 *"the happiness or misery of millions yet unborn"*: George Mason to George Mason Jr., June 1, 1787, in Farrand, *The Records of the Federal Convention of 1787*, revised edition in 4 vols., 3:33.

102 *But his absence was not unusual*: Rasmussen, *The Constitution's Penman*, 41; Stewart, *The Summer of 1787*, 50.

102 *Short, deliberate, and respected for his calm intelligence*: Tansill, *Documents Illustrative of the Formation of the Union of the American States*, 100.

102 "*Give the large states an influence in proportion to their magnitude*": Farrand, *The Records of the Federal Convention of 1787*, 1:178–79.

103 *"like a surveyor through a compass"*: Quoted in Stewart, *The Summer of 1787*, 34.

103 *"the same right or influence in the councils of the nation with Pennsylvania?"*: Farrand, *The Records of the Federal Convention of 1787*, 1:180, 183.

103 *Wilson turned south*: Stewart, *The Summer of 1787*, 66–67.

104 *Lanky, sixty-six-year-old Roger Sherman of Connecticut*: Tansill, *Documents Illustrative of the Formation of the Union of the American States*, 97–98; Bowen, *Miracle at Philadelphia*, 93.

104 *"never said a foolish thing in his life"*: Bowen, *Miracle at Philadelphia*, 93.

104 *representation should not depend on population at all*: Farrand, *The Records of the Federal Convention of 1787*, 1:196.

104 *representation must rest on "some equitable ratio"*: Ibid.

104 *"but as I find this is not to be expected"*: Ibid., 197.

104 *"the whole number of white and other free citizens"*: Ibid., 201, 205.

105 *Elbridge Gerry of Massachusetts, slight and almost birdlike*: Tansill, *Documents Illustrative of the Formation of the Union of the American States*, 97; George Athan Billias, *Elbridge Gerry, Founding Father and Republican Statesman* (McGraw-Hill, 1976), 7.

105 *"more than the cattle and horses of the North?"*: Farrand, *The Records of the Federal Convention of 1787*, 1:201, 206.

105 *When the roll was called*: Ibid., 201.

105 *a stocky, sharp-tongued lawyer*: Farrand, *The Records of the Federal Convention of 1787*, 3:92.

105 *"Even the diminutive state of Georgia"*: Farrand, *The Records of the Federal Convention of 1787*, 1:500–501.

106 *King tried to defuse the situation*: Ibid., 1:493.

106 *"Since I am up, I am concerned for what fell"*: Ibid., 1:502.

106 *"It must be apparent"*: Ibid., 1:583.

107 *"Are [enslaved people] admitted as citizens?"*: Ibid., 1:587.

107 *"I am compelled . . . to declare myself"*: Ibid., 1:588.

107 *"I was alarmed . . . at what was said yesterday"*: Ibid., 1:592.

107 *"high time now to speak out"*: Ibid., 1:593.

107 *"It has been said that it is high time to speak out"*: Ibid.

108 *The elder Pinckney from South Carolina countered*: Ibid., 1:593–94.

108 *"express security" that enslaved people would continue to count*: Ibid., 1:594.

108 *Wilson again reached for compromise*: Ibid., 1:595.

108 *But South Carolina's younger Pinckney closed the day*: Ibid., 1:596.

108 *"The Southern gentlemen . . . will not be satisfied"*: Ibid., 1:604.

108 *"The security the Southern states want"*: Ibid., 1:605.

109 *"the mere creature of the legislature"*: Farrand, *The Records of the Federal Convention of 1787*, 2:29.

109 *like asking a blind man to judge colors*: Ibid., 2:31.

110 *"should be the guardian of the people"*: Ibid., 2:52.

110 *"Corruption and some few other offenses"*: Ibid., 2:65.

110 *That Monday, Washington's enslaved coachman*: Diary entry for July 30, 1787, in Jackson and Twohig, *The Diaries of George Washington*, 5:178.

110 *The next day, Washington rode on to Valley Forge*: Diary entry for July 31, 1787, in ibid., 5:179.

110 *On August 3, the two men joined Robert and Mary Morris*: Diary entry for August 3, 1787, in ibid., 5:244.

111 *When the delegates reconvened on August 6*: Stewart, *The Summer of 1787*, 177–78.

111 *Then Morris stopped them cold*: Farrand, *The Records of the Federal Convention of 1787*, 2:201.

111 *In practice, that meant the franchise would vary wildly*: Kirk H. Porter, *A History of Suffrage in the United States* (The University of Chicago Press, 1918), 136; Rasmussen, *The Constitution's Penman*, 101.

111 *"Give the votes to people who have no property"*: Farrand, *The Records of the Federal Convention of 1787*, 2:202.

111 *"The time is not distant"*: Ibid.

112 *"the safest depositories of republican liberty"*: Ibid., 203.

112 *The last state to drop its property-owning requirement*: Porter, *A History of Suffrage in the United States*, 106.

112 *Pennsylvania and Rhode Island retained their tax-paying requirements*: Ibid., 111.

FOURTEEN: "THE MOST SACRED LAWS OF HUMANITY"

113 *"a most grating circumstance to his mind"*: Max Farrand, ed., *The Records of the Federal Convention of 1787*, 3 vols. (Yale University Press, 1911), 2:220.

113 *The trade was "iniquitous"*: Ibid.

114 *"Can it be supposed . . . that this vast country"*: Ibid., 2:221.

114 *He proposed inserting the word* free *before* inhabitants: Ibid.

114 *a "nefarious institution"*: Morris's passionate speech against slavery may be found in ibid., 2:221–23.

115 *Dayton seconded the motion*: Ibid., 2:223.

115 *"seemed to take pleasure in showing his utter disregard"*: Quoted in Paul Stephen Clarkson, *Luther Martin of Maryland* (Johns Hopkins Press, 1970), 311.

115 *"he never spoke without tiring the patience"*: Tansill, *Documents Illustrative of the Formation of the Union of the American States*, 103.

115 *"weakened one part of the Union which the other parts were bound to protect"*: Farrand, *The Records of the Federal Convention of 1787*, 2:364.

116 *Sherman counseled neutrality*: Ibid., 369–70.

116 *At Gunston Hall, Mason's plantation, hundreds of enslaved people*: These details on the men and women enslaved at Gunston Hall come from Terry K. Dunn, *Among His Slaves: George Mason's Struggle with Slavery* (Commonwealth Books of Virginia, 2017).

116 *"This infernal traffic originated in the avarice of British merchants"*: Farrand, *The Records of the Federal Convention of 1787*, 2:370.

116 *Oliver Ellsworth of Connecticut could not resist*: Ibid.

116 *"They multiply so fast in Virginia and Maryland"*: Ibid., 2:371.

117 *"If slavery be wrong, it is justified by the example of all the world"*: Ibid.

117 *"South Carolina and Georgia cannot do without slaves"*: Ibid.

117 *In that span, some 170,000 human beings*: Stewart, *The Summer of 1787*, 205.

117 *Morris proposed replacing that euphemism*: Farrand, *The Records of the Federal Convention of 1787*, 2:415–16.

118 *"the most noted antislavery men of those times"*: "Address at Cooper Institute," February 27, 1860, in Basler, *The Collected Works of Abraham Lincoln*, 3:531.

118 *"The position of the Southerners was ridiculous"*: Roosevelt, *Gouverneur Morris*, 159.

118 *he gave more speeches than any other delegate*: Rasmussen, *The Constitution's Penman*, 43.

118 *"The* finish *given to the style and arrangement of the Constitution"*: James Madison to Jared Sparks, April 8, 1831, in Sparks, *The Life of Gouverneur Morris*, 1:284–85.

118 *Hamilton was so impressed by Morris's work*: Gouverneur Morris to William Hill Wells, February 24, 1815, in Sparks, *The Life of Gouverneur Morris*, 2:339.

119 *he also made subtle changes to wording and punctuation*: A thorough examination of Morris's changes may be found in William Michael Treanor, "The Case of the Dishonest Scrivener: Gouverneur Morris and the Creation of the Federalist Constitution," *Michigan Law Review* 120, no. 1 (October 2021), 1–123.

119 *"removed the possible implication that there was justice in slavery"*: Sean Wilentz, *No Property in Man: Slavery and Antislavery at the Nation's Founding* (Harvard University Press, 2018), 111.

119 *by using a semicolon rather than a comma*: Treanor, "The Case of the Dishonest Scrivener," 100–101.

120 *"In* that *instrument I hold there is neither warrant, license, nor sanction"*: Frederick Douglass, *Oration Delivered in Corinthian Hall, Rochester, by Frederick Douglass, July 5, 1852* (Lee, Mann and Company, 1852), 36.

121 *"Who authorized them to speak the language"*: Jonathan Elliott, ed., *The Debates in the Several State Conventions on the Adoption of the Federal Constitution as Recommended by the General Convention at Philadelphia in 1787* (Burt Franklin, 1888), 22–23.

121 *"It was 'We, the people,' not 'We, the white male citizens'"*: Susan B. Anthony, "Is It a Crime for a Citizen of the United States to Vote?" (1872) in Lynn Sherr, *Failure Is Impossible: Susan B. Anthony in Her Own Words* (Times Books, 1995), 110.

121 *Franklin D. Roosevelt urged Americans to "read and reread" the Preamble*: Franklin D. Roosevelt, *Annual Message to Congress*, January 6, 1937, The American Presidency Project, https://www.presidency.ucsb.edu/node/209043.

122 *"the resumption of that noble journey"*: Martin Luther King Jr., *Why We Can't Wait* (New American Library, 1964), 25.

122 *"I have often and often in the course of the session"*: Farrand, *The Records of the Federal Convention of 1787*, 2:648.

FIFTEEN: TWO AMERICANS IN PARIS

123 *Washington wanted a gold watch from Paris*: George Washington to Gouverneur Morris, November 28, 1788, in Beatrix Cary Davenport, *A Diary of the French Revolution by Gouverneur Morris*, 2 vols. (Houghton Mifflin, 1939), 1:xxxiii–xxxiv.

124 *The forty-day winter passage was brutal*: Adams, *Gouverneur Morris: An Independent Life*, 171.

124 *Morris arrived to find France in crisis*: Simon Schama, *Citizens: A Chronicle of the French Revolution* (Vintage, 1990), 305–6.

124 *Bread prices soared*: Ibid., 306–8.

125 *Morris called on Jefferson at the elegant Hôtel de Langeac*: This description of Jefferson's Paris home comes from William Howard Adams, *The Paris Years of Thomas Jefferson* (Yale University Press, 1997), 20.

125 *For three weeks after her death*: Ibid., 34.

125 *"The only circumstance which could have brought me to Europe"*: Thomas Jefferson to Samuel Henley, November 27, 1785, in Julian P. Boyd, ed., *The Papers of Thomas Jefferson*, vol. 9, *1 November 1785–22 June 1786* (Princeton University Press, 1954), 65.

125 *Sally would become his concubine*: Adams, *Gouverneur Morris: An Independent Life*, 185.

126 *The table was set in Parisian style*: Adams, *The Paris Years of Thomas Jefferson*, 19.

126 *Morris admired the simplicity of his dark suit*: Ibid., 178.

126 *Jefferson judged individuals sharply*: Davenport, *A Diary of the French Revolution*, 1:100.

126 *The two spent many hours together exploring the city*: Miller, *Envoy to the Terror*, 18.

126 *Morris had crossed it four times without noticing it*: Davenport, *A Diary of the French Revolution*, 1:83.

126 *The city's streets, which had no sidewalks*: Matilda Betham-Edwards, ed., *Arthur Young's Travels in France During the Years 1787, 1788, 1789* (George Bell & Sons, 1892), 100.

126 *Young men of fashion*: Ibid., 103.

126 "filles *without end"*: Ibid., 100.

126 *Its arcades overflowed with wigmakers*: Schama, *Citizens*, 135–36.

127 *"such nests and hotbeds of sedition and revolt"*: Betham-Edwards, *Arthur Young's Travels in France*, 154.

127 *Soldiers strutted beside clerks*: Morris, *The Diary and Letters of Gouverneur Morris*, 1:23; Schama, *Citizens*, 136.

127 *"The city . . . is a sort of whirlwind"*: Davenport, *A Diary of the French Revolution*, 1:45.

127 *He bought a notebook, bound in apple-green vellum*: Ibid., 1:xxx.

127 *"Not being perfectly master of the language"*: Ibid., 1:4.

127 *"The manners of the nation allow them to visit"*: Thomas Jefferson to George Washington, December 4, 1788, in Julian P. Boyd, ed., *The Papers of Thomas Jefferson*, vol. 14, *8 October 1788–26 March 1789* (Princeton University Press, 1958), 330.

127 *"The tender breasts of ladies"*: Thomas Jefferson to Angelica Schuyler Church, September 21, 1788, in Julian P. Boyd, ed., *The Papers of Thomas Jefferson*, vol. 13, *March–7 October 1788* (Princeton University Press, 1956), 623.

128 *"a woman of wonderful wit"*: Davenport, *A Diary of the French Revolution*, 1:328.

128 *"very sensible and indeed a lovely woman"*: Ibid., 1:85.

128 *"perhaps the handsomest arm in France"*: Ibid., 1:76.

SIXTEEN: FRANCE IN CRISIS

129 *"no hope this side of the grave"*: Davenport, *A Diary of the French Revolution*, 1:53.

129 *France's economic agony soon ignited political revolt*: This description of the Réveillon riots comes from Jeremy D. Popkin, *A New World Begins: The History of the French Revolution* (Basic Books, 2019), 112; Schama, *Citizens*, 326–28; and Adams, *Gouverneur Morris: An Independent Life*, 187.

130 *"Oh, my country!"*: Davenport, *A Diary of the French Revolution*, 1:73.

130 *"the dear privileges of centuries long elapsed"*: Gouverneur Morris to George Washington, April 29, 1789, in ibid., 1:59–62.

130 *France would "have as full a portion of liberty"*: Thomas Jefferson to David Humphreys, March 18, 1789, in Boyd, *The Papers of Thomas Jefferson*, 14:677.

130 *Swiss Guards in embroidered coats*: Schama, *Citizens*, 337.

130 *Louis XVI was cheered repeatedly*: Davenport, *A Diary of the French Revolution*, 1:66.

131 *"It seems unmanly . . . to break a woman with unkindness"*: Ibid., 1:67.

131 *Morris attended the first meeting of the assembly*: Ibid., 1:68–70.

132 *Carpenters began dismantling the royal dais*: Schama, *Citizens*, 363.

132 *enormous of head*: Ibid., 339.

132 *"Go tell those who have sent you"*: Quoted in ibid., 363.

132 *"You are continually quoted against the good party"*: Morris describes this encounter with Lafayette in Davenport, *A Diary of the French Revolution*, 1:121.

133 *Adèle was nearly ten years his junior*: Miller, *Envoy to the Terror*, 29.

133 *The doe-eyed, chestnut-haired Adèle*: Adams, *Gouverneur Morris: An Independent Life*, 182–83.

133 *not a "sworn enemy to intrigue"*: Davenport, *A Diary of the French Revolution*, 1:17.

133 *Morris ran into Adèle in the Tuileries*: Ibid., 1:24.

133 *Two days after that, he called on her at the Louvre*: Ibid, 1:25.

134 *"a scene which imagination painted very well"*: Ibid., 1:28–29.

134 *the club-footed bishop lectured pompously*: Ibid., 1:55.

134 *his past "affairs of gallantry"*: Ibid., 1:119.

134 *"This idea will dwell on her mind"*: Ibid.

SEVENTEEN: "GRACIOUS GOD, WHAT A PEOPLE!"

135 *When a woman was caught spitting on his likeness*: Schama, *Citizens*, 373.

136 *nearly collided with a detachment of German cavalry*: Davenport, *A Diary of the French Revolution*, 1:144; Adams, *Gouverneur Morris: An Independent Life*, 190.

136 *On his way home, he saw rioters smashing the windows*: Davenport, *A Diary of the French Revolution*, 1:145.

136 *Even the notorious Marquis de Sade*: Schama, *Citizens*, 391–93.

136 *Bernard-René de Launay—born within those very walls*: Ibid., 399–401.

136 *A group climbed onto the roof*: Ibid., 402–3.

137 *de Launay raised a white handkerchief*: Ibid., 403.

137 *someone proposed tying him to a horse's tail*: Ibid., 405.

137 *"Let me die!"*: Ibid., 405.

137 *Moments later the city's provost*: Ibid.

137 *"Yesterday it was the fashion at Versailles"*: Davenport, *A Diary of the French Revolution*, 1:148.

137 *"an engagement in which the heart can take any share"*: Ibid., 1:63.

137 *his "infinite coolness and seriousness"*: Ibid., 1:157.

138 *The stench in the former prison*: Ibid., 1:158.

138 *"The people, in their enthusiastic delirium"*: Duncan, *Hero of Two Worlds*, 221.

138 *"the people will be happy if we give them hay to eat"*: Quoted in ibid., 224.

138 *"You want to kill this man without judgment!"*: Ibid.

138 *But the crowd was beyond persuasion*: Ibid., 224–25; Popkin, *A New World Begins*, 151; Schama, *Citizens*, 405–6.

139 *"This mutilated form of an old man"*: Davenport, *A Diary of the French Revolution*, 1:158–59.

139 *"I was never until now fully apprised of the mildness of American character"*: Quoted in Miller, *Envoy to the Terror*, 26–27.

139 *"The cutting off heads is become so much à la mode"*: Thomas Jefferson to Maria Cosway, July 25, 1789, in Julian P. Boyd, ed., *The Papers of Thomas Jefferson*, vol. 15, *27 March 1789–30 November 1789* (Princeton University Press, 1958), 305.

140 *claiming to have a "marriage of the heart"*: Davenport, *A Diary of the French Revolution*, 1:160.

140 *a hangover from drinking "rather too much Bordeaux"*: Ibid., 1:163.

140 *she was sitting at her vanity*: Ibid., 1:164.

140 *a "perfectly platonic" farewell*: Ibid., 1:165.

140 *"a well-meaning man but extremely weak"*: Gouverneur Morris to George Washington, July 31, 1789, in ibid., 1:170.

140 *when a London hostess asked Morris*: Ibid., 1:200.

141 *When darkness fell, he laid out a blanket*: Ibid., 1:211.

141 *When he arrived home, the first thing he did*: Ibid., 1:217–18.

141 *"a feeble health, a wretched carriage, a bad road"*: Ibid., 1:225.

141 *"celebrate the Cyprian mystery"*: Ibid., 1:261.

141 *"satisfy the sentiment"*: Ibid., 1:325.

141 *"perform the part of the first pair"*: Ibid., 1:328.

141 *"Finally, my friend, you and I will govern France"*: Ibid., 1:235.

142 *he rushed to the Hôtel de Ville*: Duncan, *Hero of Two Worlds*, 237–38.

142 *"He has marched by compulsion"*: Davenport, *A Diary of the French Revolution*, 1:243.

142 *Louis offered her smelling salts*: Schama, *Citizens*, 465.

143 *"I have come to die at the feet of Your Majesty"*: Quoted in ibid., 466.

143 *"My friends, my friends, save me"*: This account of the attack on Versailles comes from ibid., 467–68; Duncan, *Hero of Two Worlds*, 240–41.

145 *she no longer trusted Talleyrand*: Davenport, *A Diary of the French Revolution*, 1:243.

145 *The next day, October 6, she went further still*: Ibid., 244–45.

146 *Two days later, he bought her a ring*: Ibid., 247.

EIGHTEEN: A MISSION FOR THE PRESIDENT

147 *"a deep knowledge of human character"*: Davenport, *A Diary of the French Revolution*, 1:255–56.

148 *"She says we must be chaste"*: Ibid., 1:258.

148 *"I tell you that I love you because I love you"*: Ibid., 1:259.

148 *"He loves you distractedly"*: Ibid., 1:292.

148 *she greeted him from her bathtub*: Ibid., 1:300.

148 *"the pains you have taken to procure me a watch"*: George Washington to Gouverneur Morris, October 13, 1789, in Dorothy Twohig, ed., *The Papers of George Washington, Presidential Series*, vol. 4, *8 September 1789–15 January 1790* (University Press of Virginia, 1993), 176–79.

149 *The second letter was weightier*: Twohig, *The Papers of George Washington*, 4:179–83.

149 *Morris is the man*: Diary entry for October 7, 1789, in Jackson and Twohig, *The Diaries of George Washington*, 5:455.

149 *Morris's "imagination sometimes outruns his judgment"*: Diary entry for October 8, 1789, in ibid., 5:456.

149 *"Not long for a husband because a wife can follow him"*: Davenport, *A Diary of the French Revolution*, 1:413.

150 *Morris shared concerns about "our friend Lafayette"*: Gouverneur Morris to George Washington, January 22, 1790, in Dorothy Twohig, Mark A. Mastromarino, and Jack D. Warren, eds., *The Papers of George Washington, Presidential*

Series, vol. 5, *16 January 1790–30 June 1790* (University Press of Virginia, 1996), 37–40.

150 *Morris could see in the Frenchman's face*: Morris describes this encounter with Lafayette in Davenport, *A Diary of the French Revolution*, 1:306.

150 *"Madame Sara seems to have more understanding"*: Ibid., 1:452.

150 *he sought out his half brother*: Ibid., 1:460.

151 *The reception clerks eyed the wooden-legged American*: Davenport, *A Diary of the French Revolution*, 2:64.

151 *"I am very happy, Mr. Morris"*: The meeting with Leeds is described in ibid., 2:464–65; and Gouverneur Morris to George Washington, April 7, 1790, in Twohig, Mastromarino, and Warren, *The Papers of George Washington*, 5:319–23.

152 *a "confusion of language which resembles the stammering"*: Gouverneur Morris to George Washington, May 1, 1790, in ibid., 5:362–68.

152 *Leeds invited Morris back to Whitehall on May 20*: This meeting, and the one the next day with Pitt, are described in Gouverneur Morris to George Washington, May 29, 1790, in ibid., 5:430–39.

154 *"would have agreed to comply with the treaty of peace"*: Gouverneur Morris to George Washington, August 16, 1790, in Mark A. Mastromarino, ed., *The Papers of George Washington, Presidential Series*, vol. 6, *1 July 1790–30 November 1790* (University Press of Virginia, 1996), 269–72.

154 *"Those who pursuing the true interests of Great Britain"*: Gouverneur Morris to George Washington, September 18, 1790, in ibid., 6:470–77.

154 *Hamilton, who wanted America to forge closer ties to Britain*: Miller, *Envoy to the Terror*, 50, 58–64.

154 *Washington . . . remained loyal to Morris*: George Washington to Gouverneur Morris, July 7, 1790, in Davenport, *A Diary of the French Revolution*, 1:575.

154 *Jefferson . . . endorsed his tough approach*: Thomas Jefferson to Gouverneur Morris, August 12, 1790, in ibid., 1:576–77.

154 *they directed Morris to conclude his mission*: Miller, *Envoy to the Terror*, 69.

155 *a Newfoundland dog—a gift for the Duchesse d'Orléans*: Ibid., 73.

155 *she had taken up with another man*: Davenport, *A Diary of the French Revolution*, 2:48.

155 *"At the Louvre denied"*: Ibid., 2:51.

155 *Adèle sent a note summoning him to her apartment*: Ibid., 2:55.

155 *"I agree to do so* pour la dernière fois*"*: Ibid.

156 *Gouverneur took Adèle to visit her beloved English nun*: Ibid., 2:62.

156 *The niece was extremely nearsighted*: Ibid., 2:118.

156 *"There is not a man among them fitted for the great tasks"*: Gouverneur Morris to

George Washington, December 1, 1790, in Jack D. Warren, ed., *The Papers of George Washington, Presidential Series*, vol. 7, *1 December 1790–21 March 1791* (University Press of Virginia, 1998), 4–7.

NINETEEN: THE AMBASSADOR

158 *"anyone who cheers the king will be beaten"*: Duncan, *Hero of Two Worlds*, 273; Schama, *Citizens*, 558.

158 *"You, Monsieur Lafayette, will answer to the Assembly"*: Quoted in Schama, *Citizens*, 554.

158 *"half wild" with fear*: Davenport, *A Diary of the French Revolution*, 2:211.

158 *the king's flight had been "very foolish"*: Gouverneur Morris to Robert Morris, July 16, 1791, in ibid., 2:219–20.

158 *In October, the general resigned his command*: Duncan, *Hero of Two Worlds*, 280; Schama, *Citizens*, 588.

159 *the ordeal had turned the thirty-six-year-old queen's hair gray*: Davenport, *A Diary of the French Revolution*, 2:213.

159 *He feared the French lacked the "education and habit"*: Gouverneur Morris to John Jay, July 1, 1789, in Elizabeth M. Nuxoll, ed., *The Selected Papers of John Jay*, vol. 5, *1788–1794* (University of Virginia Press, 2018), 128–30.

159 *His own proposed framework for a French constitution*: Sparks, *The Life of Gouverneur Morris*, 3:481–500.

159 *a hot-air balloon trailing tricolor ribbons*: Schama, *Citizens*, 573.

159 *"It is a general and almost universal conviction"*: Davenport, *A Diary of the French Revolution*, 2:275.

160 *The thirty-seven-year-old king*: Schama, *Citizens*, 54–55.

160 *Morris called Louis a "miserable creature"*: Davenport, *A Diary of the French Revolution*, 2:212.

160 *he advised him to distribute bread to the poor*: Ibid., 2:267–68.

161 *Short dashed off a letter to Jefferson*: William Short to Thomas Jefferson, October 6, 1791, in Charles T. Cullen, ed., *The Papers of Thomas Jefferson*, vol. 22, *6 August 1791–31 December 1791* (Princeton University Press, 1986), 189–95.

161 *"Thus, he will go home with ill will"*: Davenport, *A Diary of the French Revolution*, 2:255.

161 *"one of those privileged geniuses"*: William Short to Thomas Jefferson, October 22, 1792, in John Catanzariti, ed., *The Papers of Thomas Jefferson*, vol. 24, *1 June–31 December 1792* (Princeton University Press, 1990), 513–22.

161 *The Senate debate over Morris's nomination*: These details come from Miller, *Envoy to the Terror*, 94; and Charles R. King, ed., *The Life and Correspondence of Rufus King*, vol. 1, *1755–1794* (G. P. Putnam's Sons, 1894), 419–21.

161 *"I think if you and I should chance to grow old"*: Gouverneur Morris to Rufus King, April 6, 1792, in ibid., 1:421–22.

162 *Washington stood by his choice but warned his friend to tread carefully*: George Washington to Gouverneur Morris, January 28, 1792, in Mark A. Mastromarino and Jack D. Warren, eds., *The Papers of George Washington, Presidential Series*, vol. 9, *23 September 1791–29 February 1792* (University Press of Virginia, 2000), 515–17.

162 *Morris thanked him and promised "that circumspection of conduct"*: Gouverneur Morris to George Washington, April 6, 1792, in Robert F. Haggard and Mark A. Mastromarino, eds., *The Papers of George Washington, Presidential Series*, vol. 10, *1 March 1792–15 August 1792* (University of Virginia Press, 2002), 223–25.

162 *excused from wearing a ceremonial sword*: Davenport, *A Diary of the French Revolution*, 2:429.

162 *Louis took the papers awkwardly*: Morris describes his audience with the king and queen in ibid., 2:436.

163 *They found Louis in the opulent Salon de l'Oeil-de-Boeuf*: Schama, *Citizens*, 606–7; Popkin, *A New World Begins*, 276.

163 *"The constitution . . . has this day, I think, given its last groan"*: Davenport, *A Diary of the French Revolution*, 2:453.

163 *Morris met in secret*: Ibid., 455; Miller, *Envoy to the Terror*, 147.

163 *Morris pressed Lafayette to act*: Davenport, *A Diary of the French Revolution*, 2:457.

164 *"This day the king will commence a new career"*: Gouverneur Morris to Thomas Jefferson, July 10, 1792, in Catanzariti, *The Papers of Thomas Jefferson*, 24:207–9.

164 *"Their Majesties flashed in the pan"*: Davenport, *A Diary of the French Revolution*, 2:465.

164 *Two weeks later, the king entrusted Morris with his private funds*: Ibid., 2:472, 487; Mintz, *Gouverneur Morris and the American Revolution*, 223.

164 *our "very great, good, and dear friend and ally"*: George Washington to Louis XVI, March 14, 1792, in Haggard and Mastromarino, *The Papers of George Washington*, 10:108–9.

164 *Americans thought "tenderly" of the king*: Elizabeth Wormeley Latimer, ed., *My Scrap-Book of the French Revolution* (A. C. McClurg and Company, 1898), 22–23.

165 *"The whole crisis was one so completely without precedent"*: Roosevelt, *Gouverneur Morris*, 256.

165 *it proclaimed that the allied armies did not wish to conquer France*: "The Proclamation of the Duke of Brunswick, 1792," in J. H. Robinson, ed., *Readings in*

European History, vol. 2, (Ginn, 1906), 443–45; Duncan, *Hero of Two Worlds*, 292.

165 *Louis put on his sword and descended to the courtyard*: Schama, *Citizens*, 614.

166 *"Shortly after he leaves me the cannon begin"*: Davenport, *A Diary of the French Revolution*, 2:489.

166 *Guards who surrendered were slaughtered in the courtyards*: Schama, *Citizens*, 615.

166 *"women, veritable furies"*: Louis Sebastien Mercier, *The Picture of Paris: Before and After the Revolution* (George Routledge & Sons, 1929), 205.

167 *Adèle de Flahaut and her young son sought refuge*: Davenport, *A Diary of the French Revolution*, 2:490.

167 *"The persons you have seen consider themselves in danger"*: Latimer, *My Scrap-Book of the French Revolution*, 30–31.

167 *Morris mentioned none of it*: Gouverneur Morris to Thomas Jefferson, August 16, 1792, in Davenport, *A Diary of the French Revolution*, 2:491–96.

167 *the revolutionary authorities arrested hundreds of refractory priests*: Schama, *Citizens*, 624–25.

168 *Lafayette fled across enemy lines*: Duncan, *Hero of Two Worlds*, 294.

168 *Short and other American diplomats, including Morris, were wary*: Gouverneur Morris to Thomas Pinckney, September 13, 1792, in Davenport, *A Diary of the French Revolution*, 2:557–58.

168 *"He has spent his fortune on a revolution"*: Gouverneur Morris to Thomas Jefferson, August 22, 1792, in Catanzariti, *The Papers of Thomas Jefferson*, 24:313–15.

168 *militants showed up on Morris's doorstep*: Davenport, *A Diary of the French Revolution*, 2:518–19.

168 *"a denunciation made by some blockhead or rascal"*: Gouverneur Morris to Thomas Jefferson, August 30, 1792, in ibid., 2:519–23.

168 *Dragged before an improvised tribunal*: Schama, *Citizens*, 635.

169 *When she arrived at the official's home*: This anecdote is recounted in Miller, *Envoy to the Terror*, 181; Brookhiser, *Gentleman Revolutionary*, 132; Melanie Randolph Miller, ed., *The Diaries of Gouverneur Morris: European Travels, 1794–1798* (University of Virginia Press, 2011), xxxi; Baron André de Maricourt, *Madame de Souza et Sa Famille: Les Marigny—Les Flahaut Auguste de Morny (1761–1836)* (Émile-Paul, 1907), 151–52.

169 *"Not a line from you, and yet I write"*: Adèle de Flahaut to Gouverneur Morris, January 4, 1792, in Davenport, *A Diary of the French Revolution*, 2:600–601.

TWENTY: "TERROR IS THE ORDER OF THE DAY"

170 *Horses slipped and fell on the ice-glazed streets*: Davenport, *A Diary of the French Revolution*, 2:598.

170 *"The French people accuse you"*: Quoted in Popkin, *A New World Begins*, 311.

171 *As he was led from the prison*: The abbé's first-person account of the execution of Louis XVI may be found in Charles Sneyd Edgeworth, *Memoirs of the Abbé Edgeworth: Containing His Narrative of the Last Hours of Louis XVI* (Rowland Hunter, 1815), 71–87.

173 *One of the executioners sold strands of Louis's hair*: Mercier, *The Picture of Paris*, 217.

173 *"The late king of this country has been publicly executed"*: Gouverneur Morris to Thomas Jefferson, January 25, 1793, in John Catanzariti, ed., *The Papers of Thomas Jefferson*, vol. 25, *1 January–10 May 1793* (Princeton University Press, 1992), 95–96.

173 *"The date of this letter will show you"*: Morris, *The Diary and Letters of Gouverneur Morris*, 2:28.

173 *He described his new residence to Robert Morris*: Ibid., 2:43, 57.

173 *the revolutionaries turned their attention to the hated Marie Antoinette*: Schama, *Citizens*, 798–99.

174 *"the most vulgar epithets"*: Latimer, *My Scrap-Book of the French Revolution*, 41–42.

174 Le Père Duchesne, *a radical newspaper, was disappointed*: Schama, *Citizens*, 799–800.

174 *"a despotism both in principle and practice"*: Gouverneur Morris to George Washington, October 18, 1793, in David R. Hoth, ed., *The Papers of George Washington, Presidential Series*, vol. 14, *1 September–31 December 1793* (University of Virginia Press, 2008), 229–31.

175 *Local officials with a warrant*: Miller, *An Incautious Man*, 184–85.

175 *"The difficulty (under existing circumstances) of knowing what to write"*: George Washington to Gouverneur Morris, June 19, 1794, in David R. Hoth and Carol S. Ebel, eds., *The Papers of George Washington, Presidential Series*, vol. 16, *1 May–30 September 1794* (University of Virginia Press, 2011), 248.

TWENTY-ONE: A TOUR OF THE OLD WORLD

176 *"I saw misery and affliction every day"*: Gouverneur Morris to George Washington, December 30, 1794, in Sparks, *The Life of Gouverneur Morris*, 2:456–59.

177 *"the best bread I ever saw or tasted"*: Diary entry for November 22, 1794, in Miller, *The Diaries of Gouverneur Morris: European Travels*, 33.

177 *"a gallery of paintings, if they can be called by that name"*: Diary entry for November 24, 1794, in ibid., 35.

177 *"On the road this day I saw some mules"*: Diary entry for November 26, 1794, in ibid., 37.

177 *Morris was beset by broken-down carriages and mediocre food*: Ibid., 26–28.

177 *"the best way is to pay with good humor and jog patiently on"*: Diary entry for November 30, 1794, in ibid., 41.

177 *"Another year is added to the many which have been lost"*: Diary entry for December 31, 1794, in ibid., 57.

178 *He helped her publish a semiautobiographical novel*: Françoise de Bernardy, *Son of Talleyrand: The Life of Comte Charles de Flahaut 1785–1870* (Collins, 1956), 24.

178 *her efforts to help twenty-one-year-old Louis-Philippe*: Adèle de Flahaut to Gouverneur Morris, January 27, 1795, in Sparks, *The Life of Gouverneur Morris*, 1:464–66.

178 *Adèle asked Gouverneur to give him money*: Miller, *The Diaries of Gouverneur Morris: European Travels*, 66.

178 *"Madame de Flahaut arrives this morning"*: Diary entry for April 1, 1795, in ibid., 76.

178 *On April 18, he picked some flowers for her*: Diary entry for April 18, 1795, in ibid., 78.

179 *"It surely must be love that inspires"*: Diary entry for May 6, 1795, in ibid., 83, 84.

179 *"taken with a bleeding from the breast"*: Diary entry for April 6, 1795, in ibid., 76.

179 *"We converse on her dreary situation in life"*: Diary entry for June 4, 1795, in ibid., 93.

180 *he was going to England to wrap up "some affairs"*: Gouverneur Morris to George Washington, December 30, 1794, in Sparks, *The Life of Gouverneur Morris*, 2:458.

180 *"my mind opens to a view of wealth for the interior of America"*: Diary entry for October 14, 1795, in Miller, *The Diaries of Gouverneur Morris: European Travels*, 184.

180 *Grenville presented Morris at court to King George III*: Diary entry for November 25, 1795, in ibid., 215.

181 *"whereabouts she is with her Portuguese lover"*: Diary entry for June 27, 1796, in ibid., 285.

182 *"an air of dissoluteness"*: Diary entry for July 17, 1796, in ibid., 293.

182 *a young woman came to his room selling fruit*: Diary entry for July 21, 1796, in ibid., 298.

182 *Gouverneur gawked at a polar bear*: Diary entry for December 16, 1796, in ibid., 382.

182 *toured the Medico-Surgical Joseph's Academy of Vienna*: Diary entry for October 21, 1796, in ibid., 356.

183 *cockchafer beetles preserved in sugar*: Diary entry for December 31, 1796, in ibid., 398.

183 *the British ambassador presented Morris at court*: Diary entry for September 24, 1796, in ibid., 346; Diary entry for October 26, 1796, in ibid., 359.

183 *an audience with the Austrian foreign minister*: Diary entry for December 18, 1796, in ibid., 384–85.

183 *Morris also had a brief romantic fling in Vienna*: Diary entry for December 14, 1796, in ibid., 381.

184 *Henriette offered him a ride in hers*: Diary entry for February 10, 1797, in ibid., 422–23.

184 *he went to deliver a letter from Henriette to her sister*: Diary entry for February 16, 1797, in ibid., 426.

184 *"Why conceal my passion?"*: Diary entry for February 19, 1797, in ibid., 429.

184 *"I dare not ask, I cannot expect that you will love me"*: Diary entry for March 2, 1797, in ibid., 435.

184 *she told Gouverneur she was "quite content"*: Diary entry for September 21, 1797, in ibid., 493.

TWENTY-TWO: FEDERALISTS AGAINST REPUBLICANS

186 *"a most disagreeable and impertinent fellow"*: Diary entry for September 10, 1798, in Miller, *The Diaries of Gouverneur Morris: European Travels*, 640.

187 *Hamilton updated him on the "state of our affairs"*: Diary entry for December 25, 1798, in ibid., 667.

187 *"Some of my friends have"*: Gouverneur Morris to John Parish, January 27, 1799, in Sparks, *The Life of Gouverneur Morris*, 3:117–18.

187 *"a pretty good house"*: Gouverneur Morris to John Parish, February 16, 1802, in ibid., 3:161.

188 *One traveler who crossed paths with him at an inn*: Brookhiser, *Gentleman Revolutionary*, 157; Swiggett, *The Extraordinary Mr. Morris*, 365.

188 *"I do not know but you are right in the idea"*: Gouverneur Morris to John Parish, January 27, 1799, in Sparks, *The Life of Gouverneur Morris*, 3:117–18.

188 *"I am told that his family exhibited a dreadful scene of distress"*: Quoted in Rappleye, *Robert Morris*, 507.

189 *The Prune Street Jail was part of a larger prison complex*: Ibid., 507–9.

189 *Robert did not have a bed*: This description of the conditions of Robert Morris's confinement come from ibid., 508–10.

189 *"A man that cannot hear and face misfortune should not run risks"*: Quoted in ibid., 510.

189 *Many people had turned against Robert*: Ibid., 508.

190 *the two men were "strongly affected"*: Diary entry for April 24, 1799, in Miller, *The Diaries of Gouverneur Morris: New York*, 20.

190 *"an air of firmness"*: Ibid.

190 *"a very lively strain of conversation"*: Diary entry for April 25, 1799, in ibid., 21.

190 *Gouverneur also did what he could to improve the family's financial predicament*: Rappleye, *Robert Morris*, 511.

191 *"an artificial and extraordinary force"*: Avalon Project, "Washington's Farewell Address, 1796," Lillian Goldman Law Library, accessed March 17, 2026, https://avalon.law.yale.edu/18th_century/washing.asp.

192 *"Hamilton tells me I must take an active part in our public affairs"*: Diary entry for November 28, 1799, in Miller, *The Diaries of Gouverneur Morris: New York*, 55.

192 *Morris urged Washington to return to office*: Gouverneur Morris to George Washington, December 9, 1799, in Abbot, *The Papers of George Washington, Retirement Series*, 4:452–53.

192 *"the courage of a soldier, the intrepidity of a chief, the fortitude of a hero"*: Morris, *An Oration Upon the Death of General Washington* (John Furman, 1800), 7.

192 *"He loved glory, but still more he loved his country"*: Abbot, *The Papers of George Washington, Retirement Series*, 4:9.

192 *Hamilton urged him to run for Congress*: Diary entry for March 15, 1800, in Miller, *The Diaries of Gouverneur Morris: New York*, 78–79.

192 *"Informed that I am elected senator"*: Diary entry for April 7, 1800, in ibid., 83.

193 *"The shores of Lake George are bold"*: Gouverneur Morris to John Parish, January 20, 1801, in Sparks, *The Life of Gouverneur Morris*, 3:140.

193 *his boatmen refused to shoot the Rapides du Sault Normand*: Diary entry for August 1, 1800, in Miller, *The Diaries of Gouverneur Morris: New York*, 108.

193 *"Hundreds of large ships will, in no distant period"*: Gouverneur Morris to John Parish, January 20, 1801, in Sparks, *The Life of Gouverneur Morris*, 3:143.

194 *"I congratulate the people of the United States"*: *Annals of the Congress of the United States, Sixth Congress* (Gales and Seaton, 1851), 723.

194 *Washington in 1800 was a muddy experiment*: Ron Chernow, *Alexander Hamilton* (Penguin, 2004), 635.

195 *"Two of our hardy New England men"*: Quoted in David McCullough, *John Adams* (Simon & Schuster, 2001), 553.

195 *"We want nothing here but houses, cellars and kitchens"*: Gouverneur Morris to the Princess of Thurn and Taxis, December 14, 1800, in Sparks, *The Life of Gouverneur Morris*, 3:129–30.

196 *"It was proposed . . . to prevent any election"*: Gouverneur Morris to Alexander Hamilton, December 19, 1800, in Harold C. Syrett, ed., *The Papers of Alexander Hamilton*, vol. 25, *July 1800–April 1802* (Columbia University Press, 1977), 266–69.

196 *Hamilton had played a pivotal role in the campaign*: Chernow, *Alexander Hamilton*, 622.

196 *"has no principle public or private"*: Alexander Hamilton to Gouverneur Morris, December 24, 1800, in Syrett, *The Papers of Alexander Hamilton*, 25:271–73.

197 *most of his fellow Federalists were "moved by passion only"*: Gouverneur Morris to Alexander Hamilton, January 5, 1801, in ibid., 25:298–99.

197 *During the first twenty-hour session*: Chernow, *Alexander Hamilton*, 636.

197 "*If that party wish to disorganize,* that *is the way to do it*": Quoted in Noble E. Cunningham Jr., "Election of 1800," in Arthur M. Schlesinger and Fred Israel, eds., *History of American Presidential Elections, 1789–1968*, vol. 1 (Chelsea House, 1971), 132.

197 "nil desperandum de Republica *[Don't despair of the Republic]*": Gouverneur Morris to Rufus King, June 4, 1800, in Sparks, *The Life of Gouverneur Morris*, 3:128.

197 *"this farce of life contains nothing which should put us out of humor"*: Gouverneur Morris to Robert R. Livingston, February 20, 1801, in ibid., 3:153–54.

198 *"Every difference of opinion is not a difference of principle"*: "First Inaugural Address," March 4, 1801, in Barbara B. Oberg, ed., *The Papers of Thomas Jefferson*, vol. 33, *17 February–30 April 1801* (Princeton University Press, 2006), 148–52.

198 *"The destruction of the general government"*: Diary entry for December 15, 1801, in Miller, *The Diaries of Gouverneur Morris: New York*, 201.

199 *"Did the people of America vest all powers in the Legislature?"*: The text of Morris's speech may be found in *Annals of the Congress of the United States, Seventh Congress* (Gales and Seaton, 1851), 37–41.

199 *The president was "very civil"*: Diary entry for January 8, 1802, in Miller, *The Diaries of Gouverneur Morris: New York*, 207.

199 *the "shriveled condition" of her husband*: Ibid.

200 *"remarkably erect and dignified"*: Hamilton's physical appearance and manner are described in William Sullivan, *The Public Men of the Revolution* (Carey and Hart, 1847), 260–61; and Harry MacNeill Bland and Virginia W. Northcott, "The Life Portraits of Alexander Hamilton," *The William and Mary Quarterly* 12, no. 2 (April 1955), 187–88.

200 *Both men had known hardship*: Brookhiser, *Gentleman Revolutionary*, 158–59.

200 *"Never did I see a man so completely overwhelmed with grief"*: Charles R. King, ed., *The Life and Correspondence of Rufus King*, vol. 4, *1801–1806* (G. P. Putnam's Sons, 1897), 28.

200 *"Perhaps no man in the United States"*: Alexander Hamilton to Gouverneur Morris, February 29, 1802, in Syrett, *The Papers of Alexander Hamilton*, 25:544–46.

200 *"You say I am not more a favorite than you are"*: Gouverneur Morris to Alexander Hamilton, March 11, 1802, in ibid., 25:560–61.

201 *"We have here as yet done nothing of importance"*: Gouverneur Morris to Robert R. Livingston, March 20, 1802, in Sparks, *The Life of Gouverneur Morris*, 3:165.

201 *"cold as a frog"*: Diary entry for May 4, 1802, in Miller, *The Diaries of Gouverneur Morris: New York*, 229.

201 *"[Robert] came to me lean, low-spirited, and as poor"*: Gouverneur Morris to John Parish, January 14, 1803, in Sparks, *The Life of Gouverneur Morris*, 3:178.

201 *"My political enemies have had the goodness to relieve me"*: Gouverneur Morris to John Dickinson, May 23, 1803, in ibid., 3:181.

202 *"You know there cannot be any political confidence"*: Quoted in Chernow, *Alexander Hamilton*, 678.

202 *"Hamilton is intriguing for any candidate"*: Quoted in ibid., 674.

202 *"General Hamilton did not oppose Mr. Burr because he was a* democrat": Ibid.

202 "upwards of twenty women of ill fame": Ibid., 675.

202 *Anonymous broadsides plastered on New York's taverns*: Ibid., 675–76.

203 *It was a dinner party in March*: Ibid., 680–81.

203 *When Burr read it on June 18, his fury boiled over*: Ibid., 681–85.

203 *Hamilton's reply—cool, legalistic, and evasive*: Ibid., 685–86.

203 *"Everything in Alexander Hamilton's life pointed to the fact"*: Ibid., 683.

203 *At dawn that Wednesday, two small boats slipped across the Hudson*: Ibid., 700–701.

204 *When the duelists and their seconds were on the ledge*: Ibid., 701–3.

TWENTY-THREE: THE DEATH OF HAMILTON

205 *Gouverneur's nephew brought the horrifying news to Morrisania*: Diary entry for July 11, 1804, in Miller, *The Diaries of Gouverneur Morris: New York*, 357.

205 *Hamilton was still alive*: Diary entry for July 12, 1804, in ibid.

205 *After the duel, Pendleton and Hosack had carried Hamilton down the path*: Chernow, *Alexander Hamilton*, 704.

205 *"Let the event be gradually broken to her"*: Quoted in ibid., 705.

205 *Morris rushed to Hamilton's side*: Diary entry for July 12, 1804, in Miller, *The Diaries of Gouverneur Morris: New York*, 357.

205 *more than twenty family members and friends*: Chernow, *Alexander Hamilton*, 708.

206 *Morris was so overcome by the scene*: Diary entry for July 12, 1804, in Miller, *The Diaries of Gouverneur Morris: New York*, 357.

206 *"Remember my Eliza, you are a Christian"*: Quoted in Chernow, *Alexander Hamilton*, 706.

206 *Eliza held up their two-year-old son Philip*: Ibid., 708.

206 *Morris was sitting next to him*: Diary entry for July 12, 1804, in Miller, *The Diaries of Gouverneur Morris: New York*, 357.

206 *"The big tears that flowed down Morris's cheek"*: Quoted in ibid., xxviii.

206 *"I promise to do so if I can possibly command myself enough"*: Diary entry for July 12, 1804, in ibid., 357.

206 *Morris wasn't just worried about holding himself together*: Diary entry for July 13, 1804, in ibid., 357–59.

207 *"In addition to all the difficulties of this subject"*: Ibid.

207 *On Saturday morning, mourners gathered*: This description of Hamilton's funeral comes from Chernow, *Alexander Hamilton*, 711; and "The Funeral [14 July 1804]," in Harold C. Syrett, ed., *The Papers of Alexander Hamilton*, vol. 26, *1 May 1802–23 October 1804, Additional Documents 1774–1799, Addenda and Errata* (Columbia University Press, 1979), 322–30.

207 *he was grappling with how to eulogize his friend*: Diary entry for July 14, 1804, in Miller, *The Diaries of Gouverneur Morris: New York*, 359.

208 *"Far from attempting to excite your emotions"*: "The Funeral [14 July 1804]," in Syrett, *The Papers of Alexander Hamilton*, 26:325.

208 *"so much affected . . . almost deprived him"*: Quoted in Miller, *The Diaries of Gouverneur Morris: New York*, xxix.

208 *"In signing that compact [the Constitution] he expressed his apprehension"*: "The Funeral [14 July 1804]," in Syrett, *The Papers of Alexander Hamilton*, 26:326.

209 *"I find that what I have said does not meet the general expectation"*: Diary entry for July 14, 1804, in Miller, *The Diaries of Gouverneur Morris: New York*, 359.

209 *"Nations, like individuals, are not to be reasoned out of vice"*: Gouverneur Morris to Aaron Ogden, December 28, 1804, in Sparks, *The Life of Gouverneur Morris*, 3:216.

209 *"literally like a nobleman"*: Edward J. Young, Clement Hugh Hill, and Alexander McKenzie, eds., *Proceedings of the Massachusetts Historical Society, 1885–1886*, vol. 2 (Massachusetts Historical Society, 1886), 8.

210 *"I row about nine miles on our return"*: Diary entry for August 28, 1806, in Miller, *The Diaries of Gouverneur Morris: New York*, 459.

210 *"a good deal of pain from an ugly little ulcer"*: Diary entry for August 12, 1805, in ibid., 410.

210 *"A little rain this morning which clears away at nine"*: Diary entry for July 22, 1808, in ibid., 549.

TWENTY-FOUR: MR. MORRIS TAKES A BRIDE

211 *Morris first encountered Ann Cary Randolph*: Swiggett, *The Extraordinary Mr. Morris*, 136–37; Brookhiser, *Gentleman Revolutionary*, 180; Alan Pell Crawford, *Unwise Passions: A True Story of a Remarkable Woman—and the First Great Scandal of Eighteenth-Century America* (Simon & Schuster, 2000), 53–54, 57.

211 *Richard's younger brothers, Theodorick and John*: Crawford, *Unwise Passions*, 59, 62; Brookhiser, *Gentleman Revolutionary*, 181.

212 *Nancy arrived feeling unwell*: The events at Glentivar are described in Crawford, *Unwise Passions*, 70–72.

212 *Soon, whispers spread across Virginia*: Ibid., 73.

212 *To clear his name, Richard published a letter*: Ibid., 77–78.

212 *But when he arrived at court to defend himself*: Ibid., 82.

212 *Richard turned to two of Virginia's most celebrated lawyers*: The trial is recounted in ibid., 83–98.

213 *the household at Bizarre fell into decline*: Ibid., 112.

213 *in the spring of 1805, he asked her to leave*: Ibid., 168–69.

213 *Homeless and disgraced, Nancy made her way north*: Ibid., 184–85; Miller, *The Diaries of Gouverneur Morris: New York*, li.

213 *From there, she wrote to Gouverneur Morris*: Crawford, *Unwise Passions*, 186.

213 *"Talk not of gratitude, my dear Madam"*: Quoted in ibid., 191–92.

214 *"Time, in taking away the ardor"*: Quoted in Brookhiser, *Gentleman Revolutionary*, 184.

214 *On April 28, 1809, he drove to Mrs. Pollock's boardinghouse*: Diary entry for April 28, 1809, in Miller, *The Diaries of Gouverneur Morris: New York*, 594.

214 *Morris . . . sought reassurance*: Crawford, *Unwise Passions*, 197.

214 *On Christmas Day 1809, before a gathering*: Ibid., 197–98; Diary entry for December 25, 1809, in Miller, *The Diaries of Gouverneur Morris: New York*, 621–22.

214 *"I glory that I was married in a gown patched at the elbows"*: Quoted in Crawford, *Unwise Passions*, 198.

214 *"If the world were to live with my wife"*: Quoted in Morris, *The Diary and Letters of Gouverneur Morris*, 2:516; quoted in Miller, *The Diaries of Gouverneur Morris: New York*, liii.

TWENTY-FIVE: A GRAND CANAL

215 *cramped, filthy, and filled with noisy drunks*: This description of Clinton's night at the inn comes from William W. Campbell, *The Life and Writings of De Witt Clinton* (Baker and Scribner, 1849), 70–72.

217 *It took weeks to cross the mountains on the rutted turnpike roads*: Peter L. Bernstein, *Wedding of the Waters: The Erie Canal and the Making of a Great Nation* (W. W. Norton, 2005), 102–3.

217 *Without a strong connection to the coast*: Ibid., 62–64.

217 *Morris regaled the group with descriptions of his canal*: Sparks, *The Life of Gouverneur Morris*, 1:497–98.

217 *The two men passed the evening together*: Simeon De Witt to William Darby, February 25, 1822, in *Laws of the State of New York, in Relation to the Erie and Champlain Canals*, vol. 1 (E. and E. Hosford, 1825), 38–39.

218 *Hawley was frustrated by the time and money it took*: William Chazanof, *Joseph Ellicott and the Holland Land Company: The Opening of Western New York* (Syracuse University Press, 1970), 158–69.

218 *Forman was undaunted*: Bernstein, *Wedding of the Waters*, 119.

218 *"the revenue thus liberated"*: Quoted in ibid., 109.

219 *Forman began his meeting with the president*: The meeting with Jefferson is recounted in David Hosack, *Memoir of De Witt Clinton* (J. Seymour, 1829), 346–48.

219 *"the most extensive theater for the display of skill and industry"*: Morris, *The Diary and Letters of Gouverneur Morris*, 2:518–19.

220 *They embarked from Schenectady on July 4*: Hosack, *Memoir of De Witt Clinton*, 32.

220 *They also brought along an English painter*: Katharine McCook Knox, *The Sharples: Their Portraits of George Washington and His Contemporaries* (Da Capo Press, 1972), 38–39.

220 *Gouverneur was overwhelmed*: Diary entry for July 24, 1810, in Miller, *The Diaries of Gouverneur Morris: New York*, 655.

221 *"The spray of the waters enveloped us"*: Campbell, *The Life and Writings of De Witt Clinton*, 133.

221 *"I suspect that when we come to make up our report"*: Diary entry for August 3, 1810, in Miller, *The Diaries of Gouverneur Morris: New York, 1799–1816*, 658.

221 *the Morrises visited a community of Shakers*: Diary entry for September 2, 1810, in ibid., 664–65.

221 *"too great a national interest"*: *Laws of the State of New York*, 1:68.

222 *Morris and Clinton traveled to Washington to make the case*: Burrows and Wallace, *Gotham*, 419; Diary entry for December 21, 1811, in Miller, *The Diaries of Gouverneur Morris: New York*, 722.

222 *Morris's "grand and luminous" testimony*: Sparks, *The Life of Gouverneur Morris*, 3:496–97; Harmanus Bleecker to David Hosack, December 23, 1828, in Hosack, *Memoir of De Witt Clinton*, 248.

222 *It was an increasingly chaotic place*: Marguerite Holloway, *The Measure of Manhattan: The Tumultuous Career and Surprising Legacy of John Randel, Jr., Cartographer, Surveyor, Inventor* (W. W. Norton, 2013), 48–49.

223 *The three men rode all over Manhattan*: Diary entry for July 1, 1807, in Miller, *The Diaries of Gouverneur Morris: New York*, 500.

223 *Every morning, Randel hiked from his home in lower Manhattan*: Burrows and Wallace, *Gotham*, 420; Holloway, *The Measure of Manhattan*, 57.

223 *"rocks, precipices, steep grades and other obstacles"*: Burrows and Wallace, *Gotham*, 420.

223 *Their uncompromising grid*: Ibid., 420–22; Holloway, *The Measure of Manhattan*, 51; Miller, *The Diaries of Gouverneur Morris: New York*, lix–lx.

224 *"Straight-sided and right-angled houses"*: *Remarks of the Commissioners, 1811*, accessed at https://thegreatestgrid.mcny.org/greatest-grid/key-documents/73.

224 *"The most difficult point is accomplished"*: Diary entry for January 11, 1812, in Miller, *The Diaries of Gouverneur Morris: New York*, 725–26.

224 *In a meeting with Madison two days later*: Diary entry for January 13, 1812, in Miller, *The Diaries of Gouverneur Morris: New York*, 726.

224 *the New Yorkers' "ostensible object" was the canal*: Elizabeth Donnan, ed., *Annual Report of the American Historical Association for the Year 1913*. Vol. 2, *Papers of James A. Bayard, 1796–1815* (US Government Printing Office, 1915), 188–89.

225 *There was a light dusting of snow on the ground*: Diary entry for January 16, 1812, in Miller, *The Diaries of Gouverneur Morris: New York*, 726.

225 *"the sneers and sarcasms of men"*: "Report of the Commissioners under the Act of April 8, 1811," in *Laws of the State of New York*, 1:79.

TWENTY-SIX: MR. MADISON'S WAR

226 *British troops advanced across the eastern grounds*: Walter Lord, *The Dawn's Early Light* (W. W. Norton, 1972), 162.

226 *"somewhat infected with an unseemly bias for monarchical splendor"*: Ibid., 163.

227 *"Shall this harbor of Yankee democracy be burned?"*: Peter Snow, *When Britain Burned the White House: The 1814 Invasion of Washington* (Thomas Dunne Books, 2014), 117.

227 *In the House chamber, they chopped apart doors*: This description of the burning of the Capitol comes from Walter R. Borneman, *1812: The War That Forged a Nation* (HarperCollins, 2004), 231; Fergus M. Bordewich, *Washington: The Making of the American Capital* (Amistad, 2008), 261; Lord, *The Dawn's Early Light*, 163–64; Snow, *When Britain Burned the White House*, 117–18; Pierre Berton, *Flames Across the Border: 1813–1814* (McClelland and Stewart, 1981), 372–73.

227 *British reinforcements marching toward Washington*: George Robert Gleig, *The Campaigns of the British Army at Washington and New Orleans in the Years 1814–1815* (John Murray, 1836), 132.

227 *President James Madison had galloped away*: Berton, *Flames Across the Border*, 369; Allen C. Clark, *Life and Letters of Dolley Madison* (W. F. Roberts, 1914), 164.

227 *Did she have "courage or firmness"*: Clark, *Life and Letters of Dolley Madison*, 164.

228 *At half past noon, American cannons and sharpshooters*: Berton, *Flames Across the Border*, 370–71.

228 *"at a moment's warning"*: Clark, *Life and Letters of Dolley Madison*, 164.

228 *She loaded trunks with public and private papers*: Ibid., 165.

228 *soldiers wandering aimlessly, citizens pouring across the bridge*: Gleig, *The Campaigns of the British Army*, 136; Bordewich, *Washington*, 260.

228 *When dusty messengers arrived at three o'clock*: Clark, *Life and Letters of Dolley Madison*, 165; Berton, *Flames Across the Border*, 371.

228 *She entrusted the canvas to two New Yorkers*: Clark, *Life and Letters of Dolley Madison*, 166; Berton, *Flames Across the Border*, 371.

228 *"I confess that I was so unfeminine"*: Clark, *Life and Letters of Dolley Madison*, 166.

229 *Ross politely requested supper*: Snow, *When Britain Burned the White House*, 123–24.

229 *Inside, the British found a dinner frozen in time*: Gleig, *The Campaigns of the British Army*, 134–35; Snow, *When Britain Burned the White House*, 107, 126–27; Bordewich, *Washington*, 262.

229 *Satiated, they scavenged freely*: Bordewich, *Washington*, 262; Lord, *The Dawn's Early Light*, 168–69.

229 *"Our sailors . . . were artists at the work"*: Snow, *When Britain Burned the White House*, 130; Borneman, *1812*, 231.

229 *"I never saw a scene at once more terrible or more magnificent"*: Snow, *When Britain Burned the White House*, 130.

229 *"George Washington founded this city after a seven years' war"*: Lord, *The Dawn's Early Light*, 216.

230 *Morris understood Britain had to take a tough line*: Miller, *An Incautious Man*, 202–3; James Truslow Adams, *New England in the Republic, 1776–1850* (Little, Brown and Company, 1926), 245; Borneman, *1812*, 19–20.

231 *"so hostile to freedom"*: Miller, *An Incautious Man*, 202.

231 *The economic results were catastrophic*: Adams, *New England in the Republic*, 250–52; Borneman, *1812*, 40.

231 *a fortified half-mile-long barge*: Adams, *New England in the Republic*, 253.

231 *Clay boasted that Kentucky militiamen alone*: Borneman, *1812*, 57.

232 *"a mere matter of marching"*: Thomas Jefferson to William Duane, August 4, 1812, in J. Jefferson Looney, ed., *The Papers of Thomas Jefferson, Retirement Series*, vol. 5, *1 May 1812 to 10 March 1813* (Princeton University Press, 2008), 293.

232 *"Can we hope for, shall we dare ask for mercy"*: Gouverneur Morris, "An Address to the People of the State of New York on the Present State of Affairs (1812)," in Barlow, *To Secure the Blessings of Liberty*, 543.

232 *Morris saw a pattern*: J. Jackson Barlow, "Nationalizing 'the Curse of Heaven': Gouverneur Morris on the Constitution and the Slave Power," *The Georgetown Journal of Law & Public Policy* 21, no. 1 (Winter 2023), 34.

233 *"mortal foes"*: Gouverneur Morris to Harrison Gray Otis, April 29, 1813, in Morris, *The Diary and Letters of Gouverneur Morris*, 2:552.

233 *some New England Federalists were even proposing secession*: Adams, *New England in the Republic*, 273–74.

233 *"emancipated from tyranny and oppression"*: Quoted in Borneman, *1812*, 62.

234 *The sixty-six soldiers, nine women, and eighteen children*: Ibid., 66–67.

234 *"a miscarriage, without even [the] heroism of disaster"*: Quoted in ibid., 76; Donald Hickey, *The War of 1812: A Forgotten Conflict* (University of Illinois Press, 1989), 88.

234 *Morris wondered whether the president was "out of his senses"*: Gouverneur Morris to John Parish, March 6, 1813, in Morris, *The Diary and Letters of Gouverneur Morris*, 2:548.

235 *Antiwar sentiment was spreading*: Samuel Eliot Morison, "Our Most Unpopular War," *Proceedings of the Massachusetts Historical Society*, vol. 80 (1968), 39.

235 *many citizens exercised their constitutional right to dissent*: Harvey Strum, "New York Federalists and Opposition to the War of 1812," *World Affairs* 142, no. 3 (Winter 1980), 184.

235 *Clay's Kentucky supplied only four hundred recruits*: Morison, "Our Most Unpopular War," 38.

235 *In New York, ships lay idle*: Burrows and Wallace, *Gotham*, 426.

235 *the British completed their desecration of the American capital*: Lord, *The Dawn's Early Light*, 181–82; Gleig, *The Campaigns of the British Army*, 141–42; Berton, *Flames Across the Border*, 374.

236 *The fort was a five-pointed star*: Borneman, *1812*, 239.

236 *above it flew a giant American flag*: Ibid., 244–45.

236 *"Can you see the flag?"*: Ibid., 246.

TWENTY-SEVEN: "LET US FORGET PARTY"

238 *Nancy had received a letter*: Crawford, *Unwise Passions*, 226.

238 *When Tudor arrived at Morrisania by boat*: Ibid., 227.

239 *"violent bleeding from the lungs"*: Quoted in ibid., 228.

239 *John took Nancy in his arms*: Ibid.

239 *"Remember the past"*: Quoted in ibid., 229.

240 *"the offspring of an illicit amour"*: Quoted in ibid., 231.

240 *"My brother died* suddenly": The full text of the letter may be found in ibid., 234–40.

241 *"under the wounds inflicted by relations"*: Quoted in ibid., 241.

241 *"see no use in keeping up"*: Quoted in ibid., 242.

241 *"her candor had blunted [John's] arrow"*: Quoted in ibid.

241 *"those who cried aloud against this houseless child"*: Quoted in ibid., 242.

241 *"When you entered this house"*: Quoted in ibid., 246.

241 *she had given birth at Glentivar*: Ibid, 248.

241 *"mean selfishness"*: Quoted in ibid., 247.

241 *"I loved my husband"*: Quoted in ibid., 252.

242 *British troops had occupied eastern Maine*: Adams, *New England in the Republic*, 296; Samuel Eliot Morison, *The Life and Letters of Harrison Gray Otis, Federalist*, vol. 2, *1765–1848* (Houghton Mifflin, 1913), 97.

242 *"We are in a deplorable situation"*: Borneman, *1812*, 250.

242 *"a war of party and not of the country"*: Quoted in Robert Ernst, *Rufus King: American Federalist* (The University of North Carolina Press, 1968), 314.

242 *"The enemy is at our doors"*: Quoted in ibid., 335.

242 *"I feel myself bound in duty and honor"*: Morris, *The Diary and Letters of Gouverneur Morris*, 2:570.

242 *Many New Englanders also wondered*: Morison, *The Life and Letters of Harrison Gray Otis*, 2:97; Borneman, *1812*, 252.

243 *"on the basis of fair representation"*: *A Short Account of the Hartford Convention, Taken From Official Documents, and Addressed to the Fair-Minded and the Well-Disposed* (O. Everett, 1823), 6.

243 *Connecticut accepted immediately*: Borneman, *1812*, 253.

243 *The Federalist leaders of the Hartford Convention insisted*: Morison, "Our Most Unpopular War," 47; Borneman, *1812*, 252–53.

243 *secession* was *on the minds of many New Englanders*: Morison, "Our Most Unpopular War," 47, 51; Adams, *New England in the Republic*, 292.

244 *"who wished to avoid secession at all costs"*: Morison, "Our Most Unpopular War," 47, 52.

244 *"We are going to keep you young hotheads from getting into mischief"*: Quoted in Borneman, *1812*, 253.

244 *Broad-shouldered and over six feet tall*: Samuel G. Goodrich, *Recollections of a Lifetime, or Men and Things I Have Seen,* vol. 2 (Miller, Orton, and Mulligan, 1857), 36.

244 *"a safety valve by which the steam arising"*: Quoted in Morison, *The Life and Letters of Harrison Gray Otis*, 2:110–11.

244 *His eyes were "fixed on a star in the east"*: Gouverneur Morris to Timothy Pickering, December 23, 1814, in Sparks, *The Life of Gouverneur Morris*, 3:322–24.

244 *"rescue the country from her present miserable and ridiculous condition"*: Diary entry for May 3, 1812, in Miller, *The Diaries of Gouverneur Morris: New York*, 742.

245 *"conducive to the happiness or consistent with the freedom"*: Gouverneur Morris to Harrison Gray Otis, April 29, 1813, in Morison, *The Life and Letters of Harrison Gray Otis*, 2:84.

245 *"What does it signify that men should have a written constitution"*: Gouverneur Morris to Timothy Pickering, December 23, 1814, in Sparks, *The Life of Gouverneur Morris*, 3:323.

246 *a small detachment of US troops*: Goodrich, *Recollections of a Lifetime*, 2:53.

246 *"the enemy scours the sea coast"*: The final report of the Hartford Convention may be found in *The Proceedings of a Convention of Delegates from the States of Massachusetts, Connecticut and Rhode-Island; the Counties of Cheshire and Grafton, in the State of New-Hampshire; and the County of Windham, in the State of Vermont, Convened at Hartford, in the State of Connecticut, December 15, 1814* (Wells and Lilly, 1815), 5–22.

247 *"A government without force, without money, without talent"*: Quoted in Morris, *The Diary and Letters of Gouverneur Morris*, 2:578.

247 *The Hartford delegates had been "prudent"*: Quoted in ibid, 579.

247 *Massachusetts and Connecticut dispatched representatives*: Adams, *New England in the Republic*, 299.

247 *By the time they arrived*: *A Short Account of the Hartford Convention*, 16.

247 *a crowd was enjoying an evening concert at the City Hotel*: This account of New York's reaction to the end of the War of 1812 comes from Goodrich, *Recollections of a Lifetime, or Men and Things I Have Seen*, vol. 1 (Miller, Orton, and Mulligan, 1856), 496, 503–4.

248 *He urged his fellow Federalists to move on*: Miller, *An Incautious Man*, 204.

249 *Gouverneur . . . walked a mile and a half*: Diary entry for June 10, 1815, in Miller, *The Diaries of Gouverneur Morris: New York*, 830; Crawford, *Unwise Passions*, 256; Swiggett, *The Extraordinary Mr. Morris*, 437.

249 *"How large a portion of human life!"*: Gouverneur Morris to John Parish, July 6, 1816, in Morris, *The Diary and Letters of Gouverneur Morris*, 2:600–601.

249 *he advised his party colleagues to temporarily cede the field*: Gouverneur Morris to the Committee of Correspondence, Philadelphia, August 27, 1816, in Sparks, *The Life of Gouverneur Morris*, 3:360–61.

250 *"I shall be very happy indeed to receive you here"*: Thomas Jefferson to Gouverneur Morris, October 20, 1816, in J. Jefferson Looney, ed., *The Papers of Thomas Jefferson, Retirement Series*, vol. 10, *May 1816 to 18 January 1817* (Princeton University Press, 2013), 477–78.

250 *he took advantage of the mild weather*: Diary entry for October 10, 1816, in Miller, *The Diaries of Gouverneur Morris: New York*, 881.

251 *"But, gentlemen, let us forget party"*: Gouverneur Morris to the Committee of Correspondence, Philadelphia, August 27, 1816, in Sparks, *The Life of Gouverneur Morris*, 3:361.

AFTERWORD

253 *"We are not sufficiently possessed of facts"*: "Died," *New-York Evening Post*, November 6, 1816.

253 *Nearly a century later*: "Monument to Gouverneur Morris Unveiled at Church Where He and His Brother Are Buried," *New York Times*, July 5, 1932.

254 *sites named for Morris and his family all over the Bronx*: Ian Frazier, *Paradise Bronx: The Life and Times of New York's Greatest Borough* (Picador, 2025), 41.

254 *Early in the twentieth century, some local preservationists*: Ibid., 41–42; Stephen Jenkins, *The Story of the Bronx: From the Purchase Made by the Dutch from the Indians in 1639 to the Present Day* (G. P. Putnam's Sons, 1912), 364.

254 *Morris's name is another impediment*: Frazier, *Paradise Bronx*, 41.

BIBLIOGRAPHY

MANUSCRIPT SOURCES

Boston Tea Party Historical Society

Gouverneur Morris Papers, Manuscript Division, Library of Congress

William Smith Jr. Papers, New York Public Library, Manuscripts and Archives Division

William Livingston Family Collection, Massachusetts Historical Society

SELECT BIBLIOGRAPHY

A Short Account of the Hartford Convention, Taken from Official Documents, and Addressed to the Fair-Minded and the Well-Disposed. O. Everett, 1823.

Abbot, W. W., ed. *The Papers of George Washington, Colonial Series.* Vol. 1, *1748–August 1755.* University Press of Virginia, 1983.

Abbot, W. W., ed. *The Papers of George Washington, Confederation Series.* Vol. 4, *2 April 1786–31 January 1787.* University Press of Virginia, 1995.

Abbot, W. W., ed. *The Papers of George Washington, Retirement Series.* Vol. 4, *20 April 1799–13 December 1799.* University Press of Virginia, 1999.

Acomb, Evelyn M., ed. *The Revolutionary Journal of Baron Ludwig Von Closen, 1780–1783.* The University of North Carolina Press, 1958.

Adams, Charles Francis, ed. *The Works of John Adams, Second President of the United States.* Vol. 2. Charles C. Little and James Brown, 1850.

Adams, Charles Francis, ed. *The Works of John Adams, Second President of the United States.* Vol. 3. Charles C. Little and James Brown, 1851.

Adams, James Truslow. *New England in the Republic, 1776–1850.* Little, Brown and Company, 1926.

Adams, William Howard. *Gouverneur Morris: An Independent Life.* Yale University Press, 2003.

Adams, William Howard. *The Paris Years of Thomas Jefferson.* Yale University Press, 1997.

Amar, Akhil Reed. *The Words That Made Us: America's Constitutional Conversation, 1760–1840.* New York: Basic Books, 2021.

Annals of the Congress of the United States, Sixth Congress. Gales and Seaton, 1851.

Annals of the Congress of the United States, Seventh Congress. Gales and Seaton, 1851.

Atkinson, Rick. *The British Are Coming: The War for America, Lexington to Princeton, 1775–1777.* Henry Holt and Company, 2019.

Atkinson, Rick. *The Fate of the Day: The War for America, Fort Ticonderoga to Charleston, 1777–1780.* Crown, 2025.

Bailyn, Bernard. *The Ordeal of Thomas Hutchinson.* The Belknap Press of Harvard University Press, 1974.

Balch, Thomas, ed. *Papers Relating Chiefly to the Maryland Line During the Revolutionary War.* T. K. and P. G. Collins, Printers, 1857.

Bangs, Edward, ed. *Journal of Lieutenant Isaac Bangs, April 1 to July 29, 1776.* John Wilson and Son, 1890.

Barlow, J. Jackson, ed. *To Secure the Blessings of Liberty: Selected Writings of Gouverneur Morris.* Liberty Fund, 2012.

Barlow, J. Jackson. "Nationalizing 'the Curse of Heaven': Gouverneur Morris on the Constitution and the Slave Power." *The Georgetown Journal of Law & Public Policy* 21, no. 1 (Winter 2023): 25–49.

Basler, Roy B., ed. *The Collected Works of Abraham Lincoln.* Vol. 3, *August 21, 1858–March 4, 1860.* Rutgers University Press, 1953.

Bernard, Jack F. *Talleyrand: A Biography.* New York: G. P. Putnam's Sons, 1973.

Bernardy, Françoise de. *Son of Talleyrand: The Life of Comte Charles de Flahaut 1785–1870.* Collins, 1956.

Bernstein, Peter L. *Wedding of the Waters: The Erie Canal and the Making of a Great Nation.* W. W. Norton, 2005.

Berton, Pierre. *Flames Across the Border: 1813–1814.* McClelland and Stewart, 1981.

Betham-Edwards, Matilda, ed. *Arthur Young's Travels in France During the Years 1787, 1788, 1789.* George Bell & Sons, 1892.

Billias, George Athan. *Elbridge Gerry: Founding Father and Republican Statesman.* McGraw-Hill, 1976.

Blackburn, Joyce. *George Wythe of Williamsburg.* Harper & Row, 1975.

Bland, Harry MacNeill, and Virginia W. Northcott. "The Life Portraits of Alexander Hamilton." *The William and Mary Quarterly* 12, no. 2 (April 1955): 187–98.

Bordewich, Fergus M. *Washington: The Making of the American Capital.* Amistad, 2008.

Borneman, Walter R. *1812: The War That Forged a Nation.* HarperCollins, 2004.

Boscawen, Hugh. "The Origins of the Flat-Bottomed Landing Craft 1757–1758." *Journal of the National Army Museum* (1985): 23–30.

Bowen, Catherine Drinker. *Miracle at Philadelphia: The Story of the Constitutional Convention, May to September 1787.* Little, Brown, 1966.

Boyd, Julian P., ed. *The Papers of Thomas Jefferson.* Vol. 9, *1 November 1785–22 June 1786.* Princeton University Press, 1954.

Boyd, Julian P., ed. *The Papers of Thomas Jefferson.* Vol. 12, *7 August 1787–31 March 1788.* Princeton University Press, 1955.

Boyd, Julian P., ed. *The Papers of Thomas Jefferson.* Vol. 13, *March 1788–October 1788.* Princeton University Press, 1956.

Boyd, Julian P., ed. *The Papers of Thomas Jefferson.* Vol. 14, *8 October 1788–26 March 1789.* Princeton University Press, 1958.

Boyd, Julian P., ed. *The Papers of Thomas Jefferson.* Vol. 15, *27 March 1789–30 November 1789.* Princeton University Press, 1958.

Boyd, Julian P., ed. *The Papers of Thomas Jefferson.* Vol. 17, *6 July–3 November 1790,* Princeton University Press, 1965.

Brands, H. W. *The First American: The Life and Times of Benjamin Franklin.* Doubleday, 2000.

Bridenbaugh, Carl. *Cities in Revolt: Urban Life in America, 1743–1776.* Capricorn Books, 1964.

Brookhiser, Richard. *Gentleman Revolutionary: Gouverneur Morris—The Rake Who Wrote the Constitution.* Free Press, 2003.

Brookhiser, Richard. *James Madison.* Basic Books, 2011.

Burnett, Edmund C., ed. *Letters of Members of the Continental Congress.* Vol. 2, *July 5, 1776–December 31, 1777.* The Carnegie Institution of Washington, D.C., 1923.

Burnett, Edmund C., ed. *Letters of Members of the Continental Congress.* Vol. 3, *January 1, 1778–December 31, 1778.* The Carnegie Institution of Washington, D.C., 1923.

Burrows, Edwin G., and Mike Wallace. *Gotham: A History of New York City to 1898.* Oxford University Press, 1999.

Butterfield, L. H., ed. *The Adams Papers, Diary and Autobiography of John Adams: Diary, 1771–1781.* Vol. 2. The Belknap Press of Harvard University Press, 1961.

Butterfield, Lyman Henry, ed. *Letters of Benjamin Rush.* Vol. 1. Princeton University Press, 1951.

Campbell, William W. *The Life and Writings of De Witt Clinton.* Baker and Scribner, 1849.

Catanzariti, John, ed. *The Papers of Thomas Jefferson.* Vol. 24, *1 June–31 December 1792.* Princeton University Press, 1990.

Catanzariti, John, ed. *The Papers of Thomas Jefferson.* Vol. 25, *1 January–10 May 1793.* Princeton University Press, 1992.

Chase, Eugene Parker, ed. *Our Revolutionary Forefathers: The Letters of François, Marquis de Barbé-Marbois, During His Residence in the United States as Secretary of the French Legation, 1779–1785*. Books for Libraries Press, 1969.

Chase, Philander D., ed. *The Papers of George Washington, Revolutionary War Series*. Vol. 2, *16 September 1775–31 December 1775*. University Press of Virginia, 1987.

Chazanof, William. *Joseph Ellicott and the Holland Land Company: The Opening of Western New York*. Syracuse University Press, 1970.

Chernow, Ron. *Alexander Hamilton*. Penguin, 2004.

Chernow, Ron. *Washington: A Life*. Penguin, 2010.

Clark, Allen C. *Life and Letters of Dolley Madison*. W. F. Roberts, 1914.

Clarkson, Paul Stephen. *Luther Martin of Maryland*. Johns Hopkins Press, 1970.

Cochran, John. "Reminiscences and Anecdotes." *The American Historical Register and Monthly Gazette of the Patriotic-Hereditary Societies of the United States of America*, Vol. 1 (January 1895): 432–39.

Conway, Moncure Daniel, ed. *The Writings of Thomas Paine*. Vol. 1, *1774–1779*. G. P. Putnam's Sons, 1894.

Cotner, Sharon Z. "Boning Up on Amputation." *Colonial Williamsburg Foundation Library Research Report Series*, no. 323 (1989).

Crawford, Alan Pell. *Unwise Passions: A True Story of a Remarkable Woman—and the First Great Scandal of Eighteenth-Century America*. Simon & Schuster, 2000.

Cullen, Charles T., ed. *The Papers of Thomas Jefferson*. Vol. 22, *6 August 1791–31 December 1791*. Princeton University Press, 1986.

Cullen, Charles T., ed. *The Papers of Thomas Jefferson*. Vol. 23, *1 January–31 May 1792*. Princeton University Press, 1990.

Cunningham, Noble E., Jr. "Election of 1800." In *History of American Presidential Elections, Vol. 1: 1789–1968*, edited by Arthur M. Schlesinger and Fred Israel. Chelsea House, 1971.

Cutler, William Parker, and Julia Perkins Cutler. *Life, Journals, and Correspondence of Rev. Manasseh Cutler, LL.D.* Vol. 1. Robert Clarke & Co, 1888.

Dana, Elizabeth Ellery. *The British in Boston, Being the Diary of Lieutenant John Barker of the King's Own Regiment from November 15, 1774, to May 31, 1776*. Harvard University Press, 1924.

Dann, John C., ed. *The Revolution Remembered: Eyewitness Accounts of the War for Independence*. University of Chicago Press, 1980.

Davenport, Beatrix Cary. *A Diary of the French Revolution by Gouverneur Morris*, 2 vols. Houghton Mifflin, 1939.

Davis, Thomas J. "The Great Negro Plot of 1741." *History Now* 60 (Summer 2021).

DeConde, Alexander. *The Quasi-War: The Politics and Diplomacy of the Undeclared War with France, 1797–1801*. Charles Scribner's Sons, 1966.

De Lancey, Edward Floyd, ed. *History of New York During the Revolutionary War, by*

Thomas Jones, Justice of the Supreme Court of the Province. Vol. 1. New York Historical Society, 1879.

Delafield, Julia. *Biographies of Francis Lewis and Morgan Lewis*. Anson D. F. Randolph & Company, 1877.

Doolen, Andy. "Reading and Writing Terror: The New York Conspiracy Trials of 1741." *American Literary History* 16, no. 3 (Autumn 2004): 377–406.

Donnan, Elizabeth, ed. *Annual Report of the American Historical Association for the Year 1913*. Vol. 2, *Papers of James A. Bayard, 1796–1815*. US Government Printing Office, 1915.

Dos Passos, John. "Robert Morris and the 'Art Magick.'" *American Heritage* 7, no. 6 (October 1956): 86–89; 113–15.

Douglass, Frederick. *Oration Delivered in Corinthian Hall, Rochester, by Frederick Douglass, July 5, 1852*. Lee, Mann and Company, 1852.

Duncan, Mike. *Hero of Two Worlds: The Marquis de Lafayette in the Age of Revolution*. PublicAffairs, 2021.

Dunn, Terry K. *Among His Slaves: George Mason, Slavery at Gunston Hall, and the Idealism of the American Revolution*. Commonwealth Books of Virginia, 2017.

Edgeworth, Charles Sneyd. *Memoirs of the Abbé Edgeworth: Containing His Narrative of the Last Hours of Louis XVI*. Rowland Hunter, 1815.

Elliott, Jonathan, ed. *The Debates in the Several State Conventions on the Adoption of the Federal Constitution as Recommended by the General Convention at Philadelphia in 1787*. Burt Franklin, 1888.

Ellis, Joseph J. *American Sphinx: The Character of Thomas Jefferson*. New York: Knopf, 1997.

Engelman, F. L. "Cadwallader Colden and the New York Stamp Act Riots." *The William and Mary Quarterly* 10, no. 4 (October 1953): 560–78.

Ernst, Robert. *Rufus King: American Federalist*. The University of North Carolina Press, 1968.

Farrand, Max. *The Framing of the Constitution of the United States*. Yale University Press, 1913.

Farrand, Max, ed. *The Records of the Federal Convention of 1787*, 3 vols. Yale University Press, 1911.

Farrand, Max, ed. *The Records of the Federal Convention of 1787*, revised edition in 4 vols. Yale University Press, 1937.

Ferguson, E. James. *The Power of the Purse: A History of American Public Finance 1776–1790*. The University of North Carolina Press, 1961.

Fischer, David Hackett. *Washington's Crossing*. Oxford University Press, 2004.

Fitzpatrick, John C., ed. *The Writings of George Washington from the Original Manuscript Sources, 1745–1799*. Vol. 26, *January 1, 1783–June 10, 1783*. US Government Printing Office, 1938.

Force, Peter, ed. *American Archives: A Documentary History of the United States of America.* Fifth Series, Vol. 3. M. St. Claire Clarke and Peter Force, 1853.

Ford, Worthington Chauncey, ed. *Journals of the Continental Congress, 1774–1789.* Vol. 2, *1775 May 10–September 20.* US Government Printing Office, 1905.

Ford, Worthington Chauncey, ed. *Journals of the Continental Congress, 1774–1789.* Vol. 10, *1778 January 1–May 1.* US Government Printing Office, 1908.

Ford, Worthington Chauncey, ed. *The Writings of George Washington.* Vol. 3, *1775–1776.* G. P. Putnam's Sons, 1889.

Ford, Worthington Chauncey, ed. *The Writings of George Washington.* Vol. 7, *1778–1779.* G. P. Putnam's Sons, 1890.

Fowler, William M., Jr. *The Baron of Beacon Hill: A Biography of John Hancock.* Houghton Mifflin, 1980.

Francis, John W. "Gouverneur Morris: A Fragment." *The Historical Magazine* 3, no. 4 (April 1868): 193–98.

Franks, Rebecca. "A Letter of Miss Rebecca Franks, 1778." *The Pennsylvania Magazine of History and Biography* 16, no. 2 (July 1892): 216–18.

Frazier, Ian. *Paradise Bronx: The Life and Times of New York's Greatest Borough.* Picador, 2025.

Freeman, Douglas Southall. *George Washington: A Biography.* Vol. 4. Charles Scribner's Sons, 1951.

Furet, François, and Mona Ozouf, eds. *A Critical Dictionary of the French Revolution.* The Belknap Press of Harvard University Press, 1989.

Gerber, Scott Douglas, ed. *Seriatim: The Supreme Court Before John Marshall.* NYU Press, 1998.

Glaeser, Edward L. "Urban Colossus: Why Is New York America's Largest City?" *Federal Reserve Bank of New York Economic Policy Review* (December 2005): 7–24.

Gleig, George Robert. *The Campaigns of the British Army at Washington and New Orleans in the Years 1814–1815.* John Murray, 1836.

Goodrich, Samuel G. *Recollections of a Lifetime, or Men and Things I Have Seen*, vol. 1. Miller, Orton, and Mulligan, 1856.

Goodrich, Samuel G. *Recollections of a Lifetime, or Men and Things I Have Seen*, vol. 2. Miller, Orton, and Mulligan, 1857.

Gordon, Lord Adam. "Journal of an Officer Who Travelled in America and the West Indies in 1764 and 1765." In Newton D. Mereness, *Travels in the American Colonies.* The Macmillan Company, 1916.

Graydon, Alexander. *Memoirs of His Own Time.* Edited by John Stockton Littell. Lindsay & Blackiston, 1846.

Greene, Evarts B., and Virginia D. Harrington. *American Population Before the Federal Census of 1790.* Peter Smith, 1966. First published in 1932 by Columbia University Press.

Grizzard, Frank E., Jr., and David R. Hoth, eds. *The Papers of George Washington, Revolutionary War Series.* Vol. 12, *26 October 1777–25 December 1777.* University Press of Virginia, 2002.

Haggard, Robert F., and Mark A. Mastromarino, eds. *The Papers of George Washington, Presidential Series.* Vol. 10, *1 March 1792–15 August 1792.* University of Virginia Press, 2002.

Hatch, Louis C. *The Administration of the American Revolutionary Army.* Longmans, Green, and Co., 1904.

Hickey, Donald. *The War of 1812: A Forgotten Conflict.* University of Illinois Press, 1989.

The Historical Magazine and Notes and Queries Concerning the Antiquities, History and Biography of America. Vol. 3, Second Series. Henry B. Dawson, 1868.

A History of Columbia University, 1754–1904. Columbia University Press, 1904.

Holloway, Marguerite. *The Measure of Manhattan: The Tumultuous Career and Surprising Legacy of John Randel, Jr., Cartographer, Surveyor, Inventor.* W. W. Norton, 2013.

Horne, Alistair. *La Belle France: A Short History.* Knopf, 2005.

Hosack, David. *Memoir of De Witt Clinton.* J. Seymour, 1829.

Hoth, David R., ed. *The Papers of George Washington, Presidential Series.* Vol. 14, *1 September–31 December 1793.* University of Virginia Press, 2008.

Hoth, David R., and Carol S. Ebel, eds. *The Papers of George Washington, Presidential Series.* Vol. 16, *1 May–30 September 1794.* University of Virginia Press, 2011.

Hoyt, Edwin P. *James Monroe.* Reilly & Lee Company, 1968.

Hunt, Gaillard, ed. *The Writings of James Madison.* Vol. 2, *1783–1787.* G. P. Putnam's Sons, 1901.

Hussain, Amer, and Fouzia Choukairi. "To Cool or Not to Cool: Evolution of the Treatment of Burns in the 18th Century." *International Journal of Surgery* 11, no. 7 (August 2013): 503–6.

Hutchinson, William T., and William M. E. Rachal, eds. *The Papers of James Madison.* Vol. 7, *3 May 1783–20 February 1784.* The University of Chicago Press, 1971.

Hutson, James H., ed. *Supplement to Max Farrand's The Records of the Federal Convention of 1787.* Yale University Press, 1987.

Idzerda, Stanley J., ed. *Lafayette in the Age of the American Revolution: Selected Letters and Papers, 1776–1790.* Vol. 1, *December 7, 1776–March 30, 1778.* Cornell University Press, 1977.

Irving, Washington. *The Life of George Washington.* Vol. 2. G. P. Putnam's Sons, 1889.

Isaacson, Walter. *Benjamin Franklin: An American Life.* Simon & Schuster, 2003.

Jackson, Donald, and Dorothy Twohig, eds. *The Diaries of George Washington.* Vol. 5, *1 July 1786–31 December 1789.* University Press of Virginia, 1979.

Jackson, John W. *With the British Army in Philadelphia, 1777–1778.* Presidio Press, 1979.

Jenkins, Stephen. *The Story of the Bronx: From the Purchase Made by the Dutch from the Indians in 1639 to the Present Day.* G. P. Putnam's Sons, 1912.

Johnston, Henry P. *The Campaign of 1776 Around New York and Brooklyn.* Part 2. Long Island Historical Society, 1878.

Johnston, Henry P., ed. *The Correspondence and Public Papers of John Jay.* Vol. 1, *1763–1781.* G. P. Putnam's Sons, 1890.

Journals of the Continental Congress. Vol. 22, *1782 (January 1–August 9).* US Government Printing Office, 1914.

Journals of the Provincial Congress, Provincial Convention, Committee of Safety and Council of Safety of the State of New-York, 1775–1776–1777, 2 vols. Thurlow Weed, Printer to the State, 1842.

King, Charles R., ed. *The Life and Correspondence of Rufus King.* Vol. 1, *1755–1794.* G. P. Putnam's Sons, 1894.

King, Charles R., ed. *The Life and Correspondence of Rufus King.* Vol. 4, *1801–1806.* G. P. Putnam's Sons, 1897.

King, Martin Luther, Jr. *Why We Can't Wait.* New American Library, 1964.

Kirschke, James J. *Gouverneur Morris: Author, Statesman, and Man of the World.* Thomas Dunne Books, 2005.

Knox, Katharine McCook. *The Sharples: Their Portraits of George Washington and His Contemporaries.* Da Capo Press, 1972.

Kohn, Richard H. "The Inside History of the Newburgh Conspiracy: America and the Coup d'Etat." *The William and Mary Quarterly* 27, no. 2 (1970): 187–220.

Kyriakodis, Harry. *Philadelphia's Lost Waterfront.* The History Press, 2011.

Labaree, Benjamin Woods. *The Boston Tea Party.* Northeastern University Press, 1979. First published in 1964 by Oxford University Press.

Larrabee, Harold A. *Decision at the Chesapeake.* Clarkson N. Potter, Inc., 1964.

Latimer, Elizabeth Wormeley, ed. *My Scrap-Book of the French Revolution.* A. C. McClurg and Company, 1898.

Laws of the State of New York, in Relation to the Erie and Champlain Canals, vol. 1. E. and E. Hosford, 1825.

Lengel, Edward G., ed. *The Papers of George Washington, Revolutionary War Series.* Vol. 15, *May–June 1778.* University of Virginia Press, 2006.

Lincoln, Charles Z. *The Constitutional History of New York.* Vol. 1, *1609–1822.* The Lawyers' Cooperative Publishing Company, 1906.

Looney, J. Jefferson, ed. *The Papers of Thomas Jefferson, Retirement Series.* Vol. 5, *1 May 1812 to 10 March 1813.* Princeton University Press, 2008.

Looney, J. Jefferson, ed. *The Papers of Thomas Jefferson, Retirement Series.* Vol. 10, *May 1816 to 18 January 1817.* Princeton University Press, 2013.

Lord, Walter. *The Dawn's Early Light.* W. W. Norton, 1972.

Lossing, Benson J. "Washington's Life Guard." *The Historical Magazine* 2, no. 5 (May 1858): 129–34.

Louis, Elan D. "Samuel Adams' Tremor." *Neurology* 56, no. 9 (May 2001): 1201–5.

Maclay, Edgar S., ed. *Journal of William Maclay, United States Senator from Pennsylvania, 1789–1791.* D. Appleton and Co., 1890.

Maricourt, Baron André de. *Madame de Souza et Sa Famille: Les Marign—Les Flahaut Auguste de Morny (1761–1836).* Émile-Paul, 1907.

Mastromarino, Mark A., ed. *The Papers of George Washington, Presidential Series.* Vol. 6, *1 July 1790–30 November 1790.* University Press of Virginia, 1996.

Mastromarino, Mark A., and Jack D. Warren, eds. *The Papers of George Washington, Presidential Series.* Vol. 9, *23 September 1791–29 February 1792.* University Press of Virginia, 2000.

McCullough, David. *John Adams.* Simon & Schuster, 2001.

McCullough, David. *1776.* Simon & Schuster, 2005.

McDonald, Robert M. S., ed. *Sons of the Father: George Washington and His Protégés.* University of Virginia Press, 2013.

Meltzer, Brad, and Josh Mensch. *The First Conspiracy: The Secret Plot to Kill George Washington.* Flatiron Books, 2019.

Mercier, Louis Sebastien. *The Picture of Paris: Before and After the Revolution.* George Routledge & Sons, 1929.

Miller, Melanie Randolph. *Envoy to the Terror: Gouverneur Morris and the French Revolution.* Potomac Books, 2005.

Miller, Melanie Randolph. *An Incautious Man: The Life of Gouverneur Morris.* ISI Books, 2008.

Miller, Melanie Randolph, ed. *The Diaries of Gouverneur Morris: European Travels, 1794–1798.* University of Virginia Press, 2011.

Miller, Melanie Randolph, ed. *The Diaries of Gouverneur Morris: New York, 1799–1816.* University of Virginia Press, 2018.

Miller, Melanie Randolph. "A Great Statesman: Reclaiming Gouverneur Morris." *The Georgetown Journal of Law & Public Policy*, vol. 21 (2023): 103–30.

Mintz, Max M. *Gouverneur Morris and the American Revolution.* University of Oklahoma Press, 1970.

Montross, Lynn. *The Reluctant Rebels: The Story of the Continental Congress, 1774–1789.* Harper & Brothers, 1950.

Morgan, Edmund S., and Helen M. Morgan. *The Stamp Act Crisis: Prologue to Revolution.* The University of North Carolina Press, 1953.

Morison, Samuel Eliot. *The Life and Letters of Harrison Gray Otis, Federalist.* Vol. 2, *1765–1848.* Houghton Mifflin, 1913.

Morison, Samuel Eliot. "Our Most Unpopular War." *Proceedings of the Massachusetts Historical Society*, vol. 80 (1968): 38–54, 166.

Morris, Anne Cary, ed. *The Diary and Letters of Gouverneur Morris.* 2 vols. Kegan Paul, Trench & Co., 1889.

Morris, Gouverneur. *An Oration Upon the Death of General Washington.* John Furman, 1800.

Murphy, Jim. *An American Plague: The True and Terrifying Story of the Yellow Fever Epidemic of 1793.* Scholastic, 2003.

Nuxoll, Elizabeth M., ed. *The Selected Papers of John Jay.* Vol. 1, *1760–1779.* University of Virginia Press, 2010.

Nuxoll, Elizabeth M., ed. *The Selected Papers of John Jay.* Vol. 5, *1788–1794.* University of Virginia Press, 2018.

Oberg, Barbara B. *The Papers of Thomas Jefferson.* Vol. 33, *17 February–30 April 1801.* Princeton University Press, 2006.

Palmer, R. R. *Twelve Who Ruled: The Year of Terror in the French Revolution.* Princeton, NJ: Princeton University Press, 1941.

Papas, Phillip. *Renegade Revolutionary: The Life of General Charles Lee.* New York University Press, 2014.

Patrick, Christine Sternberg, and John C. Pinheiro, eds. *The Papers of George Washington, Presidential Series.* Vol. 12, *16 January 1793–31 May 1793.* University of Virginia Press, 2005.

Pickering, Octavius. *The Life of Timothy Pickering*, vol. 1. Little, Brown, and Company, 1867.

Popkin, Jeremy D. *A New World Begins: The History of the French Revolution.* Basic Books, 2019.

Porter, Kirk H. *A History of Suffrage in the United States.* The University of Chicago Press, 1918.

Powell, John Harvey. *Bring Out Your Dead: The Great Plague of Yellow Fever in Philadelphia in 1793.* Time Life Books, 1970. First published in 1949 by University of Pennsylvania Press.

Proceedings of the Massachusetts Historical Society, 1885–1886, Vol. 2. Massachusetts Historical Society, 1886.

The Proceedings of a Convention of Delegates from the States of Massachusetts, Connecticut and Rhode-Island; the Counties of Cheshire and Grafton, in the State of New-Hampshire; and the County of Windham, in the State of Vermont, Convened at Hartford, in the State of Connecticut, December 15, 1814. Wells and Lilly, 1815.

Rappleye, Charles. *Robert Morris: Financier of the American Revolution.* Simon & Schuster, 2010.

Rasmussen, Dennis C. *The Constitution's Penman: Gouverneur Morris and the Creation of America's Basic Charter.* University Press of Kansas, 2023.

Rawle, William Brooke. "Laurel Hill and Some Colonial Dames Who Once Lived There." *The Pennsylvania Magazine of History and Biography* 35, no. 4 (1911): 385–414.

Read, Elizabeth. "The Chews of Pennsylvania." *The Magazine of American History*, vol. 4 (March 1880): 192–204.

Reardon, John J. *Edmund Randolph: A Biography*. Macmillan, 1975.

Richards, Leonard L. *Shays's Rebellion: The American Revolution's Final Battle*. University of Pennsylvania Press, 2002.

Robinson, J. H., ed. *Readings in European History*, vol. 2. Ginn, 1906.

Roosevelt, Franklin D. *Annual Message to Congress*. January 6, 1937. The American Presidency Project, https://www.presidency.ucsb.edu/node/209043.

Roosevelt, Theodore. *Gouverneur Morris*. Houghton, Mifflin and Company, 1888.

Rutland, Robert A., and William M. E. Rachal, eds. *The Papers of James Madison*. Vol. 9, *9 April 1786–24 May 1787 and supplement 1781–1784*. The University of Chicago Press, 1975.

Rutland, Robert A., ed. *The Papers of George Mason, 1725–1792*. Vol. 1, *1749–1778*. The University of North Carolina Press, 1970.

Sabine, William H. W., ed. *Historical Memoirs of William Smith*. Vol. 1. Colburn & Tegg, 1956.

Schama, Simon. *Citizens: A Chronicle of the French Revolution*. Vintage, 1990.

Schlesinger, Arthur M., and Fred Israel, eds. *History of American Presidential Elections, 1789–1968*, vol. 1. Chelsea House, 1971.

Sherr, Lynn. *Failure Is Impossible: Susan B. Anthony in Her Own Words*. Times Books, 1995.

Snow, Peter. *When Britain Burned the White House: The 1814 Invasion of Washington*. Thomas Dunne Books, 2014.

Sparks, Jared. *The Life of Gouverneur Morris, with Selections from His Correspondence and Miscellaneous Papers*. 3 vols. Gray & Bowen, 1832.

Stahr, Walter. *John Jay: Founding Father*. Hambledon and London, 2005.

Stewart, David O. *The Summer of 1787: The Men Who Invented the Constitution*. Simon & Schuster, 2007.

Still, Bayrd. *Mirror for Gotham: New York as Seen by Contemporaries from Dutch Days to the Present*. New York University Press, 1956.

Stokes, Isaac Newton Phelps. *The Iconography of Manhattan Island*, 6 vols. New York: 1915–1928.

Strum, Harvey. "New York Federalists and Opposition to the War of 1812." *World Affairs* 142, no. 3 (Winter 1980): 169–87.

Sullivan, William. *The Public Men of the Revolution*. Carey and Hart, 1847.

Swiggett, Howard. *The Extraordinary Mr. Morris*. Doubleday, 1952.

Syrett, Harold C., ed. *The Papers of Alexander Hamilton*. Vol. 1, *1768–1778*. Columbia University Press, 1961.

Syrett, Harold C., ed. *The Papers of Alexander Hamilton*. Vol. 2, *1779–1781*. Columbia University Press, 1961.

Syrett, Harold C., ed. *The Papers of Alexander Hamilton*. Vol. 25, *July 1800–April 1802*. Columbia University Press, 1977.

Syrett, Harold C., ed. *The Papers of Alexander Hamilton*. Vol. 26, *1 May 1802–23 October 1804, Additional Documents 1774–1799, Addenda and Errata*. Columbia University Press, 1979.

Szatmary, David P. *Shays' Rebellion: The Making of an Agrarian Insurrection*. University of Massachusetts Press, 1980.

Tansill, Charles C., ed. *Documents Illustrative of the Formation of the Union of the American States*. US Government Printing Office, 1927.

Taylor, Robert J., ed. *Papers of John Adams*. Vol. 3. The Belknap Press of Harvard University Press, 1979.

Thacher, James. *The American Revolution, from the Commencement to the Disbanding of the American Army; Given in the Form of a Daily Journal, With the Exact Dates of All the Important Events; Also, a Biographical Sketch of All the Most Important Generals*. Hurlbut, Kellogg & Co., 1861.

Treanor, William Michael. "The Case of the Dishonest Scrivener: Gouverneur Morris and the Creation of the Federalist Constitution." *Michigan Law Review* 120, no. 1 (October 2021): 1–124.

Treaty of Alliance with France; 2/6/1778 in *Perfected Treaties, 1778–1945*. General Records of the United States Government, Record Group 11, National Archives Building, Washington, D.C.

Twohig, Dorothy, ed. *The Papers of George Washington, Presidential Series*. Vol. 4, *8 September 1789–15 January 1790*. University Press of Virginia, 1993.

Twohig, Dorothy, Mark A. Mastromarino, and Jack D. Warren, eds. *The Papers of George Washington, Presidential Series*. Vol. 5, *16 January 1790–30 June 1790*. University Press of Virginia, 1996.

Van Doren, Carl. *Secret History of the American Revolution*. The Viking Press, 1941.

Van Doren, Carl. *Mutiny in January*. The Viking Press, 1943.

Van Schaack, Henry C. *The Life of Peter Van Schaack*. D. Appleton & Co., 1842.

Ver Steeg, Clarence L. *Robert Morris: Revolutionary Financier, with an Analysis of His Earlier Career*. Octagon Books, 1976.

Waldo, Albigence. "Valley Forge, 1777–1778: Diary of Surgeon Albigence Waldo, of the Connecticut Line." *The Pennsylvania Magazine of History and Biography* 21, no. 3 (1897): 299–323.

Warren, Jack D., ed. *The Papers of George Washington, Presidential Series*. Vol. 7, *1 December 1790–21 March 1791*. University Press of Virginia, 1998.

Weigley, Russell F., ed. *Philadelphia: A 300-Year History*. W. W. Norton, 1982.

Wheeler, Richard. "Voices of Lexington and Concord." *American Heritage* 22, no. 3 (April 1971): 8–13.

Wilentz, Sean. *No Property in Man: Slavery and Antislavery at the Nation's Founding*. Harvard University Press, 2018.

Wright, Louis B. *The Cultural Life of the American Colonies*. Dover Publications, 2002.

Young, Edward J., Clement Hugh Hill, and Alexander McKenzie, eds. *Proceedings of the Massachusetts Historical Society, 1885–1886*, Vol. 2. Massachusetts Historical Society, 1886.

ILLUSTRATION CREDITS

1. Brooklyn Museum
2. The New York Historical
3. National Portrait Gallery, Smithsonian Institution
4. National Portrait Gallery, Smithsonian Institution
5. New Orleans Museum of Art
6. Museum of the City of New York
7. Pennsylvania Academy of the Fine Arts
8. National Archives
9. Metropolitan Museum of Art
10. Wikimedia
11. Palace of Versailles
12. Museum of the History of France
13. Palace of Versailles
14. Museum of the City of New York
15. White House Historical Association
16. National Portrait Gallery, Smithsonian Institution
17. The New York Historical
18. White House Historical Association
19. Library of Congress
20. Private collection
21. The New York Public Library
22. National Portrait Gallery, Smithsonian Institution

INDEX

Note: References to "GM" refer to Gouverneur Morris.

ABOUT THE AUTHOR

SCOTT S. GREENBERGER is coauthor of the *New York Times* bestseller *Critical: What We Can Do About the Health-Care Crisis* and author of *The Unexpected President: The Life and Times of Chester A. Arthur*. Currently the executive editor of *Stateline*, he was a staff writer at the *Austin American-Statesman* and *The Boston Globe* and has written for *The New York Times*, *The Washington Post*, *Politico*, and *GQ*. Greenberger has a bachelor's degree in history from Yale University and a master's degree in international relations from George Washington University. He lives in Takoma Park, Maryland.